PURSUIT OF PLEASURE

ABOUT THE BOOK

The Edwardian age was a brief interlude, a season of opulence swept away in the holocaust that followed. It was also the crucible of the new social concepts that burst upon the Western world after the Great War.

Keith Middlemas, twentieth-century historian, brings this luxurious period vividly to life. The princes of affluence who surrounded King Edward VII basking in the Indian summer of the Victorian age pursued an ephemeral star — the sweet pleasure of a life devoted to elegance. Edward himself, the last king to give his name to an era, was a people's king and a dandy. He gave inspiration and imagination to the pursuit of pleasure.

Deauville, Biarritz, the rise of respectable theatre, the long week-ends, the great ships, the Anglo-American marriages, the cult of soft pornography — the Edwardian era displayed the superb confidence of a doomed but magnificent oligarchy.

ABOUT THE AUTHOR

Keith Middlemas was educated at Stowe School and Cambridge University. He has four children and lectures at Sussex University. Best known for his widely celebrated biographies of *Baldwin* and *Edward VII*, he has written a number of volumes of political history.

PURSUIT OF PLEASURE

High Society in
the 1900s

Keith Middlemas

GORDON & CREMONESI

Designed by Heather Gordon

Set in 11 on 13 pt Plantin
by Computacomp [UK] Ltd.,
Fort William, Scotland
and printed in Great Britain

British Library/Library of Congress
Cataloguing in Publication Data
Middlemas, Keith
The pursuit of pleasure.
1. Great Britain – Social life and customs –
20th century
1. Title
941.082'3   DA570   77–30056
ISBN 0–86033–016–8

Gordon & Cremonesi Publishers
London and New York
34 Seymour Road
London N8 0BE

To Sophie, Lucy and Annabel

Contents

The Edwardian Gentleman

Looking back from the end of the Great War, there could be no question of how much had been lost. Even the unsentimental economist John Maynard Keynes, writing his bitter indictment of the Paris peace settlement in 1919, recalled the leisured life and its unlimited gratifications with an indulgence all the more poignant for being set against harsh post-war realities: "What an extraordinary episode in the economic progress of man that age was which came to an end in August 1914! The greater part of the population, it is true, worked hard and lived at a low standard of comfort, yet were, to all appearances, reasonably contented with this lot. But escape was possible, for any man of capacity or character at all exceeding the average, into the middle and upper classes, for whom life offered, at a low cost and with the least trouble, conveniences, comforts and amenities beyond the compass of the richest and most powerful monarchs of other ages" (*The Economic Consequences of the Peace* (1919), p. 9). Later, in the years between the wars, nostalgia grew more anguished, amounting for some to a form of bereavement. In *Precious Bane*, the novelist Mary Webb wrote of "a richness on the world, so it looked what our parson used to call sumptious"; and, although she was talking of the countryside itself, the description fitted the life as well. Maurice Baring looked back to a summer, "where a constellation of beauty moved in muslin and straw hats and yellow roses on the lawns of gardens designed by Lenôtre, delicious with ripe peaches on old brick walls, with the smell of verbena and sweet geranium; and stately with large avenues, artificial lakes and wide temples; and where we bicycled in the warm night past ghostly cornfields by the light of a large full moon" (*The Puppet Show of Memory*, p. 167). At the same time, in harmony with contemporary disparagement of Victorian virtues and the supposedly stifling constraints of Victorian life, popular imagery recreated the Edwardians—and in particular their Kings—as a race of liberated individuals, drinking deep of the pleasures available only to a wealthy and secure minority. Edward VII, according to George Dangerfield, "represented in a concentrated shape those bourgeois kings whose florid forms and rather dubious escapades were all the industrialised world had left of an ancient divinity; his people saw in him the personification of something nameless, genial and phallic"; and a music-hall ballad of the 1900s carried the refrain

> The monarch to make things hum,
> The King, the runabout King.

The real intellectual break from the Victorian era came at the end of Edward's reign rather than in 1901, but this long-accepted myth serves well enough to distinguish the years between 1900 and 1914; when upper-class English society enjoyed a luxury and easiness which had not previously been known, and which can immediately be distinguished from the cost-conscious mentality of the increasingly beleaguered rich who survived into the middle of the twentieth century. The easiness of life and its unquestioned tone inspired Clermont-Tonnerre to describe them as "a race of gods and goddesses descended from Olympus upon England, living upon a golden cloud, spending their riches as indolently and naturally as the leaves grow green". Their extravagance was founded on wealth and leisure, and the almost total absence of productive effort. As the American sociologist Thorstein Veblen pointed out in 1899, "Productive labour becomes intrinsically unworthy. Prescription ends by making labour not only disreputable in the eyes of the community, but morally impossible to the noble, freeborn man, and incompatible with a worthy life" (*The Theory of the Leisure Class*, 1953 edition, p. 45). Mere idleness, then, was not enough for the leisured society: it was transformed into "the idleness of expressive discomfort, of noble vice and costly entertainment".

That privileged group enjoyed a double freedom: from economic constraints—the need to work or worry about income in the sense of actually relating earnings to expenditure—and from social or moral constraints on the pursuit of individual excellence or indulgence in pleasure. In return, they owed conformity to a code, experienced from birth, in family upbringing and at school, which was designed to inculcate a set of common assumptions about the position and role of the upper class in society, its historic mission of national leadership, and its relations with inferiors—the middle and working classes. The code carried an obligation to live in a certain style, to spend, patronise the arts, encourage good farming, horse-breeding, to fill public offices without looking for pay or perquisites, to serve in the armed forces in peace and war. And it demanded a form of conduct which, while allowing an astonishing range of aberrations in private, absolutely excluded public scandal. The screens between the rough public and the mystery of leadership in society were not to be lifted, except at the price of immediate expulsion from the group.

Such freedom allowed characters of remarkable diversity to flourish. No single description could contain the King; the rarefied scientist Lord Rayleigh; the bucolic Minister of Agriculture, Henry Chaplin; the elegant leader of the "Souls" and Prime Minister, Arthur Balfour; the socialist Bertrand Russell; and the eccentric Welsh squire George Thomas, who always carried a strap to beat the children of any friends or relatives who happened to be near at hand, who fined his servants, and his cat Sambo, if they displeased him, and who ordered for his burial a wicker coffin, since this, he believed, would prove more convenient for the Resurrection.

They were not aristocrats alone, dominating "society" as in France, Germany or Spain in the 1900s, nor yet a plutocracy like the great houses of Vanderbilt, Rockefeller, Astor and Mellon, descendants of the "robber barons" who had controlled American industry in the nineteenth century. Instead, blending birth, breeding and wealth, the Edwardian upper class proved endlessly fascinating to both extremes: to European aristocrats, who aped their customs, sports and dress; and to Americans, who married their daughters into English families, poured in their money to retrieve decayed estates, and sought, by alternate emulation and criticism, and in the end, like the novelist Henry James, by a sort of intellectual surgery, to come to terms with the attractions of a society so similar to and so different from their own.

But who were they? The Editor of Burke's *Landed Gentry* (seventh edition, 1886) had no doubts: "The Landed Gentry, the untitled aristocracy of England, Ireland and Scotland, is a class unexampled and unrivalled in Europe. Invested with no hereditary titles, but inheriting landed estates transmitted from generation to generation, this class has held, and continues to hold, the foremost place in each county."

Outside the field of chivalry, with its coats of arms and increasingly scholarly approach to pedigree, late-nineteenth-century status rested on more practical tests, principally on the holding of land. In 1881 John Bateman, author of *The Great Landowners of Britain and Ireland*, reckoned that a squire would hold from 1,000 to 2,000 acres (giving him an income of roughly £1 per acre) and that anyone with above 3,000 acres would be counted part of the "greater gentry". When Bateman was writing, before the worst of the great agricultural depression, a quarter of England was still owned by a mere 1,200 people, and another quarter by only 6,200 more. In 1900, despite enormous sales of land in the previous twenty years, 115 people still owned more than 50,000 acres each; and at least 2,500 landed proprietors received from their estates incomes of over £3,000—equivalent, in 1976 terms, to £30,000, virtually tax free.

But those land sales at the turn of the century reflected the fact that, since the extension of the franchise to all householders, and with the growth of industrial wealth, landowners, as such, had ceased to derive political power from their holdings. Peers and gentry were already to be found as shareholders and directors of businesses, industries and banks, their wealth more and more distributed away from the land itself. Old distinctions between land and industry were vanishing rapidly. Mobility into the upper class had always existed and new recruits in the nineteenth century had tended to buy country estates to provide themselves with the necessary trappings (a quarter of the 4,000 families in Burke's *Landed Gentry* in 1900 had acquired land only very recently); but by then there were many who called themselves, and were accepted as, gentlemen, who held little or no land, and whose knowledge of the horse—so essential to the country gentleman's life—was minimal.

Thus a description of the upper class of Edwardian England needs to range deliberately wider than Burke's peers and landed gentry, and to lap over the strict boundaries of chronology. Edward VII's style of life, from which many derived their habits of social behaviour, had been formed long before his accession in 1901; just as many of the best known figures of his reign, such as Arthur Balfour and Henry Chaplin, survived into the 1920s with undiminished energy.

The gentleman was not necessarily an aristocrat. True, he frequently became a peer, by creation, for public or political services, or simply because he held influence in the shires. A.J. Fox-Davies wrote in 1914, "I find myself chasing the details of some new landowner, only to see him pass on into the hands of my colleague, Mr. Ashworth Burke, for the *Peerage* volume, before I have had the opportunity of using the family in the *Landed Gentry*. Things move so rapidly nowadays." Many gentlemen were, after all, younger sons of aristocrats, deprived by the British system of primogeniture of the title which they would have had had they been French, Italian or German.

But the upper class was much wider than, and different from, the aristocracy, with its exclusive habits and vast residual wealth in land and city property. On the one hand, it behaved like a complex valve, regulating the pressures between aristocracy and middle class caused by the explosion of industrial wealth, rising birth rate, and political demands in the later nineteenth century, and admitting a steady stream of suitable candidates for social betterment, if not promotion to the peerage. On the other, the gentry, being primarily based on land, living in the counties and drawing lower incomes than the aristocrats (whose time and energies were divided between their great country houses and London) tended to be more static, provincial in outlook, and conservative in politics. If they respected and modelled their lives on any group, it was the aristocracy; and, consequently, as well as admitting new recruits, the gentry served as a buffer, preventing the sharp cleavage between aristocracy and middle class which showed so clearly in early-twentieth-century Europe, and prolonging the effective life of those above them, whom they admired but sometimes envied and resented.

This latter role, formerly a source of strength, put them at risk in the 1900s, as income from land fell sharply, following the agricultural depression. The placid pool into which new recruits had been carefully absorbed became increasingly agitated. Membership of the upper class often became an exercise in survival, as first political power in the counties slipped away, then economic independence, with the introduction of progressively steeper rates of taxation. For each new member of the gentry, one might fall out of the circle. At first the flood of new recruits added a sparkle to the somewhat bucolic layer of the county gentry: but, even before the holocaust of the 1914–18 war, there were fears that the quality of gentlemanly status had been irreparably diluted.

This unease, and frequently a sense of frustration and bitterness, can be found, paradoxically, enmeshed in the appearance of the "golden age". For those on the downward slope, it was the mid-Victorian age that was remembered with nostalgia. By contrast, the twentieth century opened on sombre notes: not only the long-term depression, but also the military disasters of the Boer War, the Black Week of December 1899, whose stains were never quite washed away by later victories. In July 1902, Lord Salisbury, Prime Minister since 1886 (except for a short break of three years) and epitome of the patrician leader in politics, resigned, and *Le Temps* of Paris commented, "What closes today with Lord Salisbury's departure is a whole historic era. It is ironic that what he hands on is a democratised, imperialised, colonialised and vulgarised England—everything that is antithetic to Toryism, the aristocratic condition and the high church he stood for. It is the England of Mr. Chamberlain, not, despite his nominal leadership, of Mr. Balfour." Salisbury's wife, who died shortly before Black Week, had said sadly, of the world she had known, "The young generation may criticise us as they like; will they ever provide anything as good as we have known?"

In spite of the unnerving sense of change, the way of life did survive, and the changes, in retrospect, seem exaggerated—as nothing compared to the disaster after 1914. Agriculture, though less prosperous than in the mid nineteenth century, improved considerably after the 1890s, and income from it, though diminished, continued to provide the staple of most gentlemen's existence. Efficient management of estates remained one of the principal justifications for the existence of the gentry, for efficiency had become an imperative for any holder of as little as 1,000 acres, if the old standards were to be maintained. As rural society began its long disintegration, fewer and fewer could follow the genial example of Tom Brown's father, old Squire Brown, who "stopped at home, and dealt out justice and mercy in a rough way, and begot sons and daughters, and hunted the fox, and grumbled at the badness of the roads and the times".

A handful of provincial squires in this mould survived; who grumbled still at the badness of the roads, and more at the fumes and noise of the first motor cars to invade the countryside, and more still at the nightmare of death duties and the land taxes of the 1909 budget—inspired, as they feared, by hatred of the landowners. But, according to Burke's editor, for most of them "the mere possession of broad acres is not the criterion of social status that once was the case". Land had become only one among several pillars of the façade of gentility. What had once been a simple distinction between upper and middle classes had been blurred, first by the introduction of industrial wealth, and then by the rise of professionally qualified men, schooled in the same system and at the same establishments as the landowning gentry. In the later nineteenth century a few industrialists, chiefly of dissenting origin, like the great railway contractor Thomas Brassey, had scorned to follow the Arkwrights, Barings and Strutts and buy estates; but Brassey's son did, and even Samuel Morley, dissenter, temperance reformer, and radical leader of the Reform League, eventually bought land and sent his sons to Trinity College, Cambridge.

Rapid social mobility in the 1900s gave the gentry the appearance of an élite, with permanent channels of entry by merit or acquisition. At the same time, more ancient families widened the almost tribal links between them—which had served both to extend their influence and to preserve it against encroachment—to embrace (often literally) the new recruits. The family as a whole, based on its ancestral estate, spaced over dower-houses, linked with others by marriage, had always been more important than the interests of its individual members— not the least reason for the frequent drift downwards of the younger sons or unmarried daughters, not merely into the clergy or professions, away from the land, but also into industry and commerce. Now the old marriage market began to include shrewd calculations about the wealth or vigour not merely of heiresses of similar degree, but of the daughters of prosperous businessmen, unknown Americans and actresses. The one remaining bar, that against association with trade, was itself discreetly overridden, at least for the second generation.

By purchase and marriage, what Bagehot had called the "plutocracy" took on the attributes of tradition. Yet, in spite of these opportunities, the status of gentleman was not to be had simply for the asking. A sort of probationary test, like a series of filters, had to be gone through before social acceptance could be granted. Something quite intangible invested the gentleman, an aura which eluded many applicants, just as it remained with those who had dropped out, no matter how far they fell. In Trollope's *Last Chronicle of Barset*, the battered, perpetual curate of Hogglestock, ill-dressed, poor and undernourished, could still face up to the formidable, well-endowed Archdeacon Grantly: "We stand on the only perfect level on which such men can meet each other. We are both gentlemen."

The code embodied honour, dignity, integrity, considerateness, chivalry and courtesy—the values inherent in an idealised rural society underpinned by deference and good neighbourliness, and from them arose the unwritten law that, although a gentleman, by definition, had no occupation, his pastimes must, in the last resort, be of value to the community. Above all, the gentleman was bound by a sense of honour. A world in which the travelling Englishman could take a gold sovereign from his belt to pay a bill in Paris, Vienna or Tehran also recognised the meaning of "the word of a gentleman"; and, if nothing else, this could be taught in schools for the sons of gentlemen (or as Chesterton slyly put it "schools for making gentlemen of sons").

The historian of late-nineteenth-century landed society has written, "Their upbringing, way of life, mannerly setting, occupations, avocations, social outlook and political beliefs, though certainly not conforming to any rigid or stereotyped pattern, were all shaped by a readily identifiable mould. They formed a loosely knit club with unwritten rules to ensure that all members were gentlemen, and it was they above all who formed the standards of gentlemanly conduct. The strength and virtue of conventions which governed behaviour, while they permitted great diversity and colourful eccentricity, very rarely produced either that hypocrisy of mere outward conformism or that brand of well-bred inhibition that had sometime been attributed to the English upper classes. The idealisation of etiquette belongs to the aspirants, the new genteel, somewhat uncertain of their position. The landed gentleman could afford to be unconventional without endangering his standing because the solid guarantee of his state lay behind him" (F.M.L. Thompson, *English Landed Society in the Nineteenth Century* (1963), p. 15). And this remained true, long after the decline of the landed interest, while the gentleman's public role survived—in local politics, estate management, service in the army, government or colonies, and patronage of sport and the arts.

It proved easier for the critics to define what a gentleman was than it was for the defence. The assault on class barriers, in particular against snobbery, "one of the most elusive but not the least powerful of the factors that influence human affairs" (G. Kitson Clark, *The Making of Victorian England* (1962), p. 289), grew to a crescendo in the Edwardian period. With a good deal of justification, radicals as well as socialists could look at the expansion of the peerage since the days of Pitt the Younger, and at late-nineteenth-century recruitment to the gentry, to verify the old saying that Lord Burghley used to repeat to his son Robert: "What is nobility but ancient riches?" A contemporary pamphlet pointed to the latent antagonism between upper and lower class: "Let things go wrong, make a false step, and in a moment it flashes out: 'Ignorant Fellow!'—'Bloody gen'leman!' " (S. Reynolds, *Seems So! A Working Class View of Politics* (1911), p. xviii). Already in 1910, at a scholarly level, the theory of a materially-based class structure ran counter to what was seen by sociologist F.G. D'aeth (in his "Present Tendencies of Class Differentiation", *Sociological Review*, III, 1910) as the mere romanticism of an organic, cross-class concept of the "gentleman".

The offensive face of class privilege—what Evelyn Waugh once called "the noise of the English aristocracy baying for broken glass"—can be seen in its more obviously snobbish outlets. *The Queen* magazine, for example, revealed what a later critic describes as "the completely prejudiced, utterly insufferable, entirely arrogant, totally self-interested, shameless and essentially British" style of the upper class (J. Stevens, quoted in Q. Crewe, *The Frontiers of Privilege*, 1963). Indeed, for the radical critics one of the worst things about the gentry was its capacity to survive into a world where in theory it should have become extinct. Old money, advantageous marriages, careful breeding, inherited talent and a spacious environment all gave inestimable advantages in a highly competitive society—to say nothing of the network of relationships, acquired through the family, at school and university, in regiment or club. All were, for obvious reasons, anathema to the egalitarian turn of mind.

Inherited privilege became harder to justify in an era which saw the formation of the Labour Party and the rise of the trade union movement to political power. Hence the attempts, then and later, to point up the virtues of a gentleman's role. Under the heading "Gentleman's Estate" in the 1971 edition of *Burke's Landed Gentry,* Anthony Lejeune put the case for the gentry thus: "They are secure in their own identity and confident of their social position. They know what is expected of them and are psychologically free to get on with the job. When the system is working properly, the result should be a degree of stability and continuity hardly to be obtained in any other way. An old landed family, belonging to its land as much as the land belongs to it, will build and plant trees for the future. People need roots, a sense of inheriting from the past and bequeathing to the future. To destroy this continuity, to prevent families from handing on what they have inherited or built, is to remove a linchpin, not just from those families, but from the whole community."

It came down to a theory of leadership, in society, politics, and the army—the public duty of the gentleman. In return for privilege, he worked, voluntarily and unpaid, on committees, as a magistrate, as an employer of agricultural labour; and, in the last resort, as a soldier in defence of his country. The protagonist of Christopher Hollis's novel *Death of a Gentleman* put it in this way: "Gentlemen were there to be shot at, when the shooting's on. That is what they are for, and whatever the other duties in which the gentlemen of England have failed throughout their history, at least they have never failed in this." The First World War, 1914–18, provided a grim, final example.

The defence rested, however, on something less clear-cut. Essential elements of the so-called English character came to be linked with gentlemanly virtues, more and more often as the tide of criticism rose. In the 1890s, John Henry Newman set his description on a level deliberately outside time: "It is almost a definition of a gentleman to say that he is one who never inflicts pain. This description is both refined and, as far as it goes, accurate .... His benefits may be considered as parallel to what are called comforts or conveniences in arrangements of a personal nature: like an easy chair or a good fire, which do their part in dispelling cold and fatigue, though nature provides both means of rest and animal heat without them. The true gentleman in like manner carefully avoids whatever may cause a jar or a jolt in the minds of those with whom he is cast. He makes light of favours when he does them, and seems to be receiving when he is conferring. He has too much good sense to be affronted at insults, he is too well employed to remember injuries, and too indolent to bear malice. If he engages in controversy of any kind, his disciplined intellect preserves him from the blundering discourtesy of better, though less educated, minds; who, like blunt weapons, tear and hack instead of cutting clean, who mistake the point in argument, waste their strength on trifles, misconceive their adversary, and leave the question more involved than they find it."

What follows is a comparison between that ideal and its practice, between public duty and private pleasures, as they were enjoyed by gentlemen in Edwardian England.

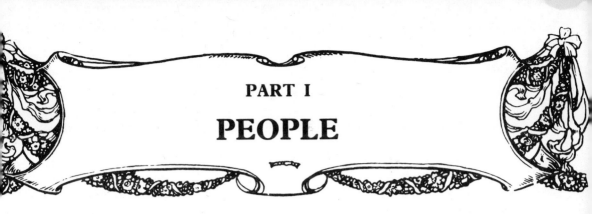

PART I

PEOPLE

CHAPTER ONE

Gentlemen at Large

Newman's portrait of the gentleman was an ideal, set in front of the privileged youth of the 1890s or 1900s much as Kipling's *Recessional* was aimed at the set ranks of unthinking imperialists during the South African War. Some perhaps lived up to it, others remembered it as a recurrent image, filtered through the formalities of headmasters' speeches or contemporary sermons. But as a description of the Edwardian upper class it can hardly fit the immense diversity of what Max Beerbohm used to call "those tall, cool, ornate people".

At the beginning of his saga of twentieth-century English social life, Anthony Powell made the narrator, Nicholas Jenkins, "brood on the complexity of writing a novel about English life, a subject difficult enough to handle with authenticity even of a crudely naturalistic sort, even more to convey the inner truth of the things observed .... Intricacies of social life make English habits unyielding to simplification ...." Jenkins concluded, "How, I asked myself, could a writer attempt to describe in a novel such a young man as Mark Members, for example, possessing so much in common with myself, yet so different?"

Here lay the essence of being a gentleman: to have had a particular type of background (in terms of birth, early training, school and so on), yet to have enjoyed, against this background, a diversity of living such as only the twelve volumes of the *Dance to the Music of Time* can depict. A gentleman of 1910 might appear in one form as a country squire, rooted in his estates, ignorant of London and the fashionable milieu, and in another as an intellectual, amateur of the arts and politics, to whom rural England comprised no more that the view from his host's lawns under the cedar trees of some great country house.

If no one can be called typical, who then, out of the 5,000 men (give or take a thousand) who made up this circle, was an exemplar? The King is usually taken as the epitome of the age, yet in his secluded upbringing he had had little of the experience common to others of the circle. As Prince of Wales, certainly as King, his life was too rarefied and remote for others, except the very rich and the aristocracy, to share. In some ways, had he not been of the royal blood, his status might have been questioned: the guttural, Germanic accent would have placed him in the always faintly suspect category of European nobility; his grossness of figure and enormous—often coarse—appetites might well have offended against the finer susceptibilities of taste or manners of a class some of whom regarded the European royal houses related to the British royal family as *parvenu*, and who disparaged the court of Queen Victoria as irremediably middle class.

But Edward VII stood out from the dismal backcloth of Queen Victoria's widowhood (part of which was, in any case, something of a caricature created by the cynics or caricaturists and the republicans) in a way which makes it impossible to ignore him as an archetype. If he often appeared a latter-day Henry VIII, who gambled, ate, drank and sported his way through life, his character was also more complex, his achievements in society more subtle, than contemporary eulogies allowed. In large measure, he possessed the classic attributes of the gentleman: sense of duty, courtesy, diplomacy, ease of manner, punctiliousness, and freedom from conventional constraints. Unlike his mother and his son, he lived a truly public life, reckoning the loss of privacy to be part of the price of his position. Even on private occasions, he rarely failed to show himself, often with disarming simplicity; as on a visit to the Isle of Man: "just a gentleman in a lounge suit and two ladies (the Queen and Princess Victoria) wearing black sailor hats, driving in an ordinary hard landau, with a few friends and officials of the island in cabs behind them and three or four local journalists bicycling by their sides". This was the obverse of the pageantry and splendour with which in 1901 he replaced the drab court life of Queen Victoria and which imported to London the flamboyance of the Second Empire he had known in the Paris of his youth.

Unlike many kings—whose jokes are always laughed at—he had a certain wit, enough at least to keep abreast of his lively contemporaries, and in private he could be genial and informal, extending the limits of decorum far beyond what his mother, or his son or younger grandson, would have thought fitting. (Once, when Lord Ampthill, the Parliamentary Private Secretary to the Colonial Secretary, Joseph Chamberlain, returned to his office, having lunched too well at his club, he found a letter waiting for transmission to the Palace. He took out the King's red box, and put in the letter—together with the butt of the cigar he had been smoking. In due course the box was returned, to be opened by Chamberlain himself. Inside was the cigar butt, and a note: "I do smoke cigars, but I don't think you meant me to finish this one.")

His courtesy impelled him always to undo the ill-effects of his frequent bouts of anger, to apologise to officials upbraided for mistakes, to thank, as few sovereigns did, the providers of services, and to go out of his way to carry out social duties. His frequent jests at the expense of his friends and his practical jokes verging on the unkind were redeemed by an overwhelming kindliness: as his Private Secretary, Sir Frederick Ponsonby wrote, "It was usual with the King, after he had let himself go and cursed someone, to smooth the matter by being especially nice to them afterwards."

Whether or not his frequent visits abroad, the long visits to related royalty, and the holidays at Marienbad, Homburg or Biarritz improved the chances of continued peace in Europe, Edward VII remained an accomplished diplomat in the technical as well as the broader sense. No Foreign Secretary had reason to complain that the King failed to represent his country in the style he would have wished; he was equally at home winning plaudits of critical audiences in Ireland by suggesting that they were experts in court etiquette, or in Paris complimenting the leading lady of the Comedie Française as "representing all the grace and spirit of France". What Sir Edward Grey called his "tactful perseverance" assimilated without anger the rough edge of hostility while professing to see only the virtues in hosts as difficult as the Kaiser or as obscure as Prince Milan of Serbia. Above all, the King had a sense of style. Fluent in German and French, he knew how to instill into an occasion magnificence. Comparing his urbane confidence with an inept performance by the French President and his wife, Ponsonby told a French official, rather grandiosely, "What can you expect? Yours are amateurs and ours are professionals at this game."

Sketches of the King's personality, however, mean little unless set against the broader picture of society. As Prince of Wales he was associated with the change in manners and ideas of the Victorian period, the *fin de siècle* revolt the forms of which ranged from the lush elegancies of Wilde and Beardsley to the brash foolery of the music halls and Pelissier's Follies. During thirty years as leader of a section of "society" he did much to make new habits acceptable to a wider audience. Then, as King, he claimed, and to some extent actually did hold, a position of social arbiter which helped to unify a class threatened with the first symptoms of disintegration.

As Prince of Wales, Edward's style of life was not consciously adopted, nor wholly a reaction against the strict discipline of his early days, prescribed by Victoria and Albert according to the rigid views of Baron Stockmar, but was rather the product of boredom at his existence in his twenties and thirties, cut off from any serious connection with affairs of state. The pleasures derived from his "fast" habits and faster friends were modified as he grew older and as he ran into a series of scandals and social misfortunes. He became by inclination what Parisians called a *boulevardier*, but he was neither degenerate nor vicious (as his unfortunate elder son, the Duke of Clarence, became). Nor did his activities mould a new "high society". They simply bestowed the royal warrant on that extravagant section of the aristocracy which had never consciously accepted the bourgeois morality of Queen Victoria's court and had existed on the fringes of society, in a latter-day dream of the eighteenth century, in some danger of becoming a redundant appendage, like a grumbling appendix.

However little this way of life appealed to the Queen, whose memories, repugnant to her, of the dissipation of George IV pervaded her whole reign and seemed to be reincarnated in her son, it performed a useful function. At an idealistic level, as Bagehot declared, the role of the heir apparent was to take "all the world and the glory of it, whatever is most attractive, whatever is most seductive". Edward's application of this maxim might have been too literal for the political philosopher, but in a practical way it helped to reconcile a still powerful group to the Crown and both to a wider public. Victoria had reprimanded her son in 1869, "there is a *very* strong feeling against the luxuriousness and and frivolity of society—and everyone comments on my simplicity"; but not all the comments were pleasing, as the republican agitation of the 1870s showed. The arid seclusion of the "Widow at Windsor" failed to appease the public taste for spectacle and grandeur, and cut off the constitutional head of state from the majority of those landed and industrially wealthy members of the élite whose power rested away from Westminster. When the Prince of Wales attached to himself a group of those whose company he most enjoyed, when he took Lord Charles Beresford and Lord Carrington to India in 1875, precisely the "independent, haughty, fault-finding, fashionable set which were most inimical to the Prince Consort and herself", he offended the Queen, but also prevented further alienation of men whose overweening arrogance, if unrelated to any public service, might have increased even more dangerously the gulf between classes.

The Prince's circle of friends numbered more than self-indulgent aristocrats. Although the Queen told him bluntly, "If you ever become King, you will find all these friends *most* inconvenient", they included financiers and bankers, the Rothschilds, Baron Hirsch, Sir Ernest Cassel and Louis Bischoffsheim, the businessmen Sir Blundell Maple and Sir Thomas Lipton, and the Sassoons, Colonel Astor and the South African millionaire J.B. Robinson. *The Times* might deprecate what it called "American cattlemen and prize fighters" in the royal entourage, but the fact that the Prince conferred his friendship on and actually stayed in the houses of such men (whose hospitality he enjoyed, and whose financial expertise gave him the shrewd advice on investment which enabled him to live the life he chose) exploded the Victorian convention that the court was a narrow circle restricted by the qualities of birth, dignity of manner and high moral reserve.

Edward's habits and pastimes, displeasing as they might be to groups of society who rejected his example, nevertheless encouraged the turn-of-the-century emancipation. Baccarat, roulette, attendance at the music hall, theatre supper parties, horse racing—everything in fact that Queen Victoria deplored as "one whirl of amusements"—brought a sort of broadside liberation from the standards she and Prince Albert had done so much to institute. Whether that was worth the price is debatable: she, after all, remembered the lurid decadence of the Regency era and the savage class hatreds of the years before 1848, which her son could not. But, as Prince of Wales and King, Edward helped, by a sort of social *Blitzkrieg*, to diminish some of the worst barriers of prejudice, just as the centrifugal attractions of his glittering court broke down much of the isolation of different sections among the upper class.

The views of those who criticised him were often less attractive than his own indiscretions. "The King", wrote Lady Paget, "as King is much more useful than he was as Prince of Wales. He has a great deal of ability but is always surrounded by a bevy of Jews and a ring of racing people. He has the same luxurious taste as the Semites, the same love of pleasure and comfort." His patronage made them socially acceptable to the old exclusive circle, and in the process weakened—though perhaps failed to destroy—their prejudices and anti-semitism. But he was not, in any sense, an egalitarian: during the visit of King Kalakua of the Sandwich Islands in 1881, he had dismissed objections to a full state reception with the two-edged comment, "Either the brute is a king, or he is a common or garden nigger; and if the latter, what's he doing here?" In such an atmosphere, the acceptance of gold and diamond millionaires, financiers and rough self-made men became perfectly fashionable and respectable. In the process, the old standards were exposed to a new, often shocking, burst of criticism.

The King's reforms extended far beyond the court to a public presentation of himself in every form of ceremonial available. State openings of Parliament, evening courts in place of "drawing rooms", public banquets, and, beyond London, events ranging from county shows to race meetings indicated that the head of state understood the value of drama in public life. As Bagehot had enjoined, "Royalty is a government in which the attention of the nation is concentrated on one person doing interesting things." Edward VII did not, however, believe in the corollary: "Its mystery is its life; we must not bring in the daylight upon magic." Instead he welcomed vicarious public interest in what he did and the broad public enthusiasm for him tinged everything and everyone around him, no matter how exclusive or wealthy their pursuits, with a sort of democratic approval. While it is true that by the 1900s "society" in the old nineteenth-century sense meant very little, because it had been so diluted, and divided from a core of purists who still tried to reject the influx of wealth and alien origins, King Edward belonged, in a sense, to all groups and gave a feeling of unity to all their confusions. His own philosophy remained remarkably out of touch with working-class opinion: in the 1880s he had told the Queen that, since the aristocracy and gentry filled such vital positions as Lords Lieutenant and county magistrates, "some pleasure cannot be denied them"; and as late as 1907, with the storms of industrial unrest building up, Ponsonby wondered whether "all this was of much use as far as the people were concerned". But to a highly critical public, fed assiduously by a new mass press and conscious of increased political power, the King's own existence served as justification for the continued privileges of the élite.

Outsiders tended to exaggerate his social leadership. Lord Northcliffe, the great newspaper proprietor, wrote in 1908, "the King has become such an immense personality in England that the space devoted to the movements of Royalty has quintupled since His Majesty came to the Throne." It was true that the King expected to be regarded as arbiter of manners and fashion, and claimed the same sort of status as First Gentleman of Europe as sycophants had bestowed on his ancestor George IV. A phrenologist who had examined the contours of his head when he was a boy reported that self-esteem was very markedly developed. In matters of protocol and taste he hated to be crossed or argued with, and he completely failed to understand the views of those who denied his authority (such as Keir Hardie, who categorically refused to attend any future royal function after his invitation to a Garden Party had been withdrawn on the grounds of his political criticism of the King's visit to Russia in 1908). But the formal structure of the court isolated him, even as he moved from country house to country house; and there were many who, during his reign, continued to echo the judgement pronounced twenty years earlier by Gladstone: "The Prince of Wales is not respected." In the spheres of religion, morality and intellectual leadership, Edward VII had no part, although few members of the élite found it necessary to put the matter quite so pointedly as did the group of high-born ladies who called themselves the "Lambeth Penitents" (the Duchess of Leeds, Lady Tavistock, Lady Aberdeen, Lady Zetland and Lady Stanhope), who when he was Prince of Wales had appealed to his wife, Princess Alexandra, to join them in promoting "the moral improvement of society".

In other ways, however, and especially in the male-dominated area of the code of manners, Edward was indeed exemplar of the age. In his youth he took for granted the double standard of sexual morality and deplored those who were found out, in the "sad affairs", as he called them, which betrayed the aristocracy into "washing dirty linen in public". But, then, rumour and scandal touched either him or his close friends in a series of cases—the Mordaunt divorce, the Aylesford–Blandford affair, and the letters of Lord Charles Beresford's mistress, Lady Brooke. Nothing publicly affected his reputation after the Brooke affair in 1891, and his own fundamental morality showed clearly in his solid attachment to his family. On the other hand, there was an undeniable contrast between his attitude as paterfamilias ("refinement of feeling in the younger generation does not exist … the age of chivalry has, alas, passed, both in social and political life", he told a correspondent in 1887) and his relationships with women across the dividing line of "respectability and reserve".

His upbringing had done nothing to dent the confidence of male superiority, which in a Latin country would have been called *machismo*. Edward unashamedly delighted in the company of women—so long as they were beautiful, amusing and deferential to his judgement in the serious matters of life. In this he was almost a caricature of contemporary attitudes towards the female sex. To observers, the Prince seemed surrounded by "a flotilla of white swans, their long necks supporting delicate jewelled heads"; and the *demi-mondaines* were quick to claim the friendship, if not more, of the heir apparent. Edward's name was linked with those of Sarah Bernhardt, Miss Chamberlayne (daughter of an American millionaire), Lily Langtry, Lady Brooke (later the Countess of Warwick), the Hon. Mrs George Keppel, and Mrs Agnes Keyser. Some were evidently mistresses, others merely inamorata or companions. Even as King he retained the habits, if not the full enjoyments, of the Prince. As Ponsonby noted, "he preferred men to books and women to either"; and, if his entourage lacked its glittering complement, as it did during the period of mourning in 1906 for the dead King of Denmark, he lamented "the tiresome evenings we shall have".

Yet it was not only the looseness of the upper echelon of society which he reflected. Gladstone, after all, had declared that most of the many Prime Ministers he had known had had mistresses, and a whole web of understandings and conventions protected reputation among the élite while permitting, even in Victorian days, a remarkable laxity of practice. In Edward two ancient strands met and intertwined: respect for, and protection of, an idealised female sex; and blind hostility to any request for a share in the world long staked out by men. Queen Victoria conformed absolutely to this standard; the independent-minded—worst of all, the suffragettes—did not. To him, the latter betrayed their womanhood, lost their charm and became viragos. Only the "professional beauties", Lily Langtry, Mrs Cornwallis-West, Mrs Luke Wheeler and Mrs Keppel, could bridge the gulf and engage his mind. Thinly disguised as Lady Roehampton, one of them meets the King in Vita Sackville-West's novel The Edwardians:

> Lady Roehampton was well known to be in the King's intimate set, and many were the looks of envy, disparagement and criticism cast upon her, as she stood easily swaying her fan and talking to the King and making him laugh. Many were the women who wished themselves in her shoes—the wives of civil servants, the young wives of territorial peers, richer in birth than in elegance, the wives of Chilean Secretaries of Legation—but those who were honest with themselves must admit that they could not make as good a job of it as Lady Roehampton was making. Confronted with the King, they would, in fact, have found themselves in extreme embarrassment. It was a delirious but fearful situation; for the King, genial as he could be, was known to lose interest, even to drum with irritable fingers on the arm of his chair or upon the dinner table. What a gulf there was between amusing the King and boring him! And, for a woman, all depended upon which side of the gulf she occupied. Life and death were in it.

The King, as foremost gentleman in the land, enjoyed to the full the life offered at the great country houses of the artistocracy, and his tastes and habits filtered down by emulation. His annual progress included visits to his friends—Lords Crewe, Carrington, Rosebery, Iveagh and Londonderry, the Gurneys, Harcourts Sassoons, and various others. The house where the King stayed had to accommodate a retinue of his servants and the host and his wife had to prepare much more than mere stately comfort. Edward feared, above all, the curse of boredom; his time had continually to be filled with stimulating conversations, games or hunting, as well as palatial meals—indugences that he shared with most of the Edwardian upper class. The King's love of good food, in quantities vast by modern standards, had ruined his figure and impaired his magnificent constitution even while he was Prince of Wales. A dinner with Lord Rosebery at Posillipo in 1903 ran to twenty courses and the King's own ordinary dinners often exceeded twelve. As he got older, he reduced his breakfasts; but before setting out of a day's shooting he would fortify himself with haddock, poached eggs, bacon, chicken and woodcock. Luncheon was a massive display, but dinner was his main meal; as late as 1910, before leaving on his last holiday at Biarritz, he gave a dinner that included turtle soup, salmon steak, grilled chicken, saddle of mutton, snipe with foie gras, asparagus, fruit, and an iced delicacy and savouries. A favourite dish was pheasant stuffed with ortolans and garnished with a rich sauce, while caviare and grilled oysters were considered the perfect introduction to a really sound meal.

In his sporting life the King set the tone, at least for those rich enough to follow and to invite him to stay. Racing was to him the most absorbing of his interests, both for the excitement of the race itself and the raffish camaraderie of racing society. In due course he became an owner, appointing Lord Marcus Beresford as manager of the royal stud. Three Derby winners and a Grand National winner gave him prestige and some financial success—and the spectacle of the King leading in Minoru through ecstatic crowds after the 1909 Derby was given immortality in a popular game akin to Racing Demon. As Prince he had dabbled in other sports—tennis, golf, fox-hunting—but shooting remained a passion with him till the end of his life. Again, it was a stylised affair, far different from the rough shoots organised by his grandson George VI in more straitened days. Whole hecatombs of birds were slaughtered on the vast estates of central Europe and the moors of Scotland, and the Norfolk fields witnessed record bags which have never been equalled since. But here, as with his yacht racing, which he eventually relinquished when the Kaiser's dedicated opposition in *Meteor* proved too much, he was self-indulgent, ill-attuned to failure. He liked "masses of pheasants driven over his head about the height of an ordinary tree, so that he never seemed to miss", Ponsonby observed, "but he never shot at a difficult bird". And the royal golf course, set out at Sandringham, was frequently replanned, to avert his unfortunate experiences in the bunkers.

Betting on horses, gambling at cards, the King, as he grew old, renewed the pleasures of his youth. He had never attempted to hide his enjoyment in these pastimes (in spite of the Tranby Croft case), and, although after 1900 he no longer played the once-scandalous game of baccarat, his fancy had gone far to make even that acceptable. In the academy of manners, on punctuality, correctness of dress, the wearing of decorations, and punctilious observance of social duties, he was the most vigorous *dominie*. The sovereign who had once gaily set his own fashions could also reprove the Duke of Devonshire for wearing an order upside down, and the immaculate Lord Rosebery for appearing at a formal reception in trousers rather than knee breeches.

Perhaps the King's greatest influence on the manners of the gentleman of his day was set by his constant travels abroad. His views about foreigners were eclectic: the Portuguese nobility he once compared to waiters in a restaurant, and his European friends ranged from the formidable Abbot of Teppel (whose shooting was unrivalled) to the eccentric French pacifist the Baron d'Estournelles. But above all he loved Paris and the Riviera, and the high society of the Third Republic responded by adopting the whims and fashions of "Le Prince de Galles". He was as well known at Longchamps as at Epsom, in the chateaux of the Greffulhes and Breteuils as at Knowsley and Mentmore. In the spring he would visit Biarritz, in

April the rather dreary court of his Danish father-in-law, and in September Marienbad (Homburg fell out of favour before he became King), for the mineral water "cure" and the company of the European aristocracy. A master of languages, a diplomat, and epitome of continental culture, he set a European tone which it was impossible for the fashionable world in Britain to ignore.

The King, as gentleman, typified many of the features of his age, but he did not necessarily originate them or stamp them on an unreceptive circle. He wholeheartedly accepted the underlying conventions of the society that he found the most attractive. Representing society, he actually lived almost wholly outside it and did not understand the forces of change altering it, politically and economically. Believing that he occupied a position of power and responsibility, he received the respect of those who did control power—but who did not necessarily follow his dictates or examples.

Leadership was of the essence of upper-class existence and politics one of the few careers wholly endorsed by the gentlemanly code. There, perhaps, among the Lords and Commons, could be found the finest aspirants to the gentlemanly ideal. One who followed the King closely and successfully was the third Lord Carrington, who in his childhood had been one of the few boys actually allowed to play with the future Edward VII at Windsor Castle, and who remained a friend of Edward's all his life. Although the majority of the King's political acquantances were Tories, party distinctions meant little to him, and Carrington, like Lord Rosebery, was a Liberal, and one with something of a social conscience. It was in his company that the Prince of Wales made his celebrated excursion, as a member of the Royal Commission on Housing of the Working Classes, into the Clerkenwell slums. (So upset was the Prince at the sickening poverty he saw that, when confronted by a woman lying in rags, surrounded by half-naked children, he made to give her a handful of sovereigns, only to be checked by an agitated Carrington, fearful of a mob rush. "We got him back safe and sound to Marlborough House in time for luncheon."

Carrington's greater experience of the outside world and his gift for social stratagems served them both well. On another occasion, seeking to associate the Prince with democratic trends, he persuaded him to watch from a balcony in Whitehall a demonstration in favour of extending the suffrage. Seeing the massed crowd below, the Prince chaffed him, "Hey Charlie, this don't look much like being a pleasant afternoon!" But Carrington had primed the organisers of the march to salute as they passed by, and, as the ranks turned to shout "God bless the Prince of Wales!", Edward's ill-humour vanished immediately. There was, of course, more between them than vanity tempered by skilful courtiership: they shared the taste for racing (Edward nourished a superstition that his horses were more likely to win if one of Carrington's daughters sat in the royal box), and, as a crony of more than forty years, Carrington was marked out for preferment as soon as Edward reached the throne.

Appointed first as Governor of Western Australia, Carrington later became

Lord Chamberlain. His most useful service, however, complemented the social side
of politics, for it was he who first rendered the Liberal leader, Sir Henry Campbell-
Bannerman, acceptable to the King, after a long period of disfavour following Sir
Henry's criticism of the conduct of the Army during the Boer War. After dining
together in Carrington's house, and meeting again in Marienbad, the King was
convinced that Campbell-Bannerman was "a gay old dog" and "quite sound on
foreign politics". "Yes", replied his friend, "if we come in, Sir Henry will make
Your Majesty a first-rate Prime Minister and will furnish you with good
government." Uneasy as the King may have been about some of the Liberal
contingent who swept the House of Commons in the the 1905 election, he was
satisfied with Campbell-Bannerman's choice of ministers, prominent among whom
was Carrington himself, Minister of Agriculture, with a seat in the Cabinet. In his
letter of thanks, Carrington encapsulated a political sentiment which served many a
gentleman politician: "I may not be very clever, but I am loyal."

Carrington, however, is hardly a representative political figure, for without royal
favour he would have been an unlikely candidate for eminence. Almost his
antithesis, certainly disliked and suspected by the King, was Arthur Balfour, leader
of the Conservative and Unionist Party, who seemed to many to sum up the place of
the gentleman in the twentieth-century political world. It is perhaps the measure of
his personal distinction that he should have risen to the Premiership, seeing that he
took, or appeared to take, so little interest in most of the problems of the people that
he governed. It is a measure also of the extent to which the House of Commons was
still "the best club in Europe", and of the degree to which personal ascendancy in
"the club" counted for more than reputation won outside. His view of politics
resembled that of the most arcadian of nineteenth-century Premiers, Lord
Melbourne, whom Lytton Strachey described as "An Autumn Rose". While critics
might disapprove of his constitutional idleness and his indifference to social duties,
they could not remain untouched by the personal fascination of the man. Beatrice
Webb thought him "A man of extraordinary grace of mind and body, delighting in
all that is beautiful and distinguished, music, literature, philosophy, religious feeling
and moral disinterestedness, aloof from all the greed and grime of common human
nature."

Juxtaposing the Fabian Mrs Webb with the high-Tory Prime Minister suggests
the contrast between the gentleman playing a part in the political arena and the
professional modern politician; one is reminded of Max Beerbohm's cartoon in
which Matthew Arnold is addressed by his niece Mrs Humphrey Ward with the
words, "Why Uncle Matthew, oh why, will you not be always wholly serious?"
Someone like Balfour could rise to great political heights, yet never be wholly rid of
the image of *poseur* among those for whom political activity was the *raison d'être* of
life. Once, when Balfour had given a particularly florid and ambiguous account of
British policy on Tariff Reform, Campbell-Bannerman rose to denounce his
statement with the ringing phrase, "Enough of this foolery!" An element of
foolery, dressed up in the utmost style and talent, lay at the heart of his method; and
perhaps the Liberal leader sounded the death-knell for this sort of political style.

Balfour's early career followed the pattern of many of his peers who entered the political arena without specific ambition, but with the ease and expectancy that marked their upbringing. A childhood at the great estate of Whittinghame in Scotland, dominated by the influence of his intellectual mother, led on to the traditional course—private tutors, private elementary school, Eton and Cambridge. Academic or sporting prowess did not mark him out, although he later wrote that "The communal life of Eton was, in itself, an education." At Cambridge he found that, "I was never taught anything I did not want to learn." Afterwards "I saw something of London society; I heard a great deal of music; I played [Real] Tennis at Lords .... I invited friends to Whittinghame; I visited them in country houses; I travelled; in short I did the sort of things that other young men do whose energies are not absorbed in learning or practising their chosen profession."

His intellectual affinity was to the group dubbed "The Souls", composed of aspiring philosphers and literary men who coalesced around him at Cambridge. The origin of the name conveys the self-consciously adulatory atmosphere. "You all sit around and talk about each other's souls", remarked Lord Charles Beresford at a dinner in 1888. "I shall call you the 'Souls'." While the Souls represented a different ideal from the "fast" set around the Prince at Marlborough House, or the "Incorruptibles" who looked down on the moral values set by the Prince, they were recognised as part of the upper stratum of London life.

The political traditions of his family, rather than conscious choice, drew Balfour into politics. His father and grandfather had sat for Scottish seats as Conservatives, and his mother's brother, father and grandfather had all held office in Conservative governments. It was at his uncle Lord Salisbury's suggestion that Balfour stood for Hertford in the 1874 election, and, since this seat was something like a property in the Cecil family, his entry into Parliament was thereafter a formality. His initial response, however, was the exhaustion fashionable among the aristocratic youth of the period, and he spent his first year as a silent Member and his second in touring round the world.

During the period of his political apprenticeship, Balfour enjoyed the immense advantage of his family connection with Lord Salisbury. In the words of Lord Willoughby de Broke, the rulers of the country "knew each other intimately, quite apart from Westminster". Nepotism became inevitable, because of shared backgrounds and personal contacts. In the Cabinet of 1895, Lord Lansdowne, the Secretary for War, was married to a sister of Lord George Hamilton, the Secretary for India, and Lansdowne's daughter was married to the nephew and heir of the Duke of Devonshire, who was Lord President of the Council. The Etonian background was indispensable, and, indeed, was calculated to produce future leaders of the right moral character, conscious of their obligations to some form of public service. Thus, it was not wholly surprising that Lord Salisbury should invite the fledgling politician to accompany him to the 1878 Congress of Berlin—Balfour's first taste of larger political life. Despite his meagre service in the House, the family could be counted upon to stand behind him. When Balfour contested Hertford in 1880 his majority of 164 on a poll of 964 corresponded exactly to the number of houses owned by Lord Salisbury in the borough.

Of course, with such connections and such a future, Balfour's career as an MP was not absolutely typical. There were others, in the Conservative Party in particular, who seemed closer to the ideal of the gentleman politician. Henry Chaplin and Walter Long, also powerful figures, cloaked their real political services in behaviour almost a caricature of the county squire. According to one genial critic, Long, President of the Board of Agriculture and, at forty-one, youngest member of the 1895 Cabinet, "Never said anything in his life that anybody remembers ... he gently dozes, his arms folded, his head sunk back upon a cushion, his ruddy October face giving a touch of colour to the scene" (A.G. Gardiner, *Pillars of Society* (1913) p. 65). Chaplin, son of a railway millionaire and banker, and Oxford friend of the Prince of Wales, was even more the representative of the English country gentleman, regarding it as his task, again in Gardiner's words, "vigorously, wakefully, alertly to guard the Empire against the knavish tricks of the Opposition" (*Prophets, Priests and Kings*). The sideburns, monocle and prominent chin of the President of the Local Government Board became familiar landmarks in the House of Commons, as well known as did his claim to advance upon any question the views of the ruling class. Undisturbed by doubt as to their correctness, he used to practise his speeches out in the open air, behind hedges, in order more easily to capture the ear of the House of Commons. "Undaunted by the most obtuse problems of government, he would tackle the tariff or the Education Bill in the same spirit as a difficult ditch in the hunting field" (Barbara Tuchman, *The Proud Tower*, p. 45), and with about as much perceptiveness. Once, after a laboured attempt to tackle, from the gentleman's point of view, the topic of bimettalism, Chaplin leant over to Balfour and asked, "How did I do, Arthur?" "Splendidly, Harry, splendidly", came Balfour's reply. "Did you understand me, Arthur?" "Not a word, Harry, not a word."

Balfour's elegant wit and graceful precision illustrate the mark of the gifted amateur. In a Cabinet meeting after the War he declared, "I think I understand. I am to try if possible to induce the French to agree to a very small battle fleet so as to leave us free to accept American proposals without modification. Having persuaded them to deprive themselves of this form of naval defence, I am then to persuade them that they really require no submarines because a war between France and England is unthinkable. This task being successfully accomplished, I am then to ask them to reduce the number of their aircraft, seeing that we cannot sleep securely in our beds lest, in a war with France, London should be burnt to the ground. For a task so complex as this I fear a trained diplomatist is required. But I will do my best." (G.M. Young, *Stanley Baldwin*, p. 36.)

He was dubbed "Bloody Balfour", the scourge of terrorists in the countryside of troubled Ireland, after the repudiation of Home Rule in 1886. Yet, despite this, Gladstone always in Parliamentary debate addressed him in the way reserved for good Liberals: "My honourable friend". For a time, Balfour joined the quartet of radical Tories of the Fourth Party, led by Lord Randolph Churchill, and he once told Margot Asquith, "My uncle [Salisbury] is a Tory .... and I am a Liberal."

Nevertheless, he was caught in the prison of his upbringing, intellectually sympathetic to the demands of working-class politicians, but wedded to the defence of the citadel of privilege. Perhaps this practical dilemma explains why he never allowed politics to distract from the social round. "What exactly is a Trade Union?" he once asked a Liberal colleague.

One evening he was one of twenty diners at Harry Cust's when the house caught fire upstairs. So absorbing was the talk that the dinner continued while the footmen passed bath towels with the port for protection against the firemen's hoses (Arnold Bennet, *Journals*, vol. 1, p. 287). On another occasion, he attended a country-house party at Cassiobury, home of Lord Essex, where Edith Wharton, arriving from London for tea, found, "Scattered on the lawn under the great cedars, the very flower and pinnacle of the London world ... so exhausted by their social labours of the past weeks ... that beyond benevolent smiles they had little to give." Meanwhile the life of the Souls continued, enhanced by the beauty of the three Wyndham sisters, to one of whom, Lady Elcho, Balfour's attentions went far enough to cause their friends some anxiety, for Hugo, Lord Elcho, was a member of the same circle. Yet Balfour remained a bachelor, and remarked of a rumour that he might have married Margot Tennant, later Asquith's wife, "No that is not so. I rather think of having a career of my own."

Intellectual conceit, albeit inoffensive, lay at the heart of his philosophy. In the modern world, it would be strange to find a future Prime Minister concerning himself with the writing of a work such as *A Defence of Philosphic Doubt* or *The Foundations of Belief* (which was much praised by the American philosopher William James), and it would be difficult to regard with anything but disquiet the rise in politics of a man who, confronted by a staircase which split in twin curves, could stand for twenty minutes trying, as he explained to an observer, to find a logical reason for taking one side rather than the other! One evening in 1901, after a rousing castigation of the capitalist system by the Labour MP Keir Hardie, "Mr. Balfour, coming back from dinner, smiled pleasantly on the Speaker, doubtless calculating that things as they were would last his time." Contemporaries who looked with favour on his advance stressed that most gentlemanly of virtues—his courage, vindicated time and again during his tenure of office as Irish Secretary. As George Wyndham put it, "Great courage being so rare a gift and so large a part of human misery being due to fear, all men are prepared to fall down before anyone wholly free from fear." Winston Churchill, then a political opponent of Balfour's, said of him that he was "The most courageous man alive. I believe if you held a pistol to his face it would not frighten him."

There still survived a sort of understanding that the political leader needed no professional expertise. Indeed, Margot Asquith insisted that Balfour's mind was metaphysical and religious, "that he had a vivid sense of the present life being of very little importance, an anti-chamber to another life....It is for that reason that he has no profound convictions about politics, they attract him only as a game which he thinks he plays well, and which amuses him much as a game of chess might do, but he does not really care for the things at stake, or believe that the happiness of mankind depends on events going this way or that" (W.S. Blunt, *Diaries* (1932), p. 559).

Balfour rarely took a detailed interest in facts and figures (an area of politics that always confused him). When dealing with a complicated Bill there was always a knowledgeable minister, such as the Home Secretary or Attorney-General, at his side. Often late for question time, even as Prime Minister, Balfour effected a major change in Parliamentary procedure by changing the Wednesday short sitting of the House of Commons to Fridays. This stemmed not from a wish to reform, but from his desire to allow more time for golf, a pastime which he did much to popularise. True, he neither shot nor hunted with any great enthusiasm, but his skills were catholic: he could be found playing in an ice-hockey match between Court and House of Commons on the lake in Buckingham Palace, while his passion for bicycling and, later, for the motor car gave an indication of the ways in which a gentleman's leisure time in the modern world might develop.

From Irish Secretary in 1887, he rose to be Leader of the House of Commons in 1891. From 1895 onwards he was First Lord of the Treasury, in the administration led by his uncle, Lord Salisbury. While more active souls, like Joseph Chamberlain, carved out a modern image for the Conservative Party and linked it inextricably to the imperial ideal, Balfour's own stature grew, despite his personal predilection for avoiding the more turbulent areas of public policy. Chamberlain could never rid himself of the stigma of his origins and the doubts felt about his political morality. Disraeli had once said that Chamberlain "looked and spoke like a cheesemonger", and Balfour, giving us a telling insight into his own assumptions, commented to Lady Elcho, "Joe, though we all love him dearly, somehow does not absolutely or completely mix, does not form a chemical combination with us." When Lord Salisbury resigned the Premiership in 1902, it was not Chamberlain or the long-doomed Lord Randolph Churchill, but his nephew Balfour who, quietly, succeeded him.

Here it is not Balfour's political record that matters, not even his part in the diehard defence of the House of Lords and the privileged status of Ulster. What made it possible for contemporaries to feel confidence in him as Prime Minister was not his inherent intellectual qualities (which were unrivalled), nor his capacity for work. His colleagues and the party managers, even if not the body of backbenchers, understood what Queen Victoria had meant when she had declared herself, after an audience with him in 1896, "Much struck by Mr. Balfour's extreme fairness, impartiality and large-mindedness. He sees all sides of a question, is wonderfully generous in his feelings towards others, and very gentle and sweet-tempered." It is the measure of Edward VII's deficiency rather than that of his Prime Minister that the King found Balfour "always so vague" and preferring the "gay old dog" Campbell-Bannerman. Churchill was far more perceptive when he called Asquith "single-minded and good. Arthur [Balfour], on the contrary, is in his nature hard; he could be cruel....The difference between him and Asquith is that Arthur is wicked and moral, Asquith is good and immoral" (Blunt, *Diaries*, p. 692).

But Balfour's weaknesses of character and leadership were revealed in the crisis faced by the Conservative Party over Tariff Reform and the tactical questions that arose over the 1909 "People's Budget", the House of Lords crisis and the 1911 Parliament Act. Long before, Salisbury had told Margot Asquith, "You may think me vain, Mrs. Asquith, but as long as I am there, nothing will happen. I understand my Lords thoroughly; but when I go, mistakes will be made: the House of Lords will come into conflict with the Commons" (Margot Asquith, *Autobiography* (1920), p. 157). Balfour's devastating defeat at the 1905 election and the difficult situation of the Conservative Party led by 1910 to the BMG ("Balfour Must Go") campaign and his eventual resignation. Even then his conduct was impeccable. As Campbell-Bannerman had quipped in 1905, he was "like a general who, having given the command to his men to attack, found them attacking one another; when informed of this, he shrugs his shoulders and says that he can't help it if they *will* misunderstand his orders!" (Margot Asquith, *Autobiography*, p. 164). Instead of fighting and dividing the party, he left for Bad Gastein, and, before the House of Lords crisis reached its climax, decided to step down. He belonged too much to the patrician age of government to face any longer the rise of new men, adventurers, like F.E. Smith and Lord Northcliffe, whose standards he despised, or the demands of government for what he called "politicians and nothing but politicians, to work the political machine as professional politicians". At a party meeting in 1911, summoned to accept his abdication, he remained cheerful and serene. Waving aside the alleged unrest among his followers, which he could not admit to being "anything exceptional", he said that he had been told that there was a danger, as the years advanced, of petrification of the faculties. He confessed he had not, at sixty-three, observed these symptoms in himself, but no man was a good judge of the progress of his own senile decay, and he was grateful to those who had called his attention to the matter. So saying, he laid down the burden of party leadership, and retired from the forefront of active politics—until the 1914 war brought him back to office as an "elder statesman". As if to mark the need for a contrast in succession, the Conservatives turned to Bonar Law. Max Beerbohm symbolised the change of leadership in a cartoon showing, on one side, the old maestro, tall and elegant, with his violin under his arm. On the other side was drawn a sour-faced little man, beating a drum. Says Balfour, "What verve! What brio! and *what* an instrument!" He was the last of the gentleman politicians to hold the leadership of a major British political party, and George Wyndham gave his fall a sardonic epitaph: "He knows that there was once an ice age, and that there will be an ice age again."

Long after the days of Surtees, and his famous creation, Jorrocks, the most popular image of the gentleman was of a hunting squire, complete with horse. When Lady Warwick described the society of the shires, she wrote of "a small select aristocracy born booted and spurred to ride, and a large dim mass born saddled and bridled to be ridden" (a reflection unconsciously plagiarised twenty years later by a "colonial gentleman", Sir Godfrey Huggins, in his analysis of the relationship between black and white in Southern Rhodesia). All those who in Wilfrid Scawen Blunt's phrase felt "My horse a thing of wings, myself a god", hacking about the countryside, riding to hounds, or steeplechasing in the local point-to-point, found their exemplar in Henry Chaplin—the bucolic President of the Local Government Board. A great gambler and lover, he contested for years with Lord Hastings the affections of Lady Florence Paget, the "pocket Venus", and his extravagances eventually ruined his fortune, as that of his rival Hastings had been after the 1868 Derby. By the 1900s, he had become only slightly more sedate and, as Master of the Blakeney Hounds, found constant difficulty dividing his time between duties in the field and in the House of Commons. "During a debate or a Cabinet, he would draw little sketches of horses on official papers. When his presence as a minister was required at Question Time, he would have a special train waiting to take him wherever the hunt was to meet next morning. Somewhere between stations it would stop, Mr. Chaplin would emerge, in white breeches and scarlet coat, climb the embankment, and find his groom and horses waiting. Weighing 250 pounds, he was constantly in search of horses big and strong enough to carry him and frequently 'got to the bottom of several in one day' " (Tuchman, *The Proud Tower*, p. 24).

Once when the field was galloping towards a narrow gap, barred by an iron cage round a young tree, "there were shouts for a chopper or a knife, when down came the Squire, forty miles an hour, with his eyeglass in his eye seeing nothing but the opening in the hedge. There was no stopping him; neither did the tree do so, for his weight and that of his horse broke it off clean and away he went without an idea that the tree had even been there" (Deon George Lambton, *Men and Horses I Have Known*, p. 133).

Of course, the country gentry comprised more than latter-day Squire Osbaldstones or sporting politicians. But there was a commonly accepted picture, endorsed by Vita Sackville-West in her description of Lord Roehampton in *The Edwardians*:

> The only people whose company he really enjoyed were his trainer at Newmarket and the keeper of his Norfolk estate. In that company he could indulge himself in the only thing—apart from his wife—he recognised as beautiful. He would, of course, have shied mistrustfully away from the word; still he got a private satisfaction out of watching his fillies entering in the paddock, and his pheasants running on the outskirts of his woods. Standing there, with trainer or keeper, he would confine his remarks to the advantages that these animals or birds were likely to bring him. "A sporting chance for the Oaks", he would say; or "We ought to equal last year's bag. But what about those damn foxes?". Nevertheless, those who appreciate the Lords Roehampton of England will readily believe that the brief grunts and utterances to the trainer and the keeper represented but a tithe of the pleasure he actually absorbed from a day spent in the paddock or trampling across the acres. Incapable though he was of saying so, he liked the green meadow with white posts, the sensitive foals, the marriage of wood and cornfield, the turnip leaves holding the rain. He got a dumb satisfaction out of these things which it never occurred to him to confide to anybody.

Others, however, were far more articulate, literate and intellectually unconventional. Wilfrid Scawen Blunt, squire of two estates in Sussex, Crabbet Park and Newtimber, had already reached the age of sixty when Queen Victoria died, but the travels which had made him a legend, even when set against those of great nineteenth-century explorers such as Burton or Speke, were by no means over then. After a tempestuous career in the Diplomatic Service, Blunt had begun seriously to travel, first through the remoter parts of Europe, the Balkans and Spain (where he performed skilfully as a bullfighter), then to North Africa, Turkey, Mesopotamia and the wastes of central Arabia. In the 1880s he had taken up vigorously the cause of Egyptian nationalism, protested against the British bombardment of Alexandria, and criticised, for years, the subsequent administration of Lord Cromer. Even more outrageous to public opinion, he had helped to defend the captured nationalist leader, Arabi Pasha, to the tune of £3,000 of his own money. He joined for a time Lord Randolph Churchill's Tory Democrats, and by the turn of the century he had become the *enfant terrible* of politics and diplomacy. Lord Houghton once said of him, "the fellow knows he has a handsome head, and he wants it to be seen on Temple Bar!" Blunt upheld the Irish Land League, and endured philosophically two months in jail, picking oakum, for protesting in favour of the right of free demonstration in Ireland. Quite unmellowed by the passing of decades, he thundered against British atrocities in India and in the Middle East in the 1900s, and even (and most unpopular of all) criticised the hanging of Roger Casement, for high treason, in 1916.

The Edwardian years opened with Blunt shipwrecked, among a horde of pilgrims, off the coast of Egypt, and until 1907 he continued to spend part of each year in that country, among his friends. To Newtimber he invited a wide range of personalities, including foreign dignitaries; the strange lyric poet Francis Thomson, whom he did much to protect and encourage; eccentric travellers such as Auberon Herbert; Churchill, a a perennial friend of his; and Maurice Baring, most charming of Edwardian diplomats and authors. High politics blended easily with rural pastimes and the genial pleasure of the "Crabbet Club", whose members had to resign and seek re-election if and when they came bishops, viceroys or ambassadors, or if they married, and whose aims were simply "to play lawn tennis, the piano, the fool and other instruments of gaiety".

But behind the gaiety, wit and intellectual brilliance of the cohorts he summoned to Newtimber, Blunt brooded over the threatening changes taking place, at home and abroad. He saw the great European war, in embryo, at the time of the Dreyfus case in 1898: "this is an event of great significance, for it means that in France as in Germany and Russia, militarism reigns supreme. It will be so in England, too, before many years are over, and then goodbye to liberty of any kind. If the nations of Europe will only cut each other's throats in a Thirty Years' war there might be some hope for the world, but they are too cowardly for that. All they dare do is to swagger hideously and talk about their Honour" (*Diaries*, p. 289).

Worse, the new century appeared in nightmare proportions: "All the nations of Europe are making the same hell upon earth in China, massacring and pillaging and raping in the captive cities as outrageously as in the Middle Ages. The Emperor of

Germany gives the word for slaughter and the Pope looks on and approves. In South Africa our troops are burning farms under Kitchener's command, and the Queen and the two Houses of Parliament and the bench of Bishops thank God publicly and vote money for the work. The Americans are spending fifty millions a year on slaughtering the Phillipinos; the King of the Belgians has invested his whole fortune on the Congo, where he is brutalizing the negroes to fill his pockets. The French and Italians at the moment are playing a less prominent part in the slaughter, but their inactivity grieves them. The whole white race is revelling openly in violence, as though it had never pretended to be Christian. God's equal curse be on them all" (*Diaries*, pp. 375–6).

At the time Blunt wrote this he was a member of a passing generation; but in the rising generation was a person, then an undergraduate at Balliol, who was every bit as strikingly individual as Blunt himself. Of Aubrey Herbert, squire of the Pixton estate in Somerset, Sir Lawrence Jones wrote, "With a small close-cropped bullet head, myopic eyes, a slight unathletic figure, drooping uncertain hands, a faintly wizened face, and untidy, inappropriate clothes, Aubrey gave one no hint, to one seeing him for the first time, of his extraordinary physical capacities. Short-sighted almost to blindness, he was the tough and dare-devil scaler of walls and precipices. There are some tall houses in King Edwards Street at Oxford, at which I still look up with a trembling of the knees when I remember how Aubrey traversed the face of them, forty feet up, with finger holds alone and a swing from ledge to ledge. But these bodily feats were by-play. Aubrey 'lived in high romance'. Every girl was a poem to him, and to most of them he wrote one. He simmered and bubbled and boiled over with enthusiasm. It might be Garibaldi, or Turkish baths, or a liqueur called Tangerino, or his brigand friends in Albania, or the bloody Bismark—his hates were as ardent as his loves—and whatever Aubrey had in his head he made at least the phrase, sometimes an epigram, often some verses. He delighted in words as some women in jewels, but he did not keep them, as most jewels are kept, for great occasions. Aubrey settling in his unbelievable hot bath at Pixton after shooting, would be lavish with his phrases, to myself waiting my turn in a bath-towel, as to his favourite girl at a dinner party. All his thoughts were open and at our service; he had no reserves with those he liked; and because his mind was singularly original and fertile, as well as romantic, there was no resisting the charm of his conversation. His activities were abreast of his mighty imagination. He became the confident of Young Turks and the hero of Albanian chieftains. One of these, whose life Aubrey had saved in some vendetta, insisted on becoming his benefactor's body servant—'Great man though I am in my own country'. He stood behind Aubrey at pheasant shoots, in kilt and embroidered jacket, and disconcerted even his master by cutting off the heads of fallen birds with a scimitar-like weapon he carried in his belt" (*An Edwardian Youth*, pp. 44–5).

Herbert had the great gift of picking up foreign languages, even tribal dialects, in a matter of weeks, and, though he travelled simply for fun or adventure, was later able to draw on his experience to effect in the House of Commons. But it was principally against the classic backcloth of Pixton that his friends remembered him:

"Later on, at midnight, muffled and greatcoated, the Balliol eleven sat on the Pixton lawn, the moon now small and silver and sailing high and the hard frost white on grass and twig; and drank hot mulled claret, heavily spiced. It was little wonder that we burst into song outside the quiet shuttered house. A cock pheasant protested, crowing from the wood that fell away below us. I had probably missed him earlier on, but I could not care" (*An Edwardian Youth* (1956), p. 49).

One of the most eccentric of all the gentlemen of the Edwardian period was Sir George Sitwell, squire of Renishaw (a Yorkshire estate held by the Sitwells for 700 years), who resembled in some ways those eighteenth-century scientifically-inclined gentlemen who had formed such famous bodies as the Lunar Society of Birmingham. Irascible and unpredictable to his children, who when at home sometimes feigned illness to avoid implication in his wilder eccentricities, he sent his sons letters "which rained in by every post on subjects ranging from the composition of the atom to the best empirical method of cutting your toe nails....'It is dangerous for you', he used to point out, 'to lose touch with me for a single day. You never know when you may not need the benefit of my experience and advice.'." But this experience often was negligible, as his son Osbert made clear.

"Now a year or two before the war my father had started to farm in a small way, and had latterly expanded the scope of his operations, into which he had thrown himself with a kind of fury. Before long the area had amounted to no less than two thousand acres, and he had founded a company, of which, since some of the land it worked belonged to me, I had been made a director .... He started, of course, with no knowledge of agriculture, but he was keen on fault-finding. I was away, and in the circumstances this new occupation afforded him the fullest outlet for it. He drove about, balanced on his British-Museum air-cushion in a pony cart—a tub, smartly painted in green and yellow, and drawn by a skewbald pony— criticising to the top of his bent. Fortunately, Maynard Hollingworth, who made the plans and carried them out, was an expert in farming; and on his advice my father had particularly specialised in pigs and potatoes. I have mentioned that recently, where certain ideas, not political or aesthetic were concerned, he had rather unexpectedly shown himself liable to be very easily influenced by the press. Thus in the years immediately preceding 1914, he had become an enthusiastic advocate of Standard Bread and paper-bag cookery, when these two objects or ideals were written up in rival daily papers. It happened that lately a correspondence had been published in *The Times*, concerning the possible benefits to be derived from reviving the medieval habit of payment in kind. My father had thoroughly enjoyed, and pondered on, these letters, and had determined that his approval of ancient ways should find a practical application. He had returned to Renishaw in January 1915, and late that month or early in February had sent a letter to my brother's housemaster at Eton, to intimate that, having been particularly hard hit by the war, he could not afford to pay the usual fees at the end of the term in money, but instead would deliver to their value pigs and potatoes. The housemaster was, it can be imagined, perturbed by the novelty of the suggestion and when the story transpired it created much interest" (*Three Lions in a Grove*, pp. 889).

Some of Sitwell's political and artistic views caricature the gruff, Blimpish backwoodsman, yet he restored with sensitivity and skill the ancient castle of Montegufoni near Florence, and spent his last years there in an assiduous sort of Indian summer.

"Henry would have to call my father at five and bring him breakfast not long afterwards. My father would then read *The Times* of two days before, and other journals and letters, till seven, when he would get up. At eight he would go round the Castle in detail, telling all the workmen to stop what they were doing, and do something else instead. Then he would consider the garden, interfere with the gardeners, and go back to write in his room, probably various severe letters. If he intended a letter to be really disagreeable, he would pen it many times, at each correction infusing into it a fresh but icy venom. After this fashion he would both perfect it, and also be able to keep a copy. Now, while we watch, for example, he must pen one so as to give his English lawyers 'a rap over the knuckles', he must dispute the item 4s. 8d. in a London chemist's bill, write to the tailor on the subject of turn-up trousers, forward hints on Florentine medieval banking to Messrs. Coutts (who would be sure to be interested), tell Hollingworth how to plant beech-trees, and he must instruct the firm from which he obtained cigarettes on divers points, such as that they used the wrong kind of paper for rolling. He must also remember to enter notes in his notebook" (Osbert Sitwell, *Laughter in the Next Room*, p. 285).

One of the distinctions between the Edwardian upper class and the aristocracies of Europe lay in the emphasis given to military education. While the officer corps of the British, like those of the German, French, Polish and Russian armies, consisted very largely of the well born, the British military élite wielded little of the power that it did in those other societies, and the education provided at the Royal Military Academy at Sandhurst in no way compared with that provided at the French military school of St Cyr (attendance at which conferred considerable social prestige) or at any of the German military academies (which all young German men were compelled to attend). There was no English equivalent of the practice of duelling at German universities, and English gentlemen regarded with a certain distaste the scarred cheeks which their German counterparts regarded as positive proof of manhood and nobility. Indeed, for many Englishmen, the Army provided merely a entertaining interlude between school and a return to civilian life.

When Lady Randolph Churchill sent the Prince of Wales a copy of her son Winston's account of military service on the North-West Frontier of India, *The Malakand Field Force*, the Prince replied, congratulating the young officer, "Everyone is reading it, and I only hear it spoken of with praise. Having now seen active service, you will wish to see more, and have as great a chance I am sure of winning the VC as Fincastle had; I hope you will not follow the example of the latter, who I regret to say intends leaving the Army in order to go into Parliament.

You have plenty of time before you, and should certainly stick to the Army before adding MP after your name."

The Prince was to be disappointed, for within two years Churchill had reached the House of Commons—to return to military life only for a brief period in the First World War. But those who made the Army a career might well have modelled their dreams on the careers of General Sir John French and Colonel Douglas Haig.

Of the two, French followed the more conventional pattern. Son of a naval officer, a justice of the peace and Deputy Lieutenant of Kent, he soon abandoned the Navy for the Army and served as a subaltern of Hussars in the 1870s, rising rapidly to major. At this stage, despite seeing some active service, his principal pursuits were riding and polo, and he never bothered to attempt the Staff College examination. He served with Sir Garnet Wolseley at Khartoum; at the age of thirty-six, after a mere nineteen years in the Army, became commander of the Nineteenth Hussars; but, in the 1890s, after serving in India, was retired on half pay—the fate of many able officers, whose promotion was blocked by the heavy ranks of aged generals. Recovered from idleness by General Redvers Buller, he jumped to Assistant Adjutant General at the War Office, where he produced the standard *Cavalry Manual*; he then commanded the First Cavalry Brigade in the South African War, and in 1902 became a major general.

For French, as for Haig, who was one of his foremost staff officers, the Boer War came as salvation, projecting the successful commanders into posts where they could take advantage of the movement for Army reform—begun by Broderick, and carried through, in the face of entrenched opposition, by Haldane, Secretary of State for War after 1906. But French, as Commander-in-Chief at Aldershot, then, from 1912, as Chief of the Imperial General Staff (CIGS), played an equivocal part: he pushed through the Haldane reforms but refused to budge over the role of cavalry in modern warfare. Caught between tradition and daring innovation, imprisoned by assumptions about the leadership of an élite qualified by birth and experience rather than by education, the future Commander of the British Expeditionary Force in 1914 seemed unable to accept, as Haig did, the implications of living in the twentieth century. Conservative, not merely over the question of cavalry, he lamentably failed to follow the Allied plan of action in 1914–15 and his career foundered in recrimination and failure.

Much of this ambiguity had already been exposed in March 1914 over the so-called "mutiny" of officers at the Curragh, the principal military station in Ireland. When it became clear that the Asquith government intended to force through Home Rule for Ireland, despite the open resistance of Ulster, many of these officers became deeply disturbed at the prospect of having to enforce, if necessary with violence, the submission of people to whom they felt far closer than they did to the southern Irish. With crass stupidity this question was put directly to the Third Cavalry Brigade; the commanding officer and fifty-seven others replied that they would rather resign. French, as CIGS, put his name to a pledge, drafted by Colonel Seeley, the Secretary for War, that British officers would not be so employed. Then the political storm broke: Asquith repudiated the pledge, and Seeley and French were forced to resign.

French had been caught defending the military caste against the impossible demands of the politicans; but he was held in such esteem that his resignation made no difference to his preferment when the real war came. Haig, too, was deeply torn by conflicting loyalties: on the day French resigned he wrote in his diary, "At 12 o'clock held meeting of [Chiefs of Staff] of Divisions and Brigades. I pointed out the danger of disruption in Army and Empire and begged them to induce regimental officers to give up dabbling in politics." But, he continued, with profound ambiguity, "we were all united to do anything short of coercing our fellow citizens who have done no wrong" (*The Private Papers of Douglas Haig, 1914–1918*, (1952), ed. Robert Blake).

In almost every other way, Haig was the reverse of French. Often called "the educated soldier" (itself a sufficiently pointed distinction), he devoted his entire energies and intellect to a military career, leaving little time for private life. He came from an ancient Border family with an estate at Bemersyde, where little had changed since in the thirteenth century Thomas the Rhymer had written,

> Tide what may, whate'er betide
> Haig shall be Haig of Bemersyde.

Son of a prominent whisky distiller, Douglas Haig was schooled, modestly enough, at Clifton and Brasenose, Oxford. At Sandhurst, he seemed aloof, uncommunicative, older than his colleagues, and unusual in having a university education; but he passed out first in order of merit, winning the Anson Memorial Sword. During nine years with the Seventh Hussars, he made a fine impression as a soldier and practically none as a regimental officer. Although he admitted to being "quite sorry" to leave for Staff College, he had achieved little distinction except at polo, at which he represented England against the United States.

Allenby, Plumer, Macdonagh, the best younger commanders of the First World War, were among his friends at Stafft College; but Haig was unique: delving always for fundamental principles of strategy and tactics on which to build his military practice. In this he emulated R.B. Haldane, his Edinburgh contemporary, later political master in the reformation of the British Army. Active service in the Nile campaign of 1899 and the Boer War gave him experience of that form of war of movement, based on railways and horse, which was to prove the grand illusion of warfare after 1914. Haig learnt almost too quickly, holding his cavalry in tight check, thinking of its long-term role, rather than loosing it like a pack of hounds after a fox. He criticised equally British gunners for their inaccuracy as compared with the Boer artillery, and British infantry for failing to operate in open formation against the sharpshooting guerillas. But Haig was much more than a goad of official incompetence: he carried part of the brunt during the unpopular latter part of the war—the period of defence of the Cape, Kitchener's drives and the institution of concentration camps—and he returned, with the praise of French in his ears, ready to teach his cavalry the use of rifles rather than lances. His austere philosophy set the new tone, which comes through in the advice he gave a young nephew in a letter written in 1901: "Don't let the lives of mediocrities about you deflect you from your determination to belong to the few who can command or guide or benefit our great Empire. Believe me, the reservoir of such men is not boundless. As our Empire grows, so there is a greater demand for them, and it behoves everyone to do his little and try and qualify for as high a position as possible. It is not ambition. This is *duty*" (John Terraine, *Douglas Haig* (1963), p. 30).

To Edwardian observers, Haig was the reformer *par excellence*. He served under Kitchener, during the remodelling of the ramshackle Indian Army after 1903, he instituted "staff rides", or tactical training without troops, and he wrote an influential manual, *Cavalry Studies*. Having once been aide-de-camp to the King, it was appropriate that he should marry one of Queen Alexandra's Maids of Honour; and in due course he became a major general—the coming man. The Liberal landslide of 1906 gave him the chance, and he became one of the five men, in the Army and the War Office, who carried out Haldane's reforms: the creation of the Expeditionary Force and, as the second line of reserve, the Territorial Army. Haig was Director of Military Training, but also within his purview came finance and military politics, a suitable introduction to the complexities of European, as opposed to colonial, welfare. He began to move far from the traditional attitudes to which he had been brought up. Preparing for war, he wrote in 1906, required "the whole resources of the nation to bring it to a successful end. Even if the proposed system costs more in peace, it should be inaugurated provided that it is more practical than war. The Swiss system seems to me to be exactly what is wanted— 'To root the army in the people' " (Terraine, *Douglas Haig*, p. 41).

At the same time, Haig helped to sweep away the leisured, idiosyncratic style of commander that had led to so much chaos in the Boer War. He sought a general acceptance for a unified system of military thinking and organisation, so that each officer would know that every other would act in concert with him (this had long been a characteristic of the German army). Brusquely, he forced through the Army Council the classic *Field Service Regulations*—to the detriment of the part-timer and the encouragement of professional soldiers. He was already leader of the group of whom Haldane enthused in 1907, "The men one comes across, the new school of young officers, entitled to the appellation of men of science just as much as engineers or chemists, were to me a revelation; and the whole question of the organisation of the army is fraught with an interest which, I think, is not behind that of the study of any other scientific problem. The new school of officers has arisen since the South African war, a thinking school of officers, who desire to see the full efficiency which comes from new organisation and no surplus energy running to waste" (Terraine, *Douglas Haig*, p. 41).

For all his lack of ability to communicate on a private level, and the superficiality of his knowledge of practically every aspect of human life outside the military sphere, Haig, when he took up the command of the First and Second Infantry Divisions and the First Cavalry Brigade (nucleus of the British Expeditionary Force) at Aldershot in 1913, to prepare them for the coming struggle, seemed the very model of the military leader. John Charteris, then serving on his staff, described as follows Haig's meticulous way of life.

"Haig set himself to the just admixture of the life of a serving officer and a country gentleman. His private means, though not great, were sufficient to enable him to meet the demands on his income. He entertained frequently, but not extravagantly ... golf replaced polo as his means of physical exercise. His attack on the citadel of golf was characteristic. He spared no pains to conquer its difficulties. He was determined to succeed. He took lessons from the professional. He practiced assiduously. Each stroke was treated as a separate, all-important problem .... The days passed evenly. The early hours of the morning he spent on horseback, supervising the training of the units of his command: when the inspection was over, he would indulge in a sharp gallop across country and took a mischievous pleasure in evading the staff officer and escort that accompanied him ... at 11 o'clock he reached his office at army headquarters and worked there until lunch time. From lunch to tea was play time—either golf or tennis as the days grew warmer—or sometimes he preferred the role of onlooker and watched the games of some section of the command. After tea two hours were devoted to reading, and this brought his day's work to a close" (Terraine, *Douglas Haig*, pp. 51–2).

Beyond the upper echelons of Army regiments, the more noted benefices of the Church, and a small number of posts in public life, the opportunities for fitting employment had widened since the later nineteenth century, when a writer could point to "the difficulty which there is in these days of finding employment in England for the numbers of young men who are growing up and who wish to earn their livelihood here as gentlemen. Every profession is overstaffed, and there are more young men (yes and capable, well-educated men) than there are places for them to fill" (Anon, *Quite a Gentleman*, 1878).

One field of public service beyond reproach offered itself to a handful of aspirants at court, among whom was Sir Frederick Ponsonby, first Lord Syonby, who rose to become Keeper of His Majesty's Privy Purse under George V, having spent some forty years in the royal service.

Ponsonby was one of the three sons of General Sir Henry Ponsonby, who had been for a short time Private Secretary to Queen Victoria. Having been educated at Eton, he received a commission in the Duke of Cornwall's Light Infantry, later transferring to the Grenadier Gueards. During service in India he served as aide-de-camp to the Viceroy in 1893–4, and then became equerry, Assistant Keeper of the Privy Purse and Assistant Private Secretary to Queen Victoria. All his life he was "a courtier to his finger tips". "His knowledge of what was done and not done, worn or not worn, said or left unsaid, was exact and comprehensive; no minor slip in etiquette or uniform escaped his notice. Anyone guilty of a breach of convention he would speak of disdainfully as 'the fellow'!" (Ponsonby, *Recollections of Three Reigns* (1951), p. xi).

In his memoirs, Ponsonby gives an intriguing insight into his training and experience as a young gentleman of the mid and late nineteenth century: "My youth was no more idiotic than most of my contemporaries; it was merely uneventful and uninteresting. 'Dans ma plus bête jeunesse', as Marcel Prevost puts it, I always followed the line of least resistance and took a great deal of trouble to be as like the other boys as possible, avoiding the things 'that were not done'."

Of course, Ponsonby shared his childhood with those who became important figures in later life. Baldwin was at Hawtrey's preparatory school with him, and as a boy he was brought into contact with Gladstone, Disraeli, Salisbury, Harcourt and others. Gladstone gave him the benefit of his views on the quantity of certain syllables in Horace; Disraeli offered a cynical comment on the amount of geographic knowledge that a British Prime Minister was supposed to possess. But what he thought more important was his sporting career. Given a choice between his examination for Sandhurst and the chance of rowing in the Eton eight at Henley, he unhesitatingly chose the latter (to such had the ideals of Arnold come!), but his father quashed the choice. Ponsonby comments that "My father who, not being an old Etonian, knew nothing of the glories of being in the Eton eight ... considered the examination for Sandhurst more important." In fact Ponsonby failed the examination ("only a few places below the last successful candidate"), but another half at Eton did the trick, and he subsequently passed into Sandhurst.

After graduation came the problem of finding a suitable regiment. Since the Grenadiers had no vacancy, he was fortunate to find an "ideal place" in the Forty-Sixth Regiment of Foot. Nothing could have been better, since the regiment had almost no men at the time, but did boast a fine mess, a band and some "charming officers". Ponsonby could confine his regimental duties to attendance one day of the week at some parade, having the rest to himself.

"It was the custom for all officers off duty to go for a walk round Plymouth every afternoon, and have a drink at every opportunity. I used to go with the youngest lot; we had a drink on the pier, then went to the Grand Hotel for a second drink, then to another hotel for a third, then to the Bodega for oysters and Chablis, and finally back to the officers' mess where we had a sherry and bitters."

Such activities proved fairly costly, so Ponsonby took up riding and hunting. He suffered a series of amusing but unfortunate experiences with a horse that he got for a bargain at Tattersalls, but which proved to be uncontrollable and wild. Then he was introduced to that other archetypal pursuit of the young gentleman—gambling. This proved even more costly than drinking and led to his decision to go to India, since "the prospect of being able to live in India on my pay offered the surest method of getting straight". Given his own description of his activities, this was indeed a wise decision. During Ascot week "It was the usual custom to gamble very heavily", and after one session of baccarat he found himself some £500 down on the evening's play. India, however, provided a gentleman's life without the financial temptations to be found in London. "Living on my wage, I could afford to keep two polo-ponies, a pony-cart, and two Indian servants, which, in England, would have been quite out of the question." Moreover, the workload was little greater, since the bulk of an adjutant's labours were performed by the private and military secretaries of the Viceroy.

It is hardly surprising that he was not delighted to receive the summons from

Queen Victoria to return to England to serve as one of her equerries. He tried to refuse, and was duly overruled. Thinking over the appointment in later life, Ponsonby could find little to recommend himself, apart from the fact that he had once acted in a French play at Osborne, and the Queen apparently thought this would be useful to her on any visits to France; but there was also his Indian experience, which enabled him, among other things, to unmask one of the more bogus of the Queen's retinue.

Apart from such intrigues, Ponsonby found the life of an equerry easy enough. Formal duties were slight, and the only real work consisted in waiting on the Queen on her excursions and being available to appear at the royal dinner table when summoned. However, Ponsonby's general background had fitted him well for what duties he was expected to fulfil, such as watching out for suspicious visitors or settling domestic disputes within the Household. True, he once arranged for plain-clothes police to watch over someone who turned out to be an eminent sculptor from Berlin—but then an English gentleman was trained to recognise his fellows, not foreign artists, who might easily turn out to be anarchists or lunatics. There were delicate moments when court protocol seemed endangered, trifling enough perhaps to the uninitiated, but felt most sensitively by a monarch as punctilious as Edward VII. By virtue of his background, Ponsonby was perfectly suited to take on difficult assignments—such as amusing the Duc de Nemours as he waited for an audience with the Queen, preventing a brawl from taking place between two antagonistic foreign diplomats, or sympathising tactfully with the sentiments of the Khedive of Egypt, who attacked the effect of Lord Cromer's reforms on the Egyptian aristocracy. "We have an aristocracy", the Khedive said, "as you have yours, and it is galling to see the heads of old families who have been there for hundreds of years ignored and trampled on."

As Assistant Private Secretary, between the end of the Boer War and the outbreak of the First World War, Ponsonby devoted himself to maintaining the dignity of the throne, both the ceremonial which guarded it, and publicity which ensured its popularity. As George V was to find, "On all social problems and matters of etiquette he was the court of first instance and the court of final appeal. His knowledge of Germany was invaluable. His resource, his conversational gifts, his faultless manners, adorned and sweetened life in the royal circle."

In case it should be thought that a courtier's life suited the indolent, Ponsonby recalled in his memoirs a day on a visit with the King to Portugal in 1903: "One of the most tiring I have ever spent in my life, for I had to stand for practically the whole day. In the morning the King received addresses in the Museum at the Geographical Society and we all stood behind him on a platform. After luncheon we went to see pigeon shooting in the garden which lasted from 2 to 5. According to the etiquette, no one was allowed to sit except the two Kings, and we had to stand in an enclosure in the hot sun, bored to death with the competition. The King of Portugal was most anxious to win, but only got third prize although he was a wonderful shot. After 5 we went to tea with the Queen Mother, but there again it was contrary to etiquette to sit and we had therefore to stand for an hour. We got back to our rooms soon after six, and as the banquet in full uniform took place at 6.30 we only just had time to dress. There were a hundred people at the banquet, and it seemed very well done, but we hardly had time to drink our coffee before we were hurried off to a gala performance at the opera. The Royal Box was in the centre of the house, and contained only three huge gilt chairs for the two Kings and the Queen Mother, and I could hardly believe my ears when I was told that according to the etiquette we all had to stand throughout the performance. I had already stood for about four hours in the afternoon and an hour in the morning and I was expected to enjoy the performance dolled up in uniform and standing to attention. I stood it for an hour and twenty minutes and then I told Lambton that I really could not stand any more and he agreed to retire quietly to the box and go and sit down outside somewhere, but when we tried to slip out quietly, the Portuguese thought we were being polite and were putting them in front of us. They said 'Please, please' and insisted on our remaining in the front row. We were so much taller than them that it was impossible to escape attention" (*Recollections of Three Reigns*, p. 156).

But Ponsonby's service went beyond the trivia of court. As a young equerry he had been reprimanded by Queen Victoria for being outspoken and expressing views which she did not wish to hear. With her son his advice proved more acceptable. Ponsonby was able to speak "man to man" and tell the King things which it would have been harder, in the best of circumstances, to say to a female sovereign. He could, in 1903, rephrase the King's indignant reply to a minister who had advised against a visit to the Pope, and thereby prevent a resignation; or deal circumspectly with "a beautiful lady from the demi-monde of Vienna, who wanted to have the honour of sleeping with the King. On being told this was out of the question, she said if it came to the worst she could sleep with me so that she should not waste the money spent on her ticket. But I told her to look elsewhere for a bed." Of more substance, he was the channel Admiral "Jackie" Fisher used to communicate to the King his outspoken views on naval reforms, and from time to time he interjected his own sensible opinions. On foreign tours, he usually acted as a sort of private press officer to the King, and on the King's most important visit abroad, to Paris in 1903, arranged for much of the ceremonial which accompanied this excursion into foreign affairs. At the court of Denmark he alone discovered how to amuse the aged King, by reminiscing of the events of the 1840s, and at the end, it was he, the self-effacing courtier, to whom Queen Alexandra confided after the King's death: "She had been turned to stone, unable to cry, unable to grasp the meaning of it all ... she would like to go and hide in the country."

Grave or amusing as occasion demanded, brave enough to face the old King's rage when he criticised the meagre nature of a gift for a French host, quick thinking, and, above all, dedicated to the perfect functioning of the monarchy, Ponsonby's public service linked the gentlemanly ideal with its most obvious protagonist, the King.

CHAPTER TWO

Angles of Vision

Edwardian society gave foremost place to three ideal types: King, soldier and gentleman politician. But to describe their careers and attributes is not necessarily to discover the indefinable thing, which was neither money, power nor status, but a blend of all three—a powerful chemical, colouring vast areas of experience. What was it that Europeans avidly copied, that Americans envied, for which Englishmen competed obsessively, and that in 1914 caused Max Beerbohm to sigh, "And oh for those old civilized and characterful days! They wring one's heart. But it's well to have lived in them"?

The view from America, and in particular from the New England states, compounded nostalgia with a subtle and often critical insight, as, to use Henry James's phrase, a host of "passionate pilgrims" invaded Europe and Britain in the late nineteenth and early twentieth centuries in a quest for history and culture, against which to measure their own Americanness, as well as for the more obvious gratifications to be found in a civilised and complex European society. They found many similarities between England and their own world, of course, and links of political sympathy dating back to the American Civil War in the 1860s, especially if they were Northerners, looking to the English liberal upper class. But, whatever the attractions of Paris, Berlin or Rome, wealthy Americans launched themselves with greater assurance on the London stage, feeling in English society a kinship with their own extravagant plutocracy. Much of what the sociologist Thorstein Veblen criticised in American life could equally be indicted across the Atlantic: conspicuous consumption and waste characterised the existence of the leisured class, elaborate ritual their simplest daily routine, and cosseting by a hierarchy of servants their contacts with the outside world. Just as Burke and Debrett assigned each to his station, so did the *Social Register* recording the *Mayflower* descent and part in the

Revolution of the original 400 families (so called because Mrs William Aster had found place for only that number in her ballroom for a celebrated party in 1892); and its editors had to contend with extravagant claims and the pretensions of those whose pinnacle of desire lay in invitation to the Philadelphia Assembly.

The novelist Henry James devoted most of his life to the interpretation of America and Americans against this British and European background, and spent his last twenty years in England, from 1898 at Rye in Sussex, where he played host to men like Edmund Gosse, A.C. Benson, Wilfrid Blunt, Maurice Baring and Hugh Walpole. As early as 1870, he had seen that "the latent preparedness of the American mind even for the most characteristic features of English life was a matter I meanwhile failed to get to the bottom of. The roots of it are indeed so deeply buried in the soil of our early culture that, without some great upheaval of feeling, we are at a loss to say exactly when and where and how it begins" (*The Reverberator*, 1908 edition, p.301). As time passed, however, and as he developed American characters in sympathy or in conflict with British and European society, in order to understand their essential Americanness, he expanded his vision of those societies. "Morally and physiologically", he wrote of England, "it is a denser air than ours. We seem loosely hung together at home, as compared with the English" (*English Hours*, 1908 edition, p.60).

James saw how the Americans' drive for worldly acquisition, their connoisseurship, contrasted with the English habit of bland detachment from material objects; likewise their vigour, flexibility and freedom from convention ran counter to what he saw as English closed formality, preciseness of mind, and stilted inability to comprehend, forgive, or forget prejudices. The dream many Americans possessed, of restoring the wilted vigour of the Old World, faded when confronted by its intricate mannered texture (the experience of the Verver family in James's *The Golden Bowl* typifies this).

In the unravelling of American themes, James penetrated deeply the veil of manners and morality in English upper-class life. Layer upon layer of documentary fiction builds up into an anatomy almost etymological in its approach to the minutiae of conversation, habit and convention. *The Sacred Fount*, as subtle a comedy of manners as Proust or Powell could write, shows a country house, circa 1900, with the weekend party playing an elaborate and increasingly fantastic charade, a social and sexual game seen at once from many angles, by an outsider aware not only of the pattern underlying the game, but also of the portents and dangers inherent in the formal comedy.

Somewhat earlier, in "The Real Thing", written in 1893, James had pinpointed an upper-class couple, in reduced circumstances, used by a magazine illustrator as models of urbane distinction, and then discarded because their appearance discounted variety:

It was in their faces, the blankness, the deep intellectual repose of the twenty years of country house visiting which had given them pleasant intonations ... I could see the rich coverts the major had helped to shoot and the wonderful garments in which, late at night, he had repaired to the smoking room to talk about them. I could imagine their leggings and waterproofs, their knowing tweeds and rugs, their rolls of sticks and cases of tackle and neat umbrellas; and I could evoke the exact appearance of their servants and the compact variety of their luggage on the platforms of country stations.

But, sadly, they were "the real thing, but always the same thing".

This theme of sterility recurs: Lord Mellifont (modelled on the painter Lord Leighton) in *The Private Life* really exists only in one— a public— dimension, even when alone with his wife. In *The Tragic Muse*, Lord Lambeth, a perfect specimen of his class, "repaid contemplation; tall, straight and strong, he was handsome as certain young Englishmen, and certain young Englishmen alone, are handsome; with a perfect finish of feature and a visible repose of mind, accessibility to questions ... it was not that he looked stupid; it was only that his perceptions didn't show in his face for restless or his imagination for imitable".

Perfectly adapted to the formal world they lived in, dry of wit, precise of thought, James's Englishmen often stand as the antithesis of his relaxed, shrewdly humorous, easy-going Americans. Thus Mr Carteret, almost the stereotype of the English gentleman politician, wealthy and authoritative:

Nick was always struck with the rare simplicity—it came out in his countenance—of one who had lived so long and seen so much of affairs that drew forth the passions and perversities of men .... It was as if experience, though coming to him in abundance, had dealt with him so clean-handedly as to leave no stain, and had moreover never provoked him to any general reflection. He had never proceeded in any ironic way from the particular to the general; certainly he had never made a reflection upon anything so unparliamentary as life. He would have questioned the taste of such an extravagance and if he had encountered it on the part of another have regarded it as an imported foreign toy with the uses of which he was unacquainted. Life, for him, was a purely practical function, not a question of more or less showy phrasing. It must be added that he had to Nick's perception his variations—his back windows opening into grounds more private. That was visible from the way his eyes grew cold and his whole polite face rather austere when he listened to anything he didn't agree with or perhaps even understand; as if his modesty didn't in strictness forbid the suspicion that a thing he didn't understand would have a probability against it. At such times there was something rather deadly in the silence in which he simply waited with a lapse in his face, not helping his interlocuter out. (*The Tragic Muse*, vol. 1, pp. 260–1.)

After twenty years in such society, it is hardly surprising that Henry James found himself in an almost alien world on his return to America; or that he should have thrown himself into the war effort, on behalf of refugees, in 1914, and become a British citizen before his death two years later. Yet his profound affection for the

English way of life did not lead him to gloss over English prejudices and the hostility that the English felt towards Americans—demonstrated in, for instance, the *Times* editorial criticising the friends of the Prince of Wales as "American cattlemen and prize-fighters". Many believed, who also laughed at Salisbury's dictum, that America was the only society that had ever passed from barbarism to decadence without an intervening period of civilisation. Edgar Jepson recorded that in the 1900s he found endless amusement in the "pretentious smugness" with which "God's Own Countrymen" blended ridiculous moral sentiments with the practical philosophy of the bucket shop. As an example of this he used to quote Senator Albert J. Beveridge's uplifting tract *The Young Man and the World*, which began, "To be an American at the beginning of the twentieth century! Ponder over those eleven words ten minutes every day!", but then broke off to add, "Of course *your first duty is to make money*." Even the equable Lawrence Jones remarked acidly that only the United States could have provided a silver cup and a brass-band reception committee as tribute to the "brainy" running of a half-miler who had been disqualified for elbowing an Englishman off the track in the 1896 Olympic Games.

Brash society climbers inspired this distaste. Jones, after recording his astonishment on finding an apparently cultured visitor keener to have her daughter introduced to his aristocratic friends than to dine amongst intellectuals at the Randolph Hotel in Oxford, concluded, "beneath all her humours and high-mindedness she was a howling snob"; and Blunt testily remarked, of the sinking of the *Titanic* in 1912, "if any large number of human beings could be better spared than another, it would be just these American millionaires with their wealth and insolence" (*Diaries*, p.800).

Yet this limited perception did not prevent the acceptance of men like James himself or the civilised travellers from the East Coast, the Bostonians and Virginians, and did not hinder the forging of marital links between aristocratic British and rich American families. The objections to the Duke of Marlborough's wedding to Consuela Vanderbilt came from the girl herself, dragooned into it by her domineering father, and condemned to years of misery. Jennie Jerome's marriage to the Duke's younger brother, Lord Randolph Churchill, made her the cynosure of London society in the last years of the 19th century and conveyed, even on her brilliant husband, the distinction of originality.

After 1900, such marriages lost some of their note, it being taken for granted that the holder of a decaying estate might look for a transatlantic heiress much as his eighteenth-century ancestors had wooed bankers' or brewers' daughters. In some ways it is harder to explain the rush of English gentlemen to marry Gibson girls, who were not necessarily endowed with the money to make a marriage of convenience work. But the old antithesis between marrying for love and marrying for money was dissolving in any case as the carapace of attitudes towards sexual life cracked in Edwardian society.

Not all Englishmen were ungrateful for the American stimulus, nor patronising towards American achievements. Compton Mackenzie first visited New York in

1912, and succumbed at once.

"Here I am and I think New York is just the most wonderful event .... It seems to me like living in a set piece at a Brock's Benefit. It is amazingly romantic. Good God, why haven't they produced a great poet here during the last twenty years? The inspiration should be tremendous.

"This hotel is astonishing. My bedroom has a bathroom, a lavatory, and a luggage room. There is a kitchen on my floor. In fact there are no hotels in England" (*My Life and Times*, Octave 4, p.156).

Lionised as he was by the literary establishment and the New York Press Club, habituated to fashionable restaurants like Sherry's and Delmonico's, entranced by ragtime, and Caruso singing in Massenet's *Manon* at the Metropolitan Opera House, he wrote home, "New York becomes more and more adorable every moment. I meet nobody who is not completely charming, and my interviewers are kind to me .... I must spend several months here every year".

In the last decade in which a truly European society still existed, Britain formed a part of the continent in a cultural as well as a political sense. With closer affiliations there than in America, the British—the upper class at least—travelled regularly across the Channel, met European friends and made European marriages. Holidays at Marienbad, sporting rivalry, shooting and hunting acquaintance with the aristocracies of France, Italy, Germany and Russia contributed to an illusion, sedulously fostered by press concentration on the doings of kings and princes, that an internationalism of society could outweigh the crude disparities between nations and classes. The British upper-class were not alone in preferring to ignore the real Germany, springing from the factories of the Ruhr, just as they failed to acknowledge the real America, the brash moneyed businessmen, who came as tourists to view rather than as acolytes to drink at cultural springs.

There were exceptions: R.B. Haldane's profound understanding of the mainsprings of German philosophy and education; Douglas Haig's close observation of the German army; Wilfred Blunt's acute perception of the state of the Second Republic in France and the meaning of the Dreyfus case; and Maurice Baring's wide knowledge of Germany (having attended Heidelberg University in the 1890s) and Russia—notably, understanding of the significance of the Russo-Japanese war and the abortive revolution of 1906. But these were exceptions to a general assumption about the intrinsic superiority of all things British, whether plumbing, fiscal policy, or the standards of the Jockey Club. Edward Marsh, one of the most civilised of younger Edwardians, and later private secretary to Churchill, noted only one sight of interest in the whole of Berlin: "it is worthwhile to see the highest and final manifestation of any quality, and it would be impossible to beat the 'Hohenzollern Museum' as an expression of the *positive* quality of want of humour for which our language doesn't yield an appropriate name" (Christopher Hassall, *Edward Marsh, a Biography* (1967), p.104).

Travel does not necessarily broaden the mind, and it is questionable how many foreigners the British actually met in their annual peregrinations to German spas, French resorts like Deauville, Nice and Biarritz, the Italian lakes and the Bay of Naples. As C.F.G. Masterman noticed, in his critique of English society, villas which were not properly fitted up with *l'installation hygienique* did not let to English clients. Cocooned in a sort of ethical superiority, fortified with gold sovereigns, free (still) of tiresome restrictions like passports, the travelling English gentleman bore some resemblance to his celebrated, predatory ancestor, *Le milord anglais*.

The Europeans he met at home presented a certain social problem because no precise equivalent to the gentleman could be found in Europe—not even in Spain, where the concept of *hidalgia* was tied to the defence of honour in a way that had died out in eighteenth-century England. The Frenchman that a gentleman might meet could be a Comte or a Baron, the German a Graf, the Italian a Principe— while he himself had a status which he believed equal to any, though resting on nothing precise or tangible. Fortunately, Europeans active in London society were mostly drawn from the diplomatic corps, which made them a special case. It was a well-known "fact" that South American diplomats were boring and not really suitable company except when occasion demanded their presence. On the other hand, there were individuals who came to be very much part of the London scene—in particular Louis de Soveral, the Portuguese ambassador. Known as the "Blue Monkey" because of his size and incipient beard, Soveral was an intimate friend of Edward VII, and, admired for his wit, a frequent guest at parties and gatherings, where, it was said, "He made love to all the most beautiful women and all the nicest men were his friends" (Francis, Countess of Warwick, *Discretions*).Princess Daisy of Pless later wrote that Soveral's enthusiasm for social distractions had much to do with a burning ambition and diplomatic calculation. What she found unacceptable was that Soveral only had affairs with highly placed women: "Most wayfaring men can quite easily fall in love with 'a little milliner', a chorus girl or anything of that sort—but to aim always at society women is wrong" (*What I Left Unsaid*, p.206).

Given the preoccupation of the upper class with its own self-consciousness, it is hardly surprising that foreign observers found the Edwardian English dominated and even obsessed by the culture of the gentleman. The fact that this became a matter for envy and imitation tended to be blandly ascribed by Englishmen to the essential inferiority of all forms of life across the Channel; but its real explanation is found rather in the political and economic situation of Britain after a century of undisputed pre-eminence. The English had grown accustomed to admiration from abroad; and the flattery of imitation more than made up for uneasiness about the actual position of Britain in the world after 1900.

Conceit was inflated by the popular image of Britain as the greatest imperial power. It was the sincere conviction of Alfred Austin, the poet laureate, that heaven could best be conceived of as sitting in a garden while receiving a flow of telegrams announcing alternately a British victory by sea and a British victory by land. But the admiration was genuine enough: in France the aristocratic "Gratin" were anglophile in manners and customs. The Greffulhes and Breteuils were intimates of the Prince of Wales, *le betting* was the custom at Longchamps, *le Derby* was held at Chantilly and *le steeplechase* at Auteuil, and an unwanted member was *black-boulé* at the Jockey Club. Charles Haas, the original of Proust's Swann, had "Mr" engraved on his calling cards. When Lord Ribblesdale visited the Salon in Paris to view his portrait painted by John Singer Sargent, he was followed from room to room by admiring crowds who, recognising the subject, pointed out to each other in whispers, "Ce grand diable de milord anglais."

Imitation, however reluctant, afflicted almost all the continental aristocracies, with the possible exception of the Russians. "German noblemen relentlessly married English wives and put on tweeds and raglan coats, while in France the life of the haute monde centred upon the Jockey Club, whose members played polo, drank whisky and had their portraits painted in hunting pink by Helleu, the French equivalent of Sargent" (Tuchman, *The Proud Tower*, p.22).

In 1911, after German territorial aims had become only too clear, Wilfrid Blunt noted, on the basis of reports by Sir Frank Lascelles, the British ambassador in Berlin, "Kaiser Wilhelm's infatuation for Lord Lonsdale, whom he regarded as the most reliable of advisers about English things. Lonsdale had told the Kaiser once that he, Lonsdale, was in King Edward's black books on account of his being unwilling to give up the Kaiser's friendship. 'I told the King, however', said Lonsdale, 'that this I would not do. I was ready to lay down my life for the Crown, as my ancestors had done, but not to betray my friends'." Blunt added, pertinently, "This is considered a good joke" (*Diaries*, p.752).

But, as a sort of penalty for success in the later nineteenth century and relative decline in the twentieth (as Britain was rapidly overhauled in the economic sphere by Germany and the United States), came exposure to an unwelcome intrusion, the boastful, hustling vigour of Germans and Americans, which evoked a response at once patronising and resentful. The British upper class found itself on the receiving end of a cultural expansionism such as they had once brashly imposed on a reluctant Europe; and they liked it no more than had eighteenth-century Italians or Austrians. Unable to come to terms directly with the phenomenon, they castigated the crudeness of American speech, the unbearable boorishness of German businessmen, and the opulent wealth of both. Significantly, Henry James's late novel *The Ambassador* is set more in the European than the British context, and the images which surround Strether, yet another American pilgrim, are of suffocating extravagance, of wealth lying heavily, like the scent of musk, across the pages.

It can be argued that German feelings of inferiority and imperial deprivation led to uncritical assertion of the value of Germanic culture (far beyond the genuine merits appreciated by such Englishmen as Haldane) and, in so far as this affected the young Kaiser Wilhelm II, may even have contributed to the crises before the outbreak of war in 1914. Except at the level of serious academic or political studies, contacts between English and Germans were limited. While the Kaiser tried to imbue a sense of what he regarded as the more admirable side of English life into his countrymen—promoting the custom of afternoon tea, and encouraging promenades in the English Garden at Munich—German society remained very different in its rigid social divisions; and, when he personally intervened to nominate a Rhodes scholar to Oxford, the unfortunate student had the temerity to shoot a deer in Magdalen College park. Such misfortunes were given wide misinterpretation. But for an insight into the real differences which lay behind superficial imitation we should turn to the great German novelist Thomas Mann. In a short story "A Railway Accident," Mann describes the archetypal gentleman, about to board a train:

> He walks in his spats, very certain of himself; he has a cold face; his eyes regard things and people with sharpness. He is not affected with traveller's fever, that is clear to see, so ordinary a matter as departing on a journey is no adventure. He is at home in life, and has no fear of its institutions and power; of the power he is himself a part. He is, in a word, a gentleman ... he passes me in the corridor, and although he bumps into me, he does not say "Beg pardon!" A gentleman!

Not so different, one might think, from the English model. But once involved in action the character behaves quite differently. Asked for his ticket by the conductor, he flies into a violent rage and throws the ticket into the conductor's face. Worse still, when the train is involved in a minor accident, the gentleman, in spite of his position, is thrown into a complete panic. Having exerted himself only to protect his own safety, he cannot bring himself to abandon the veneer of privilege, even in the face of common misfortune. Forced to share his compartment with those removed from another part of the train, all he can do is to sit there and "growl and try to protest against communism".

On British eyes, these foreign-ground lenses fitted strangely. Their own angle of vision, with its multiple reflexes and velleities of meaning, seemed sufficient for any requirements; few thought to ask how narrow the angle was. The Edwardian upper class, like its pallid descendants, seems to have been obsessed with problems of definition, usually connected with buttressing the untitled state of gentleman against a tide of claimants. For the majority of the upper class, assured in the possession of birth, breeding and landed wealth, such questions of standards and status raised no difficulties, and might be amusing to toy with, as a form of party game. But after 1900, when perhaps a twentieth of the whole population aspired to live in a way that only a hundredth could, they were posed more and more frequently.

As the bounds of "society" widened and became more fluid, lines that had once been clear were obscured. More than one Edwardian commentator feared the eclipse of pre-war standards: E.J.C. Hearnshaw considered that there was no longer any place for the traditional gentry among "the crowd of smart and moneyed Medes, Persians, Elamites and Mesopotamians, New York dandies, Chicago belles and Hebrew money-lenders". Even if they did not share Hearnshaw's feeling of doom, or his anti-semitism, most of those concerned with such problems noted a profound difference in the social texture after 1900. Frances, Countess of Warwick, could write, "When I came out, social prestige meant something ... sometimes a rich manufacturer might be able to poke his nose in, but he soon caught it for his temerity." By 1914 the old distinctions had lost precision, and she regretted it. "The men I remember were at least 'gentlemen'—a term that today is almost an apology."

A handful survived who indulged neither Lady Warwick's nostalgia nor the easy criteria of the King. The "Incorruptibles", the strict, intensely class-conscious, long-established families still living in some ways very close to the eighteenth century, are summed up in Vita Sackville-West's novel *The Edwardians* as the Duchess of D and Lady L—who regarded any deviance from the norm of behaviour (such as Lady Roehampton's appearance, dressed up and on horseback, at a *public* pageant) as a sign of fatally bad breeding, if not of actual insanity.

> Self-elected, self-imposed, Lady L and the Duchess of D assumed certain responsibilities towards society, even though the times were changing; and never forgot that they had certain standards to maintain .... Their smiles or their frowns sufficed to admit or to banish. They were the last survivors of the old regime, and they had never departed by an inch from their original standards. Their arrogance was as magnificent as it was maddening. They refused even to be introduced to people whom most people would have given their eyes to know. Their insolence was intolerable—but they could not be ignored. Fashionableness went for nothing, compared with their hearse-like state. Brilliant though a social career might be, in the long run it was always brought up short against the wall of their severity .... Sylvia took comfort in the thought that soon they would die off, and that there was no-one of quite their calibre to take their place—those old incorruptibles, in their black lace and their diamonds, who could set their disapproval even upon the choice of the King.

If their standards had been the only ones, the upper class would have been reduced to a tithe of its members. A more practical rule of thumb had, however, been evolved in the later nineteenth century to take account (where families were not already ennobled) of both pedigree and the vital new element, changes in the tenure of land. There was no problem of definition of the peerage (though plenty of snobbery about recent creations) and Debrett's *Peerage* and Burke's *Peerage and Baronetage* served as encyclopaedias of rank, in the same sense as the Almanach de Gotha did in Europe. The scholarship assiduously developed by Horace Round, the College of Heralds and the Lyon King-at-Arms could be brought to bear on pedigrees to determine not only peerages but also armigerous status, and the palmy days of romantic heraldry and charlatanry of the mid-nineteenth century, when a seat in the House of Lords could be won through the dubious revival of an ancient title, such as the barony of Strabolgi, had gone. But, since the landed gentry did not comprise a caste or lesser nobility, yet regarded themselves equally part of the upper class, the judgements made in Burke's *Landed Gentry*, though scholarly, retained an element of personal opinion which, as the editor of the 1914 edition admitted, brought him a deal of acrimonious correspondence. Faced with "many thousands of correspondents" clamouring for inclusion, he was forced to defend himself against those excluded: "In these critical days vague tradition must give place to definite and ascertained fact."

Burke's *Peerage* had been founded in 1826, but the *Landed Gentry* first appeared in 1863, three years after Edward Walford's *County Families of the United Kingdom*, and it ran through twelve editions before the First World War. It concerned itself, in Ashworth Burke's words, exclusively with "that class in Society which ranks in importance next to the privileged order—the untitled county gentleman, a class, be it remembered, not one degree below the other, in antiquated descent, personal accomplishment and national usefulness". Keeping pace with the transfer of estates (which was at its height in the period leading up to, and in the years immediately following, the First World War), it expanded steadily, but without becoming simply a record of all families currently holding land. The editors took care to impose a decent delay on the admission of new families and insisted on tracing some sort of pedigree, at least back to the eighteenth century. Even so, the majority of the families in the 1914 edition could not trace their ancestry further back than the seventeenth century, and a mere tenth could trace their lineage back to the Middle Ages.

Other works of reference, such as *Who's Who* and its various county editions, extended their columns to notables and local worthies who by no means qualified as gentry; but they showed themselves careful with the badges of rank, particularly the style "esquire" (properly applied only to officers in the Army below the rank of captain, but used with less discrimination by the *County Families* of 1860). However, the major reference works, moving slowly and discreetly, avoided altogether the most delicate questions about the upper class. Already in the nineteenth century, a kind of prescriptive status had been established for members of certain professions. Education at public school and the old-established universities, principally Oxford and Cambridge, had become a basic social test by 1900; but it had also been accepted that men such as clergymen of the Church of England and barristers were to be presumed gentlemen by reason of their profession (in most cases, of course, their education would qualify them anyway).

But then it was asked, if a claim to gentility was established by one profession, could the "professional classes" in general make such a claim, and, if so, where were *their* boundaries to be set? At once great avenues of social advancement opened up, unnerving to all new recruits who wished to draw up after them the ladder they had succeeded in climbing. There could, of course, be no question of the status of officers in the Army and Navy, holding the King's commission; and in due course, after 1914, this status was extended to officers serving only for the duration of the war, conscripted, or promoted from the ranks—"temporary gents" as they were sometimes sneeringly described. Barristers, academics, solicitors and doctors generally, surgeons, architects, civil servants of the administrative grade, and literary men (though by no means all writers) ranked as prescriptive gentlemen;

engineers formed probably the most recent cohort among them, having graduated from their position as heroes of self help and industry to the solid eminence enjoyed by such men as Sir Benjamin Baker and Sir William Garstin.

There was no mystery about it. The organisation and discipline of a profession involved a partial reconsideration of social values. In *The Making of Victorian England* (1965 edition) G. Kitson Clark wrote, "The increasing complexity of society and the complication of the services it required, enhanced the value of the men who could supply the requisite techniques, while the increasing rationality with which all but the stupidest men tended to think about these matters, encouraged the belief that men who were trained to perform difficult and responsible services, for which they were likely to be well paid, were at least as socially valuable as men who had done no more than inherit an ancient name with possibly not much money and not much sense to go with it" (p.262).

Distinguishing between the education of a gentleman and the technical qualifications of certain professional groups left a ragged line between, say, doctors on the one hand and dentists or unqualified practitioners on the other—a line the existence of which was probably due as much to the empire-building activity of the General Medical Council as to any real difference between professional and technical skills. As early as 1858, the General Medical Council had drawn up regulations to ensure that future doctors should, if possible, attend university before qualifying, in order to acquire what the Council considered to be the correct aptitudes; it was thus advocating a practice that had long been followed by those who wished to become lawyers, civil servants, or clergymen of the Established Church.

Professional men, however, comprised a large and rapidly growing class. The numbers of students at university more than doubled in the twenty years after 1900, from 20,000 to 42,000; and it could be expected that their numbers would continue to multiply. Too many fish were swimming upstream, to agitate the placid upper pools.

The ranks of aspirants could be thinned considerably by adding to the yardsticks of education and professional status the test of affiliation: chiefly by membership of clubs. *Who's Who* noted assiduously whether its entrants belonged to the Travellers, Bath or Athenaeum, or, at a lower social level, to such clubs as the Royal Automobile Club, formed in 1905. Since membership of a club depended on election, after proposal by established members and with the consent of other members, it represented the result of a selection process of uncommon severity— easily passed by the well born and bred, frequently leading to the dreaded "black-ball" for the unfortunate. The nature of the club determined the sort of screening which took place; thus the Athenaeum (founded in 1824) tended to draw its membership from among the higher clergy, academics and the legal profession, while the Garrick (1831) catered for literature, theatre and the arts. This in turn led to a subtle ranking, on a differential scale, of clubs themselves, so that a combination such as Whites and the Marylebone Cricket Club might indicate wealth and leisure, while the Travellers (civil service) or Reform (Liberal politics) suggested a more workaday professional life.

Reference books, however, merely hinted at the richness and density of behaviour among the upper class and of the complicated screens set up to preserve its charmed isolation. Nineteenth-century experience had shown beyond question that not everyone of aristocratic birth possessed the delicacy of manners and sensitivity presumed by society to go with it; and that these virtues in turn, might form the standard for a gentility which owed little to lineage and rank. With the rise of the professional class, and their association with hereditary gentry in public schools and universities, the two standards slowly merged. By 1914, it could conceivably have been said: "The fellow's ancestors may have arrived with William the Conqueror, but dammit, he's no gentleman"—a sentiment which in the eighteenth-century would have been incomprehensible.

An extraordinary profusion therefore grew up of standards and codes, sometimes general, sometimes restricted to those with a common background or experience, and sometimes confined to the private language of tiny groups such as the Souls. It was this variety which provided European or American observers with endless delight as they wandered like explorers in the lush sub-tropical jungle of English customs and behaviour. Leonard Anquetil, the fictional outsider of *The Edwardians*, an explorer and anthropologist, thus observed this world-in-a-nutshell during a tea party on the lawn at Chevron:

> Their organization puzzled him for, so far, he could perceive no common factor between all these people; neither high birth nor wealth nor brains seemed to be essential—as Anquetil in his simplicity had thought—for though Sir Adam was fabulously rich, Tommy Brand was correspondingly poor; and though the Duchess of Hull was a Duchess, Mrs Levison was by birth and marriage a nobody; and though Lord Robert Gore was a clever, ambitious young man, Sir Harry Tremaine was undeniably a ninny. Yet they all took their place with the same assurance, and upon the same footing. Anquetil knew that they and their friends formed a phalanx from which intruders were rigorously excluded; but why some people qualified and others did not, he could not determine.

The very variety of what may be seen as screens to protect upper-class life confused and made perilous the ascent of an encroaching middle-class. Something so crude as the caricature, in George Gissing's *Private Papers of Henry Ryecroft*, of a *nouveau riche* who goes into a restaurant and is then embarrassed because he does not know how to handle the cutlery represented no real social test. Nor did the pathetic attempt of a Teresa Sneddon (the doctor's suburban wife in *The Edwardians*) to ape the jargon fashionable in the upper strata. Thorstein Veblen's answers, transposed from the plutocracy of the United States, are more relevant, particularly when they concentrate on the prime manifestations of wealth and leisure—domestic service and rapidly changing fashion.

With regard to servants he observes, "The development of a special class of personal or body servants is also furthered by the very grave importance which comes to be attached to this personal service. The master's person, being the embodiment of worth and honour, is of the most serious consequence. Both for his reputable standing in the community and for his self-respect, it is a matter of moment that he should have at his call efficient, specialised servants whose attendance upon his person is not diverted from this their chief office by any by-occupation. These specialised servants are useful more for show than for service actually performed. Insofar as they are not kept for exhibition simply, they afford gratification to their master chiefly in allowing scope to his propensity for dominance. It is true, the care of the continuing increasing household apparatus may require added labour; but since the apparatus is commonly increased in order to serve as a means of good repute rather than as a means of comfort, this qualification is not of great weight. All these lines of utility are better served by a larger number of more highly specialised servants. There results, therefore, a constantly increasing differentiation and multiplication of domestic and body servants, along with a concomitant progressive exemption of such servants from productive labour" (*The Theory of the Leisure Class*, pp.53–4). How many Edwardian households bore this out!

Even more telling are Veblen's remarks on dress: "Without reflection or analysis, we feel that what is inexpensive is unworthy. 'A cheap coat makes a cheap man', 'Cheap and nasty' is recognised to hold true in dress with even less mitigation than in other lines of consumption. On the ground both of taste and of serviceability, an inexpensive article of apparel is held to be inferior, after the maxim 'cheap and nasty'. We find things beautiful, as well as serviceable, somewhat in proportion as they are costly. With few and inconsequential exceptions, we find all the costly handwrought article of apparel much preferable, in point of beauty and serviceability, to a less expensive imitation of it, however cleverly a spurious article may imitate the costly original; and what offends our sensibilities in the spurious article is not that it falls short in form or colour, or indeed in visible effect in any way. The offensive object may be so close an imitation as to defy any but the closest scrutiny; and yet as soon as the counterfeit is detected, its aesthetic value, and its commercial as well, declines precipitately" (*The Theory of the Leisure Class*, pp.119–20).

The English provided their own peculiar screens, unknown to Americans. Language especially offered a flexible means of accommodating changing fashion and, at the same time, one of the most effective barriers, because English itself fluctuated with time. When, at Eton in the 1860s, boys began to pronounce "glass" and "brass" with the long "a" instead of rhyming them with "crass", like their parents and grandparents, they were rebuked for vulgarity; and in due course they lived into an age when the short "a" became an apparently infallible guide to rough if not actually working-class origins. Maurice Baring was regularly rebuked at school for what were by then archaisms—"ain't" for "aren't", "ant" for "aunt". Edwardians with longer memories could recall the speech of Regency England, when gentlemen took "tay" out of "yaller cheyney coops under the laylock trees"; Baring's great aunt, Lady Georgiana Grey, who had played the harp to Byron, and who survived into her nineties, used to pronounce "cucumber" as "cowcumber", "soot" as "sut", and "balcony" as "balcòni". Others, from sublime conviction, simply ignored convention and continued to use the coarse speech of even earlier days. Such, in *The Edwardians*, was Sebastian's grandmother, the Dowager Duchess, "a rough, downright old woman, who said what she meant, and meant what she said, and who had no pretty, or even civilized, affectations of opinion or behaviour". Such, in reality was the sixteenth Earl of Derby, who spoke always with a strong Lancashire accent. Thirty years before the coming of the BBC and the spread of Reith's "Standard English" turned them into matters of faintly undignified comedy, dialect words and regional accents were commonplace in the conversation of rural gentry.

Fashion, with its vagaries, constantly expanded the frontiers of acceptable speech, discarding at the other end archaisms and redundant fancies. A whole new category of words came in at the apogee of Empire: words such as "verandah", "pukka", "sahib" (all from India), "posh" ("port out, starboard home" on the old P & O Line) and "taboo", and a handful of words, such as "verneukered" ("outwitted"), from the Boer War. In 1883 the *Gentleman's Magazine* had published an article, entitled "Fashionable English", criticising the misuse of epithets such as "awfully" and "screamingly", and the use of new words such as "outcome" and "folk-lore", of Americanisms such as "boss", and of the instant clichés "at large" and "irony of fate". The gentry erred as much as the vulgar.

"Men of education, some of them moving in high or the highest circles, had condescended to repeat in their daily or customary conversation the language of costermongers and of grooms and jockeys, and to use it as if it were good English. The basest slang of the streets is but too frequently heard among educated people, who ought to know better than to use it, and it has invaded the forum and the senate—if it has not yet penetrated the pulpit. 'Bloke', 'duffer' and 'cad' are words familiar to aristocratic lips. 'Who is that awfully fine filly' says Sir Fitznoodle to his companion at an evening party; 'she's dreadfully nicely groomed!' as if the fine girl had just been trotted out of the stable, after a careful currycombing, or rubbing down!"

Twenty years later, another generation of slang had passed and gone, only reinforcing the editor's sad conclusion that the malign influence of America and the slipshod morality of educated Englishmen had together combined to hasten "the undesirable consummation of rendering the pure speech of our fathers unintelligible to their degenerate descendants". What would he have made of the company at Chevron, sometime in 1906, utilising a private language which consisted in adding Italian terminations to English words? "And after dinn-are, we might have a little dans-are", a suggestion greeted by exclamations of "what a deevy idea" and "who would Sebastian bring as his partnerina?"

However admirably these screens worked to exclude the pretensions of *nouveaux riches* and social climbers, their effect was narcissistic in the extreme. Nowhere is the poverty of Edwardian upper-class thinking clearer than in its perception of those physically closest and yet most remote beings, their servants and their tradespeople.

Veblen explained the proliferation of domestic service as something mechanical, the consequence of wealth seeking a competitive and spectacularly useless outlet; and the soullessness of the relationship can be found only too often—not in Edwardian scrapbooks, or in idealised portraits of long-suffering maids and loyal retainers, but in the handful of diaries actually written by former servants (such as Hannah Cullwick, who secretly married her master, the eccentric diarist A.J. Munby, but who lived to outward appearances as though she were still the servant). This sort of judgement can only be found in private letters like that of Montagu Norman declaring: "There were the many hewers of wood and drawers of water, there were the few for whom the wood was hewn and the water drawn. If there also happened to be a minority of unfortunates who failed even to find such menial tasks to do, the failure probably lay in themselves. The unemployed were, in most cases, unemployable" (Andrew Boyle, *Montagu Norman*, p.68).

With the proliferation of servants, in all their specialised functions—valets, housemaids, parlour maids, cooks general, cooks particular, pantry boys, scullery maids, to say nothing of the armies of outdoor staff—the larger Edwardian households resembled factories in an early, patriarchal stage of industrial organisation. On the one hand, as Lady Bunting wrote in *The Contemporary Review* in 1910, the lady of the house often became more of a dependant than her servants—unable to cook her own meals, look after her children, or even pour herself a drink; on the other, the male head of the house might rarely, if ever, come into contact with the lower ranges of his employees. These, particularly the women, might be grossly overworked, lonely and exploited to a degree which the relative security of life for senior staff (those actually *known* to their employers) disguised. The latter—the butlers, head cooks, head gardeners, personal servants, gamekeepers and stalkers—fell into a quite different category, whose high peak had been reached in Victorian days in the extraordinary and privileged position given by the Queen to the egregious ex-ghillie John Brown.

Perhaps the most soulless aspect of the upper class's attitude towards servants was the bland assumption that service was due *totally*, at any place, at any time. This is well illustrated by the suggestion book of a Pall Mall club that remained open until 2 a.m. each day, with a full complement of staff attending to the end. The book is full of splenetic complaints: that not all varieties of the club's brandy were readily available at late hours; that "Sandwiches should not take *ten* minutes to prepare at 11.30 in the evening"; and, worst of all, the comment, "I hope that the closing of the club for Christmas may not be taken as a precedent" (Arthur Marshall, "Only a Suggestion", *New Statesman*, January 1976).

Lawrence Jones was honest enough to record in his memoirs, "The training of the heart ... was neglected in my day. We did not so much as notice that our servants, always about and among us, lived in basements by day and in attics by night; that on their very holidays they wore drab, funereal clothes ... we had no contacts with the working population on whose backs we lived so agreeably. Such friendships as we made with the unprivileged were with gardeners and gamekeepers, stalkers and ghillies. Those contented countrymen, who shared our pursuits, were themselves among the more fortunate. We could learn from them nothing of the lives of the industrial workers, nothing of the deadening monotony that suffocated the underlings in shops and offices" (*An Edwardian Youth*, pp.148, 248).

Real understanding of the working-class predicament was probably less substantial than in Victorian days when charity had formed a habitual part of life. Arnold Bennett and H.G. Wells might aim to enlighten the upper class, yet few authentic working-class voices seem to have penetrated the screen. E.M. Forster was ill-at-ease, even with lower middle-class characters, and one has to look a long way to find a portrait as clear as Somerset Maugham's *Lisa of Lambeth*. W.H. Davies' *Autobiography of a Super-Tramp* or Stephen Reynold's romantic vision of life among Devon fishermen—*A Poor Man's House*—skirt among minorities, rather as George Orwell was to do in the 1930s. And this whole screening process was reinforced by the operations of social censorship which allowed the upper-class a wider window on a different world: "The poor, who had little scope for the higher enjoyments of life, naturally picked up the literature that was nearest at hand." As late as 1935 a magistrate, trying an obscenity case, could ask about the passages from a book being prosecuted, "Do you consider them fit and decent for people of the working class to read?"

If the upper-class seems to have known little of the working-class world outside the ranks of a few privileged retainers, they evinced a positive contempt for the dim masses of the lower middle-class—those tradespeople and clerks who were, nevertheless, in an increasingly democratic age, one of the more conservative and therefore supportive elements of the existing social hierarchy. They rarely appear in a heroic, or even dignified, light in Edwardian fiction: only H.G. Wells attempted to do justice to the wastes of suburban London, in the *Napoleon of Notting Hill*, and with Ann Veronica and Mr Kipps. Even at the end of the decade, E.M. Forster's attempt to show the cultural self-improvement of the man of humble origin, Leonard Bast, in *Howard's End*, is deeply ambiguous. After he has been taken up by the intellectual establishment, personified in the Schlegel sisters, Bast's death is entirely in character with the attitudes of the day: he is killed, ridiculously, by the collapse of a massive bookcase—the humble aspirant crushed, literally, by the weight of the English literary heritage.

An Englishman did not have to encounter foreigners unless he chose to visit Europe; nor did he actually have to speak to servants or inferiors (indeed, one function of the butler was to preserve him from such contacts). But, unless he retired hermit-like to his country estate, he would be bound to encounter, on apparently equal terms, the "semi-English", and those "smart and moneyed

Medes, Persians ... and Hebrew money-lenders" who so distressed the purists like E.J.C. Hearnshaw.

The Irish presented him with certain difficulties. Despite violent political altercations over Irish Home Rule in the Edwardian period, with their evidence of the passionate strength of Irish nationalism and their threat to the unity of the United Kingdom, there was no widespread acceptance among the political élite that the state of being Irish — or Scots or Welsh — was something intrinsically different from membership of that kingdom. Very few had been prepared to make the parallel between Fenian leaders or Parnell and nationalists such as Garibaldi and Cavour; and, while in the 1900s Redmond and the Irish Nationalists at Westminster were acknowledged as in some sense spokesmen for Ireland, there could as yet be no recognition of the rights of Sinn Fein or of Irish socialism.

As far as observers in England were concerned, Ireland was a provincial imitation, producing at best a handful of gifted writers, poets, soldiers and a great deal of excellent hunting, fishing and shooting. The island was usually seen merely as an extension of the English upper-class world, peopled by the Protestant ascendancy; in which the real Irish had no place, except as workers on the land. Even the Anglo-Irish rated a degree lower than those whose estates were confined to England, a factor reflected in the tradition, dating back to the Union, that Irish peerages constituted a stepping stone to the full dignity of an English peerage, with its prescriptive seat in the House of Lords. (The first Lord Carrington was one who "advanced" from an Irish to an English barony; and, if the custom had fallen into disuse a century later, the habit of mind had not.) Dublin, except to Dubliners, remained a poor provincial city, and the entourage of the Viceroy in Dublin Castle was definitely lower in status than London society. Irish estates and country houses tended, in English eyes, to fall short of perfection; and Gladstone, who had looked to find in an Irish squirearchy an element of social stability, discovered instead that the most likely Irish gentleman was the Home-Ruler Charles Stewart Parnell. Many of the greater Protestant landlords had retreated from their estates in the later nineteenth century as agrarian outrages and civil disturbance threatened their peace of mind; and, while these absentees attracted a certain sympathy in England, they remained very much the poor relations of the English aristocracy.

However, the moral dilemma raised by Irish nationalism might undermine loyalty to the Crown, an essential part of the gentlemanly code. Before 1914, the "mutiny" at the Curragh, the preparations of Ulster for open rebellion, and the arming of the South divided loyalties, even for moderate Unionists like Lord Midleton (who, after 1921, served loyally the Irish Free State) or old-established families like the Plunketts. Sir Horace Plunkett later helped to save the Irish economy by organising agricultural co-operatives—scarcely a development welcome to English landlords. To take the most extreme case, a gentleman like Sir Roger Casement could decide that his loyalty was to Ireland rather than to his Anglo-Irish background—only to be hanged for treason against the United Kingdom during the First World War.

The Irish fitted uneasily into what was, primarily, an English mould—they were considered rather too unreliable, and often too entertainingly disparaging, to receive the full accolade. Significantly, in 1914, after fifty years of uniting English and Irish landowners, Burke's *Landed Gentry* divided itself into two sections; Great Britain (England, Scotland, Wales) and Ireland. To a large extent, Burke followed the trends of the society it depicted. Scottish lairds and Welsh landowners were both reliable and dignified, the former especially so, as their grouse moors and salmon rivers came into fashion in the nineteenth century, as Victorian baronial mansions sprang up to outdo the ancient strongholds of the Borders and the Highlands, and as golf, developed in Scotland, became the rage. The *Estates Gazette* noted in December 1910, "Many who used to shoot in England now take a shoot in Scotland, and go abroad much earlier than they used to, often in October or November." Although there was not as yet any accepted concept of Scottish nationalism—apart from the historical romanticism of those who approached the country through the novels of Sir Walter Scott or the tartan appurtenances of Balmoral—tolerance of Scottish habits ranged from grudging acceptance of the primacy of Scottish engineers, to a general acknowledgement of the unrivalled claims of Scotch whisky.

To be Scottish then was no disadvantage; to be a laird had a romantic tinge; and the fact that by 1900 many Scottish estates were burdened with debt, and most Scottish houses more chilly and uncomfortable than their English counterparts, did not detract from appreciation. The English, after all, did not go north in January. But it would have been eccentric, to say the least, had a Scots gentleman made a virtue of speaking Gaelic, or of attendance at the manse school in the village. The style was English, even when translated into public schools, Fettes and Loretto (which, incidentally, had no Irish equivalents). Genuine intermixing of classes, which had characterised much of earlier Scottish history, had largely disappeared in the nineteenth century, just as the minor Scottish gentry had been depressed, leaving a handful of great families who owned vast estates and presided over a subject tenantry.

Primogeniture was a principle even more rigid in Scotland than in England, and under Scottish law an entail could become almost perpetual. In Wales, the landed gentry even acquired a collective title — Benheddig (literally, "men with pedigrees"). Ownership and wealth were not, however, synonymous, even before the great agricultural depression, for much of Scotland and Wales was marginal land, suited only to sheep or deer or afforestation, which became both popular and economic in the First World War. It would be truer than for England to say that the gentry were divided into two groups: the lesser landowners, who lived on their estates (as did the second Lord Merthyr, devoted to agriculture and his Mastership of the South Pembrokeshire Hounds), and those who spent half of each year in London or abroad.

But whatever faint tinge of superiority the English upper-classes may have felt when surveying the outlying parts of the United Kingdom was nothing compared with the equivocal feelings aroused by the existence of rich, powerful (and, frequently, ennobled) Jewish families in the heart of English society; indeed the

Edwardian's attitude towards Jews is a formidable index of his understanding of himself. Even a member of an established family whose origins were in commerce might look askance. Beatrice Webb, after dining at Bath House, Piccadilly, with Sir James Wernher and a company of financial magnates, wrote that "There might have just as well have been a Goddess of Gold erected for overt worship—the impression of worship in thought, feeling and action could hardly have been stronger." Her host's driving ambition, she noticed, was to own a country mansion and ape the lifestyle of the country gentleman.

Perhaps what offended most about the intrusion of these rich was that they lacked the casual approach to money which had always been something of a prerequisite for a gentleman. It was commonly supposed that Edward Cassel had "bought" his way into the intimate circle of the Prince of Wales by his shrewd investment advice, and this was strongly resented. A gentleman might live on credit with minimal disgrace, but could a gentleman really be somebody who never needed credit? The dilemma was never resolved. Looking back from 1933, Esme Wingfield-Stratford saw the intrusion of money as *the* characteristic of the Edwardian years: "Money, the supplanter of birth, had at last with good King Edward come into its own; Cassels and Sassoons, Rothschilds and Lawsons were such men as he delighted to honour .... If the old motto had been 'noblesse oblige', the new, by imperceptible means, was coming to be 'money talks'." While in political terms Jews had been formally emancipated during the nineteenth century, there was still a great deal of hostility to their acceptance into polite society. Their number was still small in 1901—only 160,000 out of a total population of some 41.5 million—but emigration from Russia and Eastern Europe in the wake of pogroms and persecution had already enlarged the original community, and during Edwardian times this influx continued. By 1910 there were an estimated 238,000 Jews. However, the "problem" as far as the upper-classes were concerned lay not with the poverty-stricken immigrant communities in the East End of London— source of much working-class antipathy and the genesis of the Aliens Act in 1905—but with those members of the Jewish community who had now amassed enough wealth to provide themselves and their children with the life-style that had, until then, been the prerogative of the privileged Gentile.

It would probably be true to say that a Jew could never command full acceptance. There was a hollow ring to the concept "Jewish gentleman", and it is noticeable that society figures usually pointed out the racial antecedents of even close friends when they departed from the Anglo-Saxon norm. There is a good deal of truth in the picture in *The Edwardians* of Lucy, widow of an English aristocrat, considering marrying a Jew. She concludes that, "It would be a come-down to marry a Jew, and, physically, Sir Adam was not appetising, but then his millions were fabulous ... besides, Sir Adam could do what he liked with the King." At the same time the Dowager Duchess (representing an older tradition) showed scant regard for the claims of money over birth. "King or no King", she declares, "I don't like these Jews."

Explicit anti-semitism was unusual; but there were still severe restrictions on

Mark Twain, "King of American Humour," meets King Edward VII and Queen Alexandra at a garden party at Windsor Castle in 1907. (*I.L.N.*)

A garden party given at Osterley Park in 1908 by the great society hostess Lady Jersey. The men are in frock coats and the women in "tea gowns" with hats typically and elaborately decorated in ostrich plumes. (*Mansell Collection*)

Rotten Row in London's Hyde Park, where Edwardian high society met to see and be seen. From a painting by Gilbert Holiday (1910). (*Mansell Collection*)

COOKING BREAKFAST

MORNING

"ASHORE"

A BREEZE ACROSS
BREYDON WATER

A WHERRY GOING UNDER
POTTER-HEIGHAM BRIDGE

"The Sweet Life on the Norfolk Broads." Although most Edwardians took their holidays on the
Continent, the Norfolk Broads provided a fashionable escape for young people from London in the
summer season. (*Mansell Collection*)

TOWING HOME.

GOING FOR THE MILK.

HOISTING SAIL.

ON HICKLING IN A DINGHY

THE KITCHEN OF A WHERRY

An Edwardian innovation: the day trip in the new motor car. Cars were fabulously expensive and still outlandish, especially on country roads. Ladies wore hats and veils to protect them from the dust of unpaved roads. The Hut Hotel at Wisley Mere, now called Wisley Huts, is still a meeting place for motoring enthusiasts. (*Mansell Collection*)

the acceptance of Jews by public schools and for careers in the Army (there was always the example of Dreyfus in France to reinforce this prejudice on "rational" grounds). Some clubs had an explicit bar on Jewish members and the main question that social arbiters had to deal with was how far to tolerate those Jews (or individuals of Jewish ancestry) who aspired to follow the gentlemanly life-style.

On this question Edwardian high society divided. On the one hand there was a strain of explicit anti-semitism to be found—notably in the writings of G.K. Chesterton and Hilaire Belloc. They claimed that the foundations of British culture were being threatened by semitic influence, and, of course, they disliked intensely the extent of the King's patronage. Thus Belloc was prepared to tolerate frivolities in private life, but disliked the undermining of standards implied by tolerance of outsiders:

> Prince, Father Vaughan may entertain the Pope,
> And you may entertain the Jews at Tring,
> But I will entertain the larger hope,
> That Mrs James will entertain the King.

(Tring was the seat of Lord Rothschild.)

On the other hand, there was a growing readiness to accept Jews socially, which would have been unthinkable some fifty years before. Disraeli remains the most obvious exception to any rule, although it is true that the Tories, in particular Lord Bentinck, helped to alleviate prejudice by giving him the environment of a gentleman and the country seat and estate of Hughenden. But the Liberal leader Lord Rosebery married a Rothschild, and Sir Ernest Cassel became (admittedly, after declaring himself a Roman Catholic) a member of the Privy Council. Had there not been a whole series of Jewish elevations to the peerage? Moreover, with the sense that British society rested upon justice, there was considerable sympathy with the sufferings of Dreyfus and with the long campaign for his rehabilitation, to say nothing of the sufferings of the Jewish population in Russia during the years of the pogroms. But liberal sympathy paled into insignificance when set beside the simple fact that Jewish bankers and stockbrokers were a valuable source of investment tips and financial assistance to an aristocratic caste increasingly aware of the value of a positive bank balance. Furthermore, as Frances, Countess of Warwick, makes clear in a story she tells in her memoirs, Jewish guests at dinner or weekend parties might turn our to be much more witty and amusing than the stuffier sections of the traditional élite.

"At a luncheon party at Warwick many years ago my husband and another man were talking of their pedigrees. My husband was proving his descent from the 'King-Maker' through the female line, and the other man was bragging that his family were still older, as he was directly descended from the Plantagenets. Presently a faint voice from the end of the table piped, 'I am descended from Benjamin!' For a moment there was silence, and all eyes turned to the speaker. It was Guggenheim, the copper king. Then the party rocked with laughter. English

Earls, even Plantagenets' descendants, seemed trumpery moderns compared with the claims of the old Jew."

There is something very apposite here: the Jew dines with the English aristocracy, not as an ordinary man, but as a "copper king". He sits at the end of the table, and speaks in a "faint voice"—but when he does he dispels at a stroke the pretensions that had dominated aristocratic society. Even more significant is the reaction to what would once have been considered gross impertinence.

CHAPTER THREE

The Way Up

The elaborate texture of upper-class life before 1914 and the unfettered individualism of those who enjoyed it rested on a firm base of shared experience, secure assumptions and something approaching a common culture. The freedom it gave from the constraints of work and social pressures encountered by those outside was assured precisely because the walls protecting it were not (or were only very rarely) assaulted from within. Newcomers qualified by wealth, background and adherence to the code observed by those within were discreetly admitted.

Initiation came not in early childhood, but at school. Nannies dominated the earliest years of all those destined for membership of the upper and the professional middle-classes; but their very variety, from the serene substitute mother (like Winston Churchill's Mrs Everest—"Womaney", as he called her even in his school days) to uncaring or sinister figures, made it unlikely that their charges would be aware of anything more in common with other children than a basic training in table manners and the habit of separation from their parents for all but a tiny, formal part of the day.

The introduction to conformity came at around the age of thirteen, or earlier for those who were taught at preparatory school, rather than by a private tutor. Suddenly, the boy was faced with two dissimilar but complementary codes of behaviour, to be learnt with utmost speed and on pain of punishment which must often have seemed extreme: the code prescribed by the establishment of head and housemasters, and the boys' own code, equally binding, often subversive of the first, and handed down by prefects or monitors—figures almost as remote and awe-inspiring as masters themselves. From the very first days at public school, the boy would be taught to accommodate himself or risk rejection as an outsider; and only when he had been fully indoctrinated into the codes and the experience of living in such a community could he benefit from its opportunities and finally enjoy the privileges himself.

Seventy years later, and half a century after the Edwardian wave of nostalgic reminiscence about public-school days had been swamped by the bitter parodies and critiques of the inter-war years, there remain two opposite views about what happened after the great reforming age of Victorian headmasters had died away, in the 1880s and 1890s. The paradox can be seen in Churchill himself, a stubborn, sometimes angular personality often bitterly unhappy during his career at Harrow; who at fourteen could write to his mother, "I hope you don't imagine that I am happy here. It's all very well for monitors and cricket captains but it is quite a different thing for fourth form boys. Of course what I should like best would be to leave this hell of a place but I cannot expect that at present" (Randolph Churchill, *Winston S. Churchill*, vol.1, 1874–1900, p.128), yet who in his later years attended Speech Day enthusiastically, and sang the Harrow song "Forty Years On" with tears in his eyes.

In 1864, during the heyday of the public school, the Royal Commission appointed to examine the nature and working of such establishments had reported of them, in much the same way as Edwardian advocates of the system later did, that "Among the services which they have rendered is undoubtedly the maintenance of classical literature as the staple of English education, a service which far outweighs the error of having clung to these studies too exclusively. A second, and a greater still, is the creation of a system of government and discipline for boys, the excellence of which has been universally recognised, and which is admitted to have been most important in its effects on national character and social life. It is not easy to estimate the degree to which the English people are indebted to these schools for the qualities on which they pique themselves most—for their capacity to govern others and control themselves, their aptitude for combining freedom with order, and public spirit, their vigour and manliness of character, their strong but not slavish respect for public opinion, their love of healthy sport and exercise. These schools have been the chief nurseries of our statesmen; in them, and in schools modelled after them, men of all the various classes that make up English society, destined for every profession and career, have been brought up on a footing of social equality and have contracted the most enduring friendships, and some of the ruling habits of their lives; and they have had perhaps the largest share in moulding the character of an English Gentleman" (*Report of the Royal Commission on Public Schools*, vol.1, p.65).

At their best the public schools of ancient foundation (Harrow, Eton, Rugby, Winchester, Charterhouse, Shrewsbury and so on) and the great range of those founded in the wake of Dr Thomas Arnold's reforming career at Rugby (such as Marlborough and Haileybury) still provided something unique in Europe: an education which allowed for the unscholarly entrant by placing no inordinate stress on competitive examinations. In his *A Schoolmaster's Apology*, Alington, headmaster of Shrewsbury in 1913, countered the critics with his assertion that his school had made more progress than they realised; and contemporaries at Charterhouse of the later reforming headmaster J.F. Roxburgh recalled the brilliant products of the sixth, who went up to Oxford and Cambridge in triumph, as well as the great mass who despised work as a grind and met no outside examinations at any point in their careers. Both Maurice Baring and Lawrence Jones left affectionate portraits of their careers at Eton, making light the toils of fagging, the inordinate emphasis put on athleticism, and the obsessive concentration on Greek grammar and Latin hexameters. "The whole of my first half was like Paradise", Baring wrote, and described his first summer as "a period of unmixed enjoyment: rows up to Hurley every afternoon and gingerbeer in the garden there, bathes in the evening at Cuckoo Weir, teas at Littlebrowns, where one ordered new potatoes and asparagus, or cold salmon and cucumber, gooseberries and cream, raspberries and cream, and every fresh delicacy of the season in turn" (*The Puppet Show of Memory* (1922), p.95). Eton provided something almost unique, a chance of individual excellence outside the conventional stream: Baring learnt to play the organ, wrote lyric poetry, and shrugged off total failure as an oarsman — three occupations which at other schools might have earned him the epithet of "wet" and endless ragging. Yet Eton was no different in the quality of the memories, redolent of vanished triumphs and invincible nostalgia.

"Goodbye to the school library, my favourite haunt at Eton, the scene of so much hurried, scrambled work, of such minute consultations of ecclesiastical authorities for Sunday questions, or of translations of Virgil and Horace, and the Greeks; of such long and serious discussions of future and present plans and literary topics, schemes and dreams, poems, plays, operas, novels, romances, with Willy Coventry and Gerald Cornish. Goodbye to the leather tables, where numberless poems had been copied out on the grey library foolscap paper, which for some reason we used to call electric light paper; tables over which we leapt in wild steeplechases, where so many construes had been prepared, and so many punishments scribbled, and where the great poets of England had been surreptitiously discovered, and the accents of Milton and Keats overheard for the first time, and the visions of Shelley and Coleridge discerned through the dust of the daily work and above the din of chattering boys. Goodbye to the playing fields, to South Meadow, the Field, to Upper School, and to William's inner room, where I had so often dreamt of getting prizes and wondered what I should choose if I ever managed to get the Prince Consort's prize. Goodbye to the Brocas, to Upper Hope, and Athens and Romney Weir and to all the stretches of the river. Goodbye to Windsor and Norman Tower, and to the chimes of the inexorable school clock; to my little room with its sock cupboard, bureau and ottoman, to Littlebrowns and to Phoebe, and then to one's friends: to my dame and to my tutor, and to Arthur Benson, and the unforgettable readings and talks in his house" (*The Puppet Show of Memory*, p.116).

Others saw it differently. Something of the deep Edwardian unease showed through in, for example, H.A. Vachells's novel of Harrow life, *The Hill*, set ostensibly in the 1880s but actually written in 1904—a book which revelled in traditionalism and the preservation of older values, the classics against modern studies, the privilege of prefects against the intrusion of the "removes", and of the gentlemanly code against bounders and the sons of the new rich. Harrow, by that standard, was unchanged, encased in amber, perfect but sterile.

As the great nineteenth-century upheaval died away, the public school stopped moving. The generation of headmasters who succeeded Arnold, Hawtrey and Moberley tended to be strong-willed administrators who consolidated their power over the whole school—men like Dr Warre at Eton, Moss at Shrewsbury, Ridding at Winchester, Welldon at Harrow: stern, usually humourless, autocrats. William Haig-Brown ruled at Charterhouse for thirty-four years and in that time quadrupled the size of the school—a good indicator of the parental demand which underpinned his success. But the headmasters' authority depended on the acquiescence of housemasters of equally long tenure, and on the allegiance of prefects, whose claim to a form of self-government ran back to the previous century. In the relatively huge public schools of the 1900s, with four or five hundred boys, few ever encountered the remote headmaster: authority was divided between the housemaster and prefects, between the boys' code, celebrated, in a distinctly subversive way, by Kipling in *Stalky and Co.*, and the dignified version, applied by housemasters whose ideas had often ceased to correspond to the changing world outside, and whose temperament, almost unchecked, shaped the lives of the boys in their charge.

The new boy's daily life was bounded by rules of enormous complexity, couched in an esoteric school language which had to be learnt. Infringement meant punishment; and, however sound an introduction this might be to a society which repeated, mirror-like, the mysterious gradations and privileges of schoolboy existence, it tended to stifle originality or drive it into resentment and opposition. No wonder the young Churchill was sometimes miserable at Harrow, without the one escape, excellence at games.

> Oh we are the bloods of the place,
> We shine with superior grace
> At the goal or the wicket, at footer or cricket,
> And nothing our pride can efface.
> The worms of the sixth we despise.
> We count them as dirt in our eyes.

ran the Charterhouse parody of Aristophanes. Obsession with competitive sports may have been inspired by a haunting fear, on the part of Victorian masters, of what would follow if boys were left idle: indolence or, worst, immorality; but by the 1900s athleticism had become a cult. Instead of simply providing a compensation for the less scholarly, prestige from success at games threatened to cut off intellectual ability altogether, except in schools like Winchester and Eton, or where the sixth form retained its former standards.

If he did not suffuse his memories with the golden haze of romanticism, an

Edwardian would recall that his youth had been formed by the rigorous discipline of the classics, the pursuit of sporting excellence, and the society of other boys. The interpretation he put on these things would vary: many honestly believed in the theme developed by Gladstone in a memorable lecture at Eton in 1891.

"But this, Mr. Provost, I venture to say, and say with confidence, and it is not a fancy of youth nor a whim of the moment, but the conviction forced upon me even more by the experience of life than by any reasoning quality, that if the purpose of education need to fit the human mind for the efficient performance of the great functions, the ancient culture, and above all the Greek culture, it is by far the best and strongest, the most lasting, and the most elastic instrument that could possibly be applied to it" (Baring, *The Puppet Show of Memory*, p.108).

On the other hand, as the phlegmatic Dr Warre, headmaster of Eton, revealed in some of his sermons, such concentration on the classics allowed little time for other, mundane but useful, pursuits: "And you boys—whatever you may be in after life — whether you may be great statesmen—or whether you may be lawyers — or whether you may be writers—or *even* if you are only *engineers*" (Hassall, *Edward Marsh*, p.105)—a descending scale of merit, too close to the truth to be parody.

Later, after the Great War, and a generation too late, the new wave of reformers—Roxburgh at Stowe, Coade at Bryanston, Kurt Hahn at Gordonstoun—would alter this curriculum. Only at Stowe, however, was the obsession with games challenged; and it took more than all the reformers' efforts to overcome the inherent obstacles to normal development in bringing up boys in a wholly segregated environment. Nowhere in the Edwardian period was the disparity between the dignified version and the real life of boys greater, for boys themselves conspired, unconsciously, not to tell the truth to their parents or to their own children about the quite understandable prevalence of homosexuality in public schools. Alec Waugh remembered that a friend to whom he gave, in 1916, a copy of his book *The Loom of Youth* (which touched gently and sympathetically on the question of romantic affection between older and younger boys and caused a sensation when it was published) greatly enjoyed it, but returned it saying he must "never let his wife see it". What mattered was not the thing itself, natural enough when boys matured at eighteen among thirteen year olds, but the obsessive secrecy and shame which surrounded "immorality", the almost total lack of sexual education, and the consequent muddle of feelings, which lasted into early adult life—a form of conditioning which affected the position of women, and wives, and contributed to some of the more curious excesses of Edwardian sensibility. Such sexual education as existed followed the pattern set by the Reverend Edward Lyttleton, author of *The Training of the Young in the Laws of Sex* (1900), who went so far as to acknowledge the existence of homosexuality (after Wilde's trial it could hardly be denied), while offloading responsibility from the public schools to "the common predisposition to vicious conception which is the result of parental neglect". Even more curious, in the light of the Freudian knowledge then available, was his injunction virtually to ignore the father's role in sexual upbringing and to concentrate on the boy's feelings for his mother: "With emphasis laid on the suffering involved to his mother, and the wonderful part given as a reason why the mother so dearly loves her son". There was, he admitted, a pressing need for change—not because of abysmal sexual ignorance, but because of the country's imminent social decline. "Sanity and upright manliness", Lyttleton wrote to *The Times* as headmaster of Eton in 1913, "are destroyed, not only by the reading of obscene stuff, but by a premature interest in sex matters, however it be excited." All this formed part of the extraordinary double standard which survived the Victorian period, and was in some ways intensified before the Great War. The high public line on morality barely corresponded to private practice—and the public schools did no more than reflect the paradoxes of society as a whole.

Initiation and preparation were completed long before the age of eighteen; those who went on to university would find sports reduced to sounder proportions, and the hermetic environment of school opened to the view of a galaxy of girls, billowing in silk and satin, descending on the ancient colleges like Zuleika Dobson herself. Max Beerbohm's famous portrait of Oxford, delicate, rococo, whimsical and gently mocking the absurdities of college protocol, or the dandyness of its undergraduates, depicted the university as he had known it, the mellow buildings, the broad streets, the interplay of dons and donnish schemes, scholars and college servants, against a fanciful preposterous plot: Zuleika, the most beautiful girl in the world—and a professional conjurer into the bargain—arriving at the start of Eights Week and winning the love of every single undergraduate, all of whom decided to drown themselves for her after the races were over.

Slightly more seriously, Maurice Baring reflected on the delicious life offered by Trinity, Cambridge, where he belonged to the debating societies, the Magpie and Stump, and the Decemviri, skirted the rarified world inhabited by the "Apostles", and shed his Christian principles: "I did little work at Cambridge, and from the Cambridge curriculum I learnt nothing. I attended lectures on mathematics which might just as well have been, for the good they did me, in Hebrew. I spent hours with a coach who wearily explained to me things which I didn't and couldn't understand"; but then, "Inspite of having learnt nothing, in an academic sense at Cambridge, I am glad I went there, and I think I learnt a good deal in other ways. I look back on it and I see the tall trees just coming out in the parks, behind Kings College; a picnic in canoes on the Cam; bookshops, especially a dark, long bookshop in Trinity Street; little dinner parties in my rooms in Trinity Street, the food arriving on a tray from the college kitchen where the cook made crême brûlé better than anyone in the world, and one night fireworks on the window-sill and the thin curtains ablaze; rehearsals for the ADC; long idle mornings in Trinity and Kings; literary discussions in rooms at Trinity; debates of the Decemviri in Carr-Bosanquet's room on the ground floor of the Great Court; summer afternoons in Kings College gardens, and the light streaming through the gorgeous glass of the west window in Kings Chapel ... gossip at the Pitt Club in the mornings, crowds of youths with well brushed hair, straw hats, telling stories in front of the fireplace; the Sunday evening receptions in Oscar Browning's rooms full of Arundel prints and crowds of long haired bohemians; the present Provost of Eton mimicking the dons; and the endless laughter of those who could say:

> We were young, we were merry, we were very, very wise,
> And the door stood open to our feast."

(*The Puppet Show of Memory*, p.153.)

At both Oxford and Cambridge the emphasis was overwhelmingly on the classics (of the fifteen Cambridge finals papers of 1910, nine were devoted wholly to Latin and Greek translation and composition, one to grammar and two more partly to linguistics), but that it was possible to strike a balance between this and other areas of education can be seen from the memoirs of J.F. Roxburgh, who found himself debating at the Cambridge Union against Hugh Dalton, a future Labour Chancellor of the Exchequer, and Norman Birkett, later the greatest advocate of his day. "A man could then always find a niche for himself in the activities of the place. The clever and ambitious would work for the hallmark of a First, but no sort of stigma attached to the average, the lax or the stupid: their passport to the world could be stamped with a Blue or by making their mark in the Union or some university club. Those who wished worked hard, others just scraped an honours degree, many still read for pass degrees, doing the bare minimum as they rode to hounds, played games and made friends" (Noel Annan, *Roxburgh of Stowe* (1965), p.30).

Of course, there were critics of a system which bred its governing class in the habit of throwing buns at each other, and pats of butter at the ceiling, or piling chairs up on top of those who had already passed out, in order to pour ink on them from a great height. "Port was drunk, and thrown about the room," Baring remembered: "Indeed we had a special brand of port called *throwing port*, for the purpose." The critics resented the way the system then reserved for them the highest positions in political and professional life. If a youth of eighteen sought scientific or technical training, he would look elsewhere, to new universities such as Birmingham, granted its charter in 1900, or to such institutions as Imperial College, formed in 1908. Stafford Cripps, a member of the Parmoor family, who were traditionally landed gentry, was most unusual in turning down a scholarship at Cambridge in order to read Chemistry at University College, London, under the tutorship of Sir William Ramsay. Yet even among these foundations the intake remained narrow, and the total government aid to institutes of higher education amounted to no more than the German state lavished on each of its twenty-two universities. Nothing existed in Britain comparable to the *grand écoles* in France, remorselessly training a professional élite for government service, without recourse to the classics or to competitive games. Yet the Edwardians liked things as they were; so long as parents were satisfied—and diplomacy ranked high among the qualifications expected of a headmaster—and so long as the examiners at the ancient universities saw the high classical and philosophical standards maintained, the drive for change remained weak.

The educational system also performed a most valuable social function. Before the 1840s it had not necessarily been part of a gentleman's upbringing to have attended public school, and he was even less likely to have attended university; but, if he had been formally educated other than by private tutor, he would have attended one of the handful of ancient schools (Eton, Harrow, Rugby, and so on) and, if he had gone on to university, Oxford, Cambridge, one of the three Scottish universities or Trinity College, Dublin (depending on where he came from). By the 1900s, a revolution had taken place: "If to be a gentleman implied a certain refinement of motive, a certain liberality of spirit, which took a larger view of human affairs than the narrowness of view and meanness of motives which were the probable results of experience confined by the walls of country house or factory, then it was right and desirable that the natural instincts of a born gentleman should have been fostered by an appropriately liberal education. Therefore it came to be increasingly assumed that a gentleman would have had the education of a gentleman ... and that someone who had had the education of a gentleman was likely to *be* a gentleman" (Kitson Clark, *The Making of Victorian England*, p.255).

It can probably be said that the overwhelming majority of adult gentlemen in Edwardian England had so benefited; and increasing demand in the previous fifty years, together with the sudden and absolute rise in numbers, both of old and of new gentry, caused first the reform of the ancient, and frequently decayed, public schools.

In keeping with the main reason for their origin, the staff and religious teaching of these schools were closely bound up with the Church of England, and entry to them was far from easy for the sons of dissenters or practising Jews. But, once entry had been achieved, the prospects were remarkable. As early as 1878 it could be said, "In the present day, it appears undoubted that the largest fortunes are being made by the shopkeeping class, and if these give their children the good education which we have found to be necessary to produce gentlefolk, then these children will become the gentlefolk of the next generation" (Anon, *Quite a Gentleman*, p.50).

During the last part of the nineteenth century, the professional classes followed this hint almost to a man. Towards 1900, a public-school education had become part of the common experience of the rulers of the country. They had become, if not actually cheap, at least no longer expensive to the new elite. Fees had barely increased in fifty years: Eton in 1913 was £167 a year, Harrow £153, Winchester and Rugby £126, Charterhouse and Radley £116; while lesser known schools charged much less—Blundells and Haileybury a mere £84 a year and Dulwich £88. These sums represented roughly the wages of a good cook, housekeeper or a trainee butler. Moreover there were now plenty of places available. The founding of new schools in the 1890s had been matched by building and rebuilding everywhere else. But expansion only added new rungs to an old ladder: distinctions were being formalised in the new Headmasters' Conference. Many old endowed schools ceased to be classed as "public", and fashionable grading came to rest almost entirely on the *boarding* school, among which only twenty four were admitted to the Public Schools' Club when it was founded in 1909.

Very many of the sons of the industrial interest were by then attending public school, among them, for example, Austen and Neville, the sons of Joseph Chamberlain, at Rugby. Remote from the towns of their origin, learning subjects far removed from the mechanical or scientific world, in an environment where plebeian language or manners could lead to instant ostracism, if not actual brutality, they conformed, and in turn began the process of assimilation.

For those who went on to university, the process was completed. There was a steep rise in admissions to Oxford and Cambridge, where certain colleges had been marked out as the nurseries of great men: Balliol as a source of intellectuals; Christ Church for high-Tory statesmen; Trinity, Cambridge, for the sons of the Whig nobility; and Queens, Oxford, for the Evangelicals. Many of the rigid barriers persisted: a narrow curriculum, aggressive Anglicanism, and the social dominance of the landowning class; and the majority still tended to mistrust the brilliance of intellectual groups such as the Cambridge Apostles (which included Clive Bell, John Maynard Keynes, E.M. Forster and Roger Fry and was the seed-bed of the "Bloomsbury group") and, in a more general sense, the luminaries of Balliol. There was a suspicion that such leading lights, even in the age of Alfred Marshall, George Moore, Bertrand Russell and Wittgenstein, were up to no good; as Gladstone reflected in his old age, "Liberty was regarded with jealousy and fear, something which could not wholly be dispensed with, but which was to be continually watched for fear of excesses."

Whatever its faults, the system worked, giving not merely status but also the entry to power. A.H.H. MacLean worked out in 1900 that, of the incumbents of office in the main walks of professional life since 1837, 71 per cent of those in government service, 52 per cent of teachers, 29 per cent of ministers of religion, 27 per cent of lawyers, and 16 per cent of soldiers (most of whom went to crammers) had been to public school; and that, of the schools that they had attended, the leaders, in terms of the number who had attended them, had been Eton (which accounted for three times as many as any other school), Harrow, Rugby, Westminster, Winchester and Charterhouse, in that order. Of 208 Cabinet Ministers in the half-century 1886-1936, 115 were public school men, of whom 50 had been to Eton and 23 to Harrow.

In the social scale, a characteristic ascent was that of James George Burke (cousin of the editor of the *Landed Gentry*), who bought the house and estate of Auberies in 1857. Six of his seven sons went to Eton or Harrow, Christ Church or Trinity, had careers in the Army and became justices of the peace, and rated a place in the *Landed Gentry*, from which their father had been excluded until 1880. On the other hand, public school did not provide a mere rubber stamp of respectability. Parents with money, but lacking perception, might choose an academy beyond the pale, the Edwardian equivalent of Evelyn Waugh's Llanabbas Hall (in *Decline and Fall*), in the charge of a "failed gentleman" like the immortal and odious Captain Grimes—and find their sons, instead of being admitted to the élite, sneered at forever for having fluffed the vital test of "belonging".

The secret, then, for social advancement was intelligent choice, backed by cash—an opportunity which had not existed so openly before, and would not occur in quite the same way again. The long fall in returns from land after 1890 helped bring about a change in the attitude that upper-class society took to money, especially industrial money; induced a great transfer of wealth from land to other forms of investment; and encouraged a revival, in which, as we have seen, American heiresses played a leading part, of the eighteenth-century marriage market. "The novelty and glamour of these moves to call in young and vigorous dollar stock to refresh the old and sometimes decaying English aristocracy naturally attracted attention", says F.M.L. Thompson (*English Landed Society*, p.302), and newly ennobled families and rich industrialists behaved in similar fashion. Viscount Peel's eldest son married Ella Wilkinson, daughter of Lord Ashton the linoleum manufacturer; and Sir Stafford Northcote married the daughter of a Canadian railway millionaire, who became, in turn, an English peer, Lord Mount Stephen. Such injections of money revealed the new tone and rested on a sound appreciation of the principles of economic survival, but they also brought with them a weakening of the iron bands of privilege. The rich, rather than the gentry or the aristocracy, dominated the picture of Edwardian England; never before in English history had so many of the rewards of life been available for sale.

A vast yearning for these sweet delicacies existed—ridiculous, perhaps, to the assured upper-class, who mocked the absurdities of the *nouveaux riches* and regarded their vulnerabilities as matter for comedy, but tangible and important to the up-and-coming. These too, had a vision of life; and their desire to realise the ideal picture their fancy painted helped them endure the innumerable pinpricks and humiliations consequent on attempts at social climbing.

Opportunity to acquire began at birth. The combined introduction of antiseptics and anaesthesia improved the conditions of childbirth, and the chances of infant survival improved enormously in the last decade of the nineteenth century. At a time when no general form of state health provision existed, the advantages of skilled care or surgery accrued primarily to the rich. Childbirth in upper-class families normally took place at home (thereby avoiding the high risk of contagion at hospital), attended by a doctor and a monthly nurse. Then, during infancy, the child would be in the hands of a nanny, quite probably one of the new Norland nurses, trained and professionally qualified; it would be dressed in expensive and scrupulously clean clothes, would be vaccinated against smallpox, and would be at risk only through the elaborate and fattening patent foods or excessive cream which total ignorance of diet still prescribed for the nursery regime.

In youth, too, the child, especially if a boy, would receive every advantage: elaborate toys and games to keep his mind alert, servants in the house, light and air in the spacious rooms, central heating in winter, and exercise and games at school at least to the age of eighteen—five or six years after his working-class contemporary had begun heavy manual labour. It is far from fanciful to ascribe upper-class physique to upper-class upbringing, as opposed to a youth spent among the insanitary hovels of agricultural labourers or the dismal rows of back-to-back tenements in worn-out industrial slums. Figures for infant mortality up to the age of five, for 1900, give 18 per cent for the West End, 55 per cent for the East End of London; 96 per 1,000 for the wealthier suburbs of Blackburn, 315 for the poorest. The Medical Officer of Health for Glasgow, the worst-congested city in Britain, noted the appalling distinction between Pollock, a favoured residential area, and Blackfriars, possibly the most noisome slum in Europe; yet there were members of the city council who solemnly affirmed that the difference—the two districts were two miles apart—was due to "climatic variations".

A survey of schoolchildren showed that, on average, working-class schoolboys were five inches shorter and eleven pounds lighter at the age of thirteen than were their contemporaries at public schools; and statistics gave the recruiting authorities, and ultimately the government, an unpleasant shock when a third of volunteers for the Boer War had to be turned away as medically unfit. (In a famous article in the *Contemporary Review* in 1902, General Sir Frederick Maurice quoted the incredible figure of 60 per cent. The reality, at 37 per cent, was, however, serious enough for a War Office already alarmed at the quality of volunteers.) No gentleman ever had to submit to manual labour like shifting twenty-four bushels of stone, for parish road-mending, for two shillings, or to work for employers like Suffolk farmers "famous for their meanness. They took all they could from the men and boys who worked their land. They bought their life's strength for as little as they could. They wore us out without a thought because, with big families, there was a continuous supply of labour" (Ronald Blythe, *Akenfield*, 1972 edition, pp.37, 40). They scarcely knew what it was that drove men, when the recruiting came, simply to "change their sky". Leonard Thompson, farmworker, put on nearly a stone in weight while in the Army. "They said it was the food but it was really because for the first time in my life there had been no strenuous work. I want to say this simply as a fact, that village people in Suffolk in my day were worked to death. It literally happened. It is not a figure of speech. I was worked mercilessly" (*Akenfield*, p.41).

At the end of life, the contrast between upper and working class showed even more deplorably: "Five at least of the leading ministers in Lord Salisbury's government were over six feet tall, far above the normal stature of the time. Of the nineteen members of the Cabinet, all but two lived to be over seventy, seven exceeded eighty, and two exceeded ninety, at a time when the average life expectancy of a male at birth was forty-four, and of a man who had reached twenty-one was sixty-two. On their diet of privilege, they acquired a certain quality which Lady Warwick could define only in the words, 'they have an air!' " (Tuchman, *The Proud Tower*, p.29).

To see how conditions had changed since the eighteenth century and widened the class gulf, one need only recall that none of Queen Anne's numerous children survived childhood, and that, of the seven children born to his parents, who belonged to the gentry, the historian Edward Gibbon was the only one to reach adulthood. Once cholera and smallpox had receded, the remaining killer diseases, tuberculosis, typhoid, diptheria, scarlet fever, whooping cough and measles, struck more harshly, and frequently at those very households that, because of their poverty, were least able to counter them. Those who had money thus started on an equal footing with the upper class; and the educational system by then provided them with the same ladder of opportunity and qualifications.

Later, qualified by attendance at public school, and perhaps at Oxford or Cambridge, the new gentleman was able to take his place in society. He still needed, however, the trappings of position: land, a house suitably furnished, and perhaps a title (things that were doubly necessary to any aspirant who had not had the benefit of an upper-class education). To these wealth was the key.

The long "rise of the gentry" which had been an underlying feature of English history in the seventeenth and eighteenth centuries had always been complemented by a decline in more ancient families. When one old family sold land, a new one was likely to buy it; but this gradual form of transfer diminished after the Napoleonic wars. In the nineteenth century it became more expensive to enjoy the delights of manorial property, "without which", as Sir Christopher Sykes wrote in 1792, "it is impossible to be at ease and quiet in the country". Between 1790 and 1860 the price of a thousand-acre estate rose from about £12,000 to about £40,000—a rise unmatched by increases in rents. Too many wanted to buy; too few wished to sell; and consequently many merchant families in the 1860s settled for a fairly modest holding with a small country house. At the same time, as J.B. Burke noticed, "the aim of the prosperous trader is to fix himself on some estate in his immediate neighbourhood" (*The Vicissitudes of Families* (1861), p.4), and this parochial tendency increased the time that he might have to wait. A common country saying was that "three generations made the gentleman"; and it is probable that the entry of new families was almost balanced by the decline of old. Something like a quarter of those entered in the first edition of *The Landed Gentry* had disappeared by 1891; and slightly more new families had made an appearance.

After the 1870s, however, the import of American wheat revolutionised the economics of landowning. Despite their appeals for protection on the lines of the German tariff, the landowning interest was rejected—by Disraeli and a Conservative Cabinet. Rents and income fell, and landowners saw the need to realise their capital and to transfer their investment. A great wave of sales followed, with the breaking of entails, accompanied by a steep fall in price, until in the 1890s land was fetching not much more than half of its 1860 value. Worse, landowning had ceased to be a major source of political advantage or to guarantee a secure annual income.

But the advantages of status remained; and from that point of view, land had become relatively cheap. Buyers could pick and choose their area, and buy in large parcels all at once, rather than wait decades to build up a sizable holding. Men such as the Canadian millionaire H. McCalmont, the coalmine-owner James Joicey, the mustard king, J. Colman, and J.B. Robinson, brewer, dominated the year 1890; and after 1900 the pace quickened. Among the buyers were Thomas Brassey's grandson, who acquired Apethorpe from Lord Westmoreland in 1904; the cotton spinner John Wood, who acquired Hargrave Hall from Lady Gage; Sir Ernest Cassel, Sir Edward Guinness (Lord Iveagh), W.H. Smith (Lord Hambleton), Sir

W.G. Armstrong and Samuel Cunliffe-Lister; Lord Cowdray, who acquired 21,000 acres during the Edwardian period; and Sir Julius Wernher, who purchased Luton Hoo—according to Beatrice Webb because "part of the minor convention of his life has been the acquisition of a great country mansion, with an historic name as counterpart of Bath House, Piccadilly, his London seat. This was no doubt to please his 'society' loving wife—a hard vainglorious woman, talkative and badly bred, but not otherwise objectionable" (*Our Partnership*, p.412). What John Bright had sought after the repeal of the Corn Laws in 1846, "a free trade in land", had come into being, well before the panic sales of 1910–14, which seem to have been sparked off by the land taxes of the 1909 Liberal budget.

A similar market developed in the even more restricted field of works of art, as the great eighteenth-century collections were opened up to disgorge a few masterpieces. The monumental sale of the Duke of Buckingham's collection at Stowe, in 1847, imposed on him by bankruptcy after a lifetime of conspicuous spending, had been unusual. Even in the 1880s, the famous Marlborough and Hamilton Palace sales were characterised by sluggish bidding. Thirty years later, however, competition for old-master paintings had reached an all-time peak, and the master dealer, Joseph Duveen (later to reach the peerage himself, as Lord Millbank), was busy supplying the varied tastes of English customers and of American millionaires such as Benjamin Altman and Henry Clay Frick, at prices he judged appropriate to their wealth and self-esteem. Owners still shunned publicity, and disposed of their paintings and furniture through such discreet intermediaries; or sent them labelled "Property of a Gentleman" to salerooms such as Christie's, patronised chiefly by well-known private clients and a handful of dealers. The would-be owner might, therefore, buy at auction, but he was much more likely to put himself in the hands of a knowledgeable dealer, to furnish his country house and decorate its walls with portraits which—if not examined too closely—gave an aura of civilised ancestry. This is not to say that the new rich were not discriminating (Lady Cowdray amassed a remarkable collection of eighteenth-century French furniture, and Sir John Aird patronised contemporary masters), but signifies only that the means to acquire an instant collection now existed.

Much the same was true of honours. The younger Pitt's creations had scarcely allowed trade to penetrate the House of Lords. Even in the 1880s, when party subscriptions from landowners fell off, and Sir Stafford Northcote let it be know that a man who bore the not inconsiderable expenses of a contested election (probably about £4,000) would have a "great claim on the gratitude of the Conservative Party", the aspirant expected to work hard and wait for several years. The first real "sale" of honours dates from 1891, when the Liberal Chief Whip persuaded Gladstone to promise peerages to two candidates, James Williamson and Lord de Stern (a Portuguese title), whose merit was the size of their subscriptions. Rosebery, somewhat distastefully, redeemed the pledge in 1895. Thereafter, the decline continued, in proportion to the need to raise political capital, especially for the two elections of 1910. The awards of knighthoods, baronetcies and peerages were arranged by Akers-Douglas and Gulland, the Conservative and Liberal Chief

Whips; yet a certain discretion was preserved. A decent time had still to elapse, and some identifiable public service begun, before elevation. Only after 1918 did the system fall into disrepute, when under Lloyd George's premiership, and in the disreputable hands of Maundy Gregory, "baronetcies were hawked around the clubs, with the prices clearly marked".

Everyone—among the political élite—knew what went on. In his novel *The Ivory Child*, H. Rider Haggard shows his hero, Allan Quatermain, still naïve after years in the African bush, meeting an old enemy and fraudulent speculator, Van Koop, and finding that he now goes under the style of Sir Junius Fortescue, Bart. " 'How did a man like Van Koop become a baronet ?' I inquired. 'By purchase, I believe', Lord Ragnell replied. 'By purchase! Are honours in England purchased?' 'You are delightfully innocent, Mr. Quatermain, as a hunter from Africa should be .... This individual subscribed largely to the funds of his party. I am telling you what I know to be true, though the amount I do not know. It has been variously stated to be from fifteen to fifty thousand pounds, and perhaps by coincidence, subsequently was somehow created a baronet'."

Not everyone who was ennobled in these years lacked merit; but the greater part of the industrial section of new titles must be accounted a return on political investment—often made with the wealth amassed by the founding father. Thomas Brassey's descendant became Lord Brassey of Apethorpe; Cowdray's title can hardly be separated from his magnificent support of the Liberal Party; Henry Allsop, the Burton brewer (Lord Handlip) was an ardent Conservative, and Michael Burton (Lord Burton) a Liberal. Between 1886 and 1914, 246 titles were granted, of which 200 were wholly new; roughly seventy-five of them went to trade and industry. What was new—and to contemporaries shocking—was that fifty titles at least went direct to self-made men, rather than to their descendants. The old conventions surrounding assimilation were, indeed, breaking down, and, whereas Lord Salisbury had sought to keep a balance between industry, political or public service, and the landed interest, after 1906 the Liberal government abandoned caution, perhaps deliberately. Of 570 hereditary members of the Lords at the time of the Parliament Act crisis of 1911, ninety-odd were newly created peers from non-landed families, and a further hundred or so were newly ennobled members of the civil service, Army, legal profession, and other sections of the professional élite.

There were, however, some, such as the Birmingham manufacturer Sir Richard Tangye, who refused to use their wealth to earn a place in the upper-class establishment. Tangye, inventor of the hydraulic press, was a Dissenter, son of a grocer who had been fined repeatedly for failing to pay church tithes, and his antipathy for the establishment and all it represented showed itself in his hero-worship of Oliver Cromwell, whose relics he collected and whose actions he took to be the foundation of English liberty. Such sympathies were, of course, uncommon in Edwardian England, where the emphasis was on the race for wealth and privilege.

Naturally, resentment welled up, especially among those who, like the backwoods peers who left their rural exile, the *ultima Thule* of an increasingly impoverished class, to mount an attack on the 1909 budget, had lost access to the high life. Faced with the threat posed by rapid social mobility, Edwardian society responded by developing a code of elaborate formality, in order to guard against the encroachments of men who wanted to gain the rewards of society in their own lifetime and on their own terms. Old standards and assumptions had to be recast if they were not simply to be abandoned.

Though the majority of them would have concurred in what he said, few defenders of the citadel were so outspoken as Lord Charles Beresford, fulminating on "The Future of the Anglo-Saxon Race" in the *North American Review* in 1900: "British society has been eaten into by the canker of money. From the top downwards, the tree is rotten. The most immoral pose before the public as the most philanthropic, and as doers of all good works. Beauty is the slave of gold, and intellect, led by beauty, unknowingly dances to the strings which are pulled by Plutocracy" (quoted in Hynes, The *Edwardian Turn of Mind* (1968), p.61).

But a guiding principle was evolved: that a gentleman grew, like a rare plant, only in certain conditions, where breeding, upbringing, education, manners, wealth in land, and appearance all combined in the correct proportions. "Politicians, industrialists and other dubious persons can be instantly ennobled at a stroke of the Prime Minister's pen", a later commentator wrote in the *Landed Gentry*, "but nobody can make the instant gentleman" (Anthony Lejeune, "Gentlemen's Estate", *Burke's Landed Gentry*, 1958 edition). In saying this he was echoing the sentiments of George III at the ennoblement of Robert Smith, first Lord Carrington, which, as Lord Aberdeen remarked, brought into the House of Lords "a new description of person".

It was easier, even in the 1900s, to bridge the gap at the level of works of reference than to penetrate the screens of manners. In 1860 the *County Families* had noted, "In a country like our own ... mainly owing to the influence of trade and commerce, individuals and families are continually crossing and recrossing the narrow line which severs the aristocracy from the commonalty." Such was Lord Allerton, ennobled in 1902 after a lifetime devoted to the tanning industry and the Great Western Railway. But was he accepted among his neighbours? There would of course be no problem with a man like John Wynford Philipps, the son of a clergyman, and a baronet in his own right, who drifted into business more or less by accident, made a fortune, and ended up as director of twenty-nine companies, chairman of twenty, with the title of Lord St Davids in 1905, and a viscountcy in 1918. It may have been true that the period 1890 to 1914 was a sort of Indian summer in which many of the industrialised peers entered society in the grand manner and brought a new vitality to ancient houses and country pursuits. But the "taint of Industry and Trade" could never quite be removed within one generation. *The Queen* magazine lamented, "nowadays often it is sufficient merely to acquire these symbols (yacht, house, grouse moor, race horses, cars) to be admitted to Society", and launched strong attacks on the *parvenu* class, who, despite their wealth, represented a very different pattern of behaviour: "Parvenus of both sexes are notorious for their insolence and tyranny to all servants and social inferiors. The intellectual pretentions of a parvenu are as colossal as his knowledge is small ... a parvenu, out and out, is as selfish as he is pretentious ... as undignified as he is ungrateful."

To allow such a man to pose as "gentleman" might have dire consequences for the social fabric: "In the country the British Workman likes and respects every Squire and Parson who is really worthy of affection and veneration [but] the founder of most large businesses has generally been placed by birth but a little, if at all, above those under him in trade. The Englishman, despite his demands for equal political rights, is yet far more willing to serve under what he calls a real gentleman than under a successful member of his own class."

However, when it came to pinpointing the offenders, the same handful of names recurred, suggesting that the actual number of moneyed men was less significant than their intrusion into the higher reaches of the social order. Most obvious, of course, was the enthusiasm that the King seemed to find in entertaining and consorting with the business community. A shared interest in yachting brought him into contact with John Lawson-Johnson, the inventor of Bovril, and Edward did not scruple to sell him the royal yacht *Britannia*. The presence of three of Britain's newest millionaires at a house party at Sandringham in 1895 caused a sensation in fashionable society, but, so far as Edward was concerned, money was a practical and convenient social yardstick. It mattered not a whit that W.W. Astor, Colonel John North and J.B. Robinson had none of the ordinary pedigree qualifications; and on becoming King he was quite prepared to honour men whose backgrounds would have debarred them even in the palmy days of Pitt. Thus Horace Farquhar was made an earl, Thomas Lipton was knighted, and the election of Sir Blundell Maple to the Jockey Club was encouraged.

The "money men", bankers, financiers (of the reputable sort) and stockbrokers, seem to have been found much more acceptable than were their industrial counterparts, a reflection of the ancient connection between county families and their younger scions, who, for lack of inheritance in a world formed by primogeniture, had made their fortunes in the City. The career of Charles Henry Mills, senior partner in Glyn's Bank, son of a banker, educated at Eton and Christchurch, and for twenty years Tory MP for West Kent, is typical of the upper reaches of Edwardian banking. Mills owned a splendid town house, Camelford House in Park Lane, used to invite his staff down to his estate of Wildernesse for cricket in the summer, and was one of the first of city families to abandon the simpler, often puritanical, nineteenth-century tradition and copy the more opulent Edwardian plutocrats. Even before he became Lord Hillingdon, his wife's entertainments were proverbial, and she was popularly supposed to have been the model for the Duchess in *The Edwardians*.

Traditionally, city men had not aspired so high. Bertram Currie, another of Glyn's partners, who retired in 1896, summed up his career with the jingle,

> A city banker born and bred
> Sufficient for my fame

If those who know me best have said
I tarnished not the name.

But most Edwardians wanted more. Montagu Norman, later Governor of the
Bank of England, shocked the staid partners of Martins Bank by jumping across to
Brown Shipley as a junior partner, even before he had qualified, and then shocked
Brown Shipley by decamping to Wall Street—all before he was twenty-five. As well
as mercurial ability, Norman had family connections, and his only alternative to
banking would have been a career in the Army (which he despised, particularly after
his experience in the Boer War) or the Church (which was unsuitable, since he had
no strong belief).

A particularly illuminating example of the way in which the Edwardians differed
from their Victorian fathers in their attitudes and expectations comes, appropriately,
from the world of industry. The greatest of nineteenth-century entrepreneurs, the
railway contractor Thomas Brassey, who by 1870 had laid one-twentieth of all the
railway in the world (in terms of track mileage), scorned the hope of a title and the
lures of the fashionable world. Forty years later, William Lewis, having risen, in the
words of The Times obituary in August 1914, "through sheer hard work and force
of character from a humble position to one of great power and wealth", expected
his due, and in 1911 was ennobled as Lord Merthyr.

The Victorian engineer had been a hero in public esteem, and his successors, the
great public contractors who built the world's railways, harbours, dams and bridges,
form an interesting counterpart to the bankers and City gentlemen. Two in
particular reached the apogee of their careers after 1900: Sir John Aird and
Weetman Pearson, first Lord Cowdray. Both came from very humble
backgrounds; both sought a measure of social prestige, Aird in London, Cowdray in
Sussex; and both were only partially successful.

Aird was the grandson of a Scots crofter who had walked from Ross-shire to
London to find work and was killed by a cave-in of earth during the digging of the
Regents Canal. His father began work for the Phoenix Gas Company in the
1840s—"A very squalid part of London with a knackers yard adjoining for the
preparation of cat's meat from dead horses"—but, being cast in the very mould of
Samuel Smiles's Self Help, rose to become manager, and then one of the foremost
water and gas contractors in Southern England. John, the second son, began work
for his father laying main drains in Berlin in the 1850s. He married a girl whose
father was a wharfinger from Deptford Green, a man of power along the river
Thames; and, while his father constructed the main London sewer for Sir Joseph
Balzagette, and sections of the London Underground in the 1860s, John Aird built
Millwall Docks and Beckton gasworks, and then took over the whole firm in 1870.

It was hardly a propitious social background. But he began with the advantages
of security and some inherited capital; and he possessed friends higher in the social
sphere—his partners, the Lucas family, also contractors but established at

Warnham Park in Sussex. Also his character set him apart from the rest of the family. His brother Charles observed "an extraordinary force of character, a mastery over all about him; even men of great position in the busy world who had far more culture and education, would be glad to associate with him and seek his advice. He showed a marvellous grasp of the ins and outs of different work but more marvellous still was his power over men older than himself and of greater position in life. He firmly believed in himself and whatever might arise, he stuck to that opinion."

A tall florid giant, with prominent features, blue eyes, a deep and commanding voice, and a beard which he wore longer and more splendid as he grew older, John Aird looked not unlike an Old Testament patriarch. In fact, he modelled himself consciously on the ideal of the Renaissance prince. He believed a man of his position should appear to be three times as rich as he actually was and live always in the greatest magnificence. To the end of his life he remained a superb showman, his façade the expression of a crude but remarkable vitality.

In pursuit of this ideal, he moved the firm's office to a huge baroque building in Great George Street, opposite the Foreign Office, and took the lease of Wilton Park near Beaconsfield, while he had installed in his own large town house in Hyde Park Terrace a private theatre, to which plays were brought in order to save him the journey and inconvenience of going to the theatre. Almost meticulous in his pursuit of the grand manner, he would at his many dinner parties present every woman with a carefully chosen and expensive gift, such as an exquisite fan. Always he loved to be at the centre of parties; yet he did not aspire to enter high society—partly because he was never really rich enough, but mainly because he was not interested. He cared instead for his own circle of brilliant and intelligent friends, many of whom certainly were numbered among the Edwardian gentry.

In habits he set his own individual standards. He played the flute and showed off his skill at the traditional Scottish sword dance. He restored Wilton with taste and made it comfortable, having electric lighting and central heating installed. He enjoyed the company of the artists of the day, such as Alma-Tadema and Dixey, and his picture gallery was well-known; he patronised contemporary masters (so long as they were generally accepted by fashionable tastes) and made it almost a point of honour to buy the painting or sculpture of the year at the Royal Academy. He took Alma-Tadema to Egypt for no other reason than to have him paint him a picture of Moses in the Bullrushes.

Intellectual pride was Aird's greatest extravagance, and his real, if unconventional, qualities gave him a position in the cultural life of London equal to that that his great wealth and commercial weight could afford him. Although he bought Highcliffe Castle in 1900 and gave large parties there, he was not interested in estates or the country and its sports. Making a hobby out of politics, in 1887 he became Member of Parliament for North Paddington, where such acts of his as giving every child in the constituency a commemorative book, in celebration of the Diamond Jubilee, were long remembered. He held the seat until 1905, a staunch Conservative (although his father had been a Liberal) and a follower of Disraeli—

more out of temperament than from any profound political conviction. During his early years in Parliament, he spoke frequently on employers' liabilities, showing himself fair if somewhat illiberal; but, growing bored, he rarely addressed the House after 1890. He remained a backbencher, silent on the important issues of the day.

In the 1900s his business interests, more than his social predilections, led him into the highest reaches of Edwardian society. In the years 1898 to 1902, the project to build a dam across the Nile at Aswan brought him into association with Lord Cromer, first Consul-General for Egypt, Lord Revelstoke of Baring Brothers, General Sir Herbert Kitchener, Lord Salisbury, the engineer Sir Benjamin Baker (who in the 1900s represented what the Stephensons had in the mid-nineteenth century), and the brilliant son of a Jewish banking family from Cologne, Ernest Cassel, who had come to England in 1870 and became a close friend and business adviser to the Prince of Wales. After four years of meticulously planned construction, the completion of what was perhaps the greatest single work ever planned and executed by British engineers and contractors was followed by a characteristically opulent inauguration. The Khedive Abbas came in his royal barge, the Duke and Duchess of Connaught in their yacht, and among the hundred or so other guests was Winston Churchill, fresh from the Boer War.

Aird was crippled by a paralytic stroke in the same year as that in which the King himself died. Even his last years, however, bore witness to the style he had created for the Edwardian entrepreneur. When he could no longer walk, he retired to Wilton Park, and his butler would push him through the gardens in a bath-chair, occasionally stopping to take from the back of the machine his medicine—a bottle of champagne on a bed of ice. There were no regrets; he had lived exceedingly well and his name in Egypt at least was such a symbol of magnificence that when his daughter was travelling there after the First World War she had to alter her name to avoid being charged double as an Aird. Finally he escaped the collapse of the world he had helped to build, dying peacefully at Wilton in January 1911.

Unlike Aird, Weetman Pearson chose the country rather than the town as foil for his rise in society. Conventionally schooled at Harrogate, from 1874 he worked for his father, in charge of the family brickyard in Bradford. He married Annie, daughter of a well-known Bradford mill-owner, Sir John Cass, but early aspired to break out of the provincial society of the West Riding. After fifteen years of grindingly hard work, he had raised himself to a position as commanding as that attained by Sir John Aird, both at home and abroad.

His works in Mexico—the drainage of Mexico City, the building of the Tehuantepec Railway and the creation of the Mexican Eagle Oil Company—made him by 1914 probably the foremost contractor in the world. A short, round little man, Pearson had none of the physical characteristics usually ascribed to empire builders, yet his power and command and dominant personality surmounted his physical deficiencies. Because of his habit of intense concentration, chit chat, gossip and the leisured conversation of the salons meant nothing to him, and a certain measured aloofness cut him off intellectually except from the company of other professionals. If he had been a socialite or a pursuer of gentlemanly hobbies, there could hardly have been time for the enormous quantity of construction and other work with which he filled half a century. Some of the arts appealed to him, though he never really appreciated music and spent the hours at Covent Garden, which his wife loved, abstractedly working out the answers to the next day's problems. When later he could afford it, he bought fine pictures in fashionable taste, but the real collector was his wife. His interest in Mexican antiquities, of which he assembled a fine collection, was derived from his work.

But the setting which he chose had to reflect his sense of dignity. When his baronetcy came in 1895, he bought from Sir Edgar Whitehead (inventor of the torpedo) the house and estate of Paddockhurst in Sussex, and spent all his time out of London there, draining and levelling, laying out new gardens, busying himself engineering the water supply and refurbishing in granite, marble and bronze. His wife, a striking personality, who resented and eventually triumphed over Sussex landowners' latent hostility to this incursion from industry, was a radical who sided with the suffragettes. Pearson, for his part, entered the House of Commons as a Liberal imperialist; he was a friend of Rosebery and a constant, indeed essential, support to Liberal Party funds.

It was no fault of his that he remained a quiet backbencher. His business left him little for what he regarded as the time-wasting fuss and protocol of the Commons. He was once cartooned as being turned away by a doorkeeper, who thought him a stranger; but, popular in the constituency, he held his seat for fourteen years and on rare occasions his industrial knowledge proved effective in debate. In the inner circles of the Liberal Party, however, his wealth and experience made him, like his friend Lord Inchcape, the shipping magnate, a notable asset to Rosebery, Asquith and Sir Edward Grey. They trusted his business sense and his advice on labour and trade unions, to which they were largely strangers. He was known not to be ambitious for high office; and his London house could be used for party functions and private political gatherings.

In 1908, a year before his peerage, Pearson paid £340,000 for Cowdray Park, with its magnificent Elizabethan ruins and a Victorian mansion; in Scotland he first leased, then bought, the vast estate of Dunecht near Aberdeen—moor and forest, with a battlemented baronial house. Later he crossed swords with the preservers of ancient monuments, who complained bitterly when he bought the crumbling ruins of Dunottar Castle and propped them against falling into the sea. But even these lands, adding 13,000 acres to the 6,000 of Paddockhurst, failed to bring him complete acceptance. It was not surprising that his close friends lay outside high society, among his business colleagues in political life, such as Sir Alfred Mond, or like-minded Americans, such as H.W. Taft and Judge Gerard, treasurer of the Democratic Party.

The close-knit, self-sufficient Cowdray family was in many ways in advance of its time—liberal, enlightened about women and divorce; but these views were wedded to a sense of what was fitting, high Victorian in its insistence on certain standards in life. A tinge of puritanism, antithesis of elaborate Edwardian entertainment, marked their houses. Cowdray hated gambling and would never allow it at his parties. Cocktails were never served; at Dunecht, guests would creep into the pantry, where the butler, a sound racing man, would supply their needs. Good wine appeared at dinner, but "beer is no' served in the house of Dunecht". Just as his tastes expressed an independent turn of mind, these standards helped to make Cowdray less vulnerable to social distinctions, less reliant than, say, Sir Thomas Lipton on royal favour as a guarantee of status. The man who befriended President Porfirio Díaz of Mexico, and who could decline when enthusiastic Albanians offered him, in 1919, the throne of that uneasy country, scarcely needed acceptance by "society" to satisfy the restless creativity of the entrepreneur.

Edwardian society held many compartments: some for those who already possessed everything that the most discriminating arbiter of taste and gentility could require; others for those who chose to become stereotypes in order to gain entry; and others for men who wished simply to be what they were and had the money and temperament to be so and enjoy it. Yet, even among the most independent or critical, there were very few who were prepared to (or could) live without thought for the opinions of others—that curious, repeatedly refined compound which dissolved pretensions and exposed mere veneering and gilding for what they were.

CHAPTER FOUR

The Way Down

The high peaks of Edwardian society offered glittering rewards to assiduous or lucky mountaineers; and, if many who set out to scale them failed to quench their yearning, there were at least staging-posts on the way up, where they could watch their sons reach higher, and their well-endowed daughters marry well. Outright failure could not easily be compensated, succeeded as it must have been by frustration and resentment, but it was, by nineteenth-century standards, rare. Yet something much worse was always present, like the sombre figure standing behind the Roman emperor at his feast, intoning, *"Memento mori"*; the up-and-coming and the long-established equally were faced with the threat of scandal and loss of respectability. It was as if, in a decade of jaded palates, a harsh sauce was needed: the faster the roundabout spun, the more exciting the chase, then the greater the risk of accident, exposure, dishonour.

The theme of loss and the catastrophic consequences of social ostracism runs like a black band of mourning through many Edwardian plays and novels. Scandal and the just rewards of sin formed a rich vein to be mined by preachers and the editors of Sunday papers. The titillating but old-fashioned mixture of vice, adultery and retribution which still gives immense popularity to the *News of the World* could be found in half a dozen Edwardian papers, such as Horatio Bottomley's *John Bull*, Frank Harris's *The Candid Friend*, and (sometimes) *Vanity Fair*. Headlines were never broader or blacker than when scandal touched "society".

In earlier days, before the opportunities of acceptable employment opened up, younger sons of poorer gentry families had often had a hard struggle to retain their position. Many drifted, inevitably, downwards, into business and perhaps into the ranks of the working class. The narrator in the small tract *Quite a Gentleman*, published in 1878, laments the lack of openings for young men, who must therefore emigrate to the Colonies or "go into trade and lines of business here which would have been thought most derogatory—impossible—to a gentleman's son half a century ago". But the broader area occupied by old and new gentry alike in the 1900s permitted those with diminished fortunes or estates to survive—even at the price of perpetual exile in the provinces.

Expulsion thus became the penalty not so much of incompetence or overbreeding, but of offences against the code. So far had manners and motives superseded birth that the once-common tolerance of violence and criminal behaviour among the upper classes vanished; Edwardian society expelled those who offended—or, at least, who did so in public.

The decade opened in the long shadows cast by the trial and imprisonment (in 1895) of Oscar Wilde, for sodomy. A society which could scarcely bear to be reminded in public of its "normal" sexual frailties recoiled at the exposure of an apparently homosexual relationship between two of its most gilded denizens. Wilde was not merely imprisoned, but his plays were suppressed, and on release he was forced into exile and death in France. While a revival of his writings took place later, the lines of what was or was not permissible were redrawn, often harshly. Censorship of plays by the Lord Chamberlain, and prosecution of books by the Director of Public Prosecutions reached a state absurd even by the standards of the later nineteenth century; thus reinforcing and actually extending the old, pernicious double standard of private and public morality. Terrible things might happen, but, so long as they were hidden from a supposedly prying and prurient public, it was as if they had never happened; if they came out into the open, then the offenders, like Wilde, suffered the double penalty, by legal and social judgement.

Thus Lord Alfred Douglas ("Bosie"), Wilde's presumed paramour, could, as the one "offended", return to society: Desmond MacCarthy met him when Wilfred Blunt gave a party at Newtimber "purposely to rehabilitate him. Douglas had married, and he thought it was really time people ceased to cut him." In the intervening years, however, Douglas had learned much: "true to his type, the outlaw aristocrat, he was a very dirty fighter, not caring what weapons he used, and also caring precious little what means he took to get his way when in a tight place or wanting money" (Desmond MacCarthy, *Memories* (1953), pp.203–4).

More unfortunate than Douglas, and rather more deserving of sympathy, was Lord Arthur Somerset. "Podge", as he was known to his friends, the Prince of Wales among them, was implicated in the Cleveland Street scandal in 1889, when a messenger boy, arrested for stealing, betrayed the existence of a male-brothel, run by a Mr Hammond, using the services of post-office clerks. Investigations by the Metropolitan Police revealed that regular clients included, among several high-ranking names, the Earl of Euston and Lord Arthur—a younger son of the Duke of Beaufort, and equerry, as well as close friend, to the Prince. A characteristically muddled attempt at cover-up followed. Euston escaped completely, vindicating himself later in a suit for criminal libel against a journalist who had dared to publish his name. The Department of Public Prosecutions passed Somerset's case to the

Prime Minister, Lord Salisbury, who evaded comment by sending it to the Lord Chancellor, Lord Halsbury; and Halsbury actually recommended that the prosecution should be dropped. Meanwhile, Somerset, the "unfortunate lunatic", as the Prince of Wales called him, was allowed to slip across the Channel, and the minor participants were given ludicrously light sentences. But, when Labouchère, W.T. Stead and the radical press began to ask unpleasant questions, the whole scandal was exposed; and, even if nothing else had mattered, the hounding given to the Tory Ministry made it impossible for Somerset ever to return. For nearly thirty years, with stoic endurance, he lived in exile, first on the run in Southern Europe and Turkey, taking bizarre and menial jobs, and then, after a partial reconciliation with his family (in sharp contrast to the unremitted hounding of the homosexual Lord Beauchamp by his brother in law, the Duke of Westminster), in the south of France, where he eventually died, a forgotten man, in 1926.

One reason for the urgency of efforts to cover up in the Cleveland Street case was the fear that the Prince of Wales's eldest son, Prince Albert Victor, a dissolute and vacuous youth, might also be exposed; and Somerset's claim to a certain sort of martyrdom may have been justified. Prince Albert's debauchery was successfully hidden until his death in 1892, as were many other incipient scandals, unrelated to royalty. What counted most, after the fact itself—and many of his friends simply could not believe Somerset to be guilty—was that public judgement was irrevocable.

One potential scandal that did not break concerned the Irish Crown Jewels, which in 1907 vanished from a safe in which they were being kept in Dublin Castle, in the care of Sir Arthur Vicars. The Secretary of State for Ireland, Augustine Birrell, was away on holiday; in his absence, the police pursued their routine investigations and in due course found that a well-known pawnbroker in the city had them in his safe. Unfortunately, he had acquired them apparently in good faith, having laid out £10,000 to the three men who had brought them in, and whom he clearly identified as the son of a leading Liberal politician, a member of a distinguished Anglo-Irish family, and an official of Dublin Castle itself. He offered, however, to hand the jewels over, for the £10,000 and a week's interest.

What followed blended farce and panic. The three thieves divided the money, and, counting on their position and Liberal Party funds to keep them from prosecution, simply spent it. Meanwhile, the embarrassed Irish police, caught between the wish to prosecute criminals and a prohibition apparently imposed by Dublin Castle, the seat of Liberal rule, asked for £10,000 to redeem the pledge. But the Liberal politician could not raise it himself, nor could he extract it from party funds, without inviting too many awkward questions. Eventually, as the second week ran out, the problem was solved in a way entirely characteristic of the period: a prominent Liberal supporter, on the roll of industrialists seeking honours, was offered an immediate knighthood. In return he subscribed the £10,000, the interest on it and sufficient extra to buy silence from the pawnbroker. Sir Arthur Vicars was dismissed, and on Birrell's return a closed inquiry was initiated. Vicars named Tim Healey and another Irish advocate as his defence, but both withdrew when the press was excluded. No report was published, and a blanket of silence lay over the case for some years, while the unfortunate Vicars retired, unable to vindicate his name.

The King, as George Wyndham, Irish Chief Secretary, told Wilfred Blunt, "was furious at the idea of there being a scandal like the one in Berlin, and it cannot be kept secret as everybody at Dublin knows it". Nevertheless, it remained a secret for long enough, and even those in the know, who publicised the story in the 1920s, kept the names of the participants to themselves.

The ancient legal distinction between misdemeanours (which might under certain circumstances be venial) and felonies (which were not) was rarely questioned. Prison and hard labour were stains no gentleman could throw off, even if there were a conspiracy of silence to protect him from the worst possible consequences. Arthur Ponsonby recalled, from his golfing days at Marienbad, "During a competition I received an anonymous letter to the effect that one of the competitors, an American, had done seven years' imprisonment for forgery. He was a good-looking, youngish man and extremely popular with everyone. I put the letter in the fire, but a few days later I received another letter, and again a third; but it was clearly no business of mine to enquire into the past history of the members and I therefore paid no attention. My correspondent proved to be a lady whom the American had jilted, and finding I would do nothing she told another lady the story in the strictest confidence. Needless to say it was all over Marienbad in about two hours. It was apparently true that as a youth he had forged and been sent to prison, but he had made good and was in quite a good position somewhere. The wretched man thought it useless to fight the case and bolted by the next train" (*Memories of Three Reigns*, p.243).

The price of offences against the code of gentlemanly respectability could be appallingly high. An element of representativeness, of holding the privileged order responsible for public morality, lay behind the awfulness of being found out in public. "When a peer of high rank drags his dignity in the dirt ... he stains his order", *The Times* pronounced after the disgrace and death of the last Marquis of Hastings in 1868; and Edward VII, whose own character was brushed by scandal in the Mordaunt divorce case, and in the card-sharping affair at Tranby Croft, never hid his repugnance at what he called "the washing of dirty linen in public". As far as the public were concerned, the upper-class were duty-bound to maintain an appearance of respectability; and to this end the golden rule was, as the Duchess in *The Edwardians* was clearly aware, "Prevent a scandal .... Within the closed circle of their own set, anybody might do as they pleased, but no scandal must leak out to the uninitiated. Appearances must be respected, though morals might be neglected."

The corollary of this was that mistakes could not easily be put right. Ponsonby tells a terrible story of what the imputation of cowardice—one of the most serious offences against the code—could involve. During the South African War, a captain (unnamed) in command of a company at Sanna's Post had surrendered to the Boers, having lost over half his men in action; and this surrender had led to the capitulation of the whole force, commanded by Colonel Adye. When the prisoners were released after the war, this officer was court-martialled, acquitted of cowardice, but reprimanded for an error of judgement. The Commander-in-Chief, Lord Roberts, agreed with the findings, but "Lord Wolseley, who was Commander-in-Chief at home, took the view that it was necessary to make an example as the white flag had been used too freely in South Africa. He therefore reversed the decision and ordered Captain X to be cashiered for cowardice. He persuaded St John Brodrick, the Secretary of State for War, to support him and give his approval."

On his return, the Captain appealed, quite properly, to the highest authorities, and, with the aid of an experienced military lawyer, won the approval of both the King and Lord Roberts, now Commander-in-Chief, to a remission allowing him merely to resign—a strategy which was later approved by a special court of inquiry composed of generals who had been in South Africa. Unfortunately, Brodrick took a high line, claiming that he was bound by the previous decision; in face of the King's insistence, he threatened to resign.

"The King was furious and apparently contemplated accepting Brodrick's resignation. Then suddenly the whole principle of constitutional monarchy was at stake and Brodrick appealed to Balfour, the Prime Minister. Balfour took the view that he was bound to support one of his Cabinet and wrote to the King that if Brodrick resigned, he feared the whole Cabinet would tender their resignation. Here was a very awkward situation for the King, because if the Government resigned and had an election with the cry that His Majesty was acting autocratically and was overriding the decisions of his responsible Ministers, the whole country would support them. The King quickly grasped this and told Balfour he would leave the matter in the hands of the Cabinet and would abide by their advice. This was considered by the Cabinet a very adroit way on the King's part of extricating himself from a delicate and dangerous situation. The King always prided himself on being entirely a constitutional monarch, but at heart he was a born autocrat. The matter came before the Cabinet, but of course it was a very one-sided affair, for Brodrick presented his case and there was no one to represent the other point of view. The Cabinet supported Brodrick: Captain X was cashiered and disgraced, and the British Constitution saved at his expense" (*Recollections of Three Reigns*, pp. 126–7).

It is hard to avoid the conclusion that the face of the War Office, rather than the Constitution, was at stake. But subjective interpretation of the offence was only too common. At its most extreme, it can be seen when applied to Ireland, and the destructive conflict of loyalties between North and South and between Irish and English nationalism. The so-called "mutiny" of the Curragh was, to a degree, punished—French and Seeley were forced to resign in 1913. But this was no bar to French's career, for on the outbreak of war he was granted command of the Expeditionary Force in France. Sir Roger Casement, on the other hand, was accused of high treason for planning rebellion in Ireland during the war, with German aid; and a man whom some Irishmen have claimed as a great patriot was stripped of his knighthood, hanged in Pentonville Prison in August 1916 and buried in an unmarked grave. What a biographer of Haig wrote applies in historical perspective to Casement as well: "There is no easy escape from the conflict of loyalties which must arise when a lawfully elected government passes measures genuinely repugnant to the consciences of those who have to enforce them" (Robert Blake, *The Private Papers of Douglas Haig*, p.16), but this could hardly have been said before the 1950s.

Leaving aside what could be proved criminal, the pitfalls were clear enough. "There were certain things which you did not do, and there was an end to it", reflected Lord Roehampton, in *The Edwardians*. "You did not take the best place at your own shoot, you did not look over your neighbour's hand at cards, you did not open his letters, or put up with his committing adultery with your wife. These were things which everybody knew, and which consequently might be taken for granted." The sequence is interesting: the first three are, after all, no more than conventions of manners. Yet the code of gambling was as strict as that of sexual habits. The original Tranby Croft affair, in which Sir William Gordon-Cumming was accused of cheating, had as its sequel a libel action brought by Gordon-Cumming in 1881, in order to clear his name. When, largely on the testimony of the Prince of Wales, the defendant won, Gordon-Cumming was promptly expelled from the Army, his club and society in general. Sport raised the same passions. At Marienbad, Ponsonby often acted as golfing arbiter during the King's visits to the spa. One year an Englishman claiming a handicap of eighteen turned up. In public he played badly, but Ponsonby and the club professional once saw him playing excellent shots when out of sight. Ponsonby therefore graded him at plus-four, and, when the man objected, told him what had occurred. "He spluttered at first, but suddenly shut up like an umbrella and left the Club. He never played again at Marienbad" (*Recollections of Three Reigns*, p.244).

But the scandals of Edwardian England centred chiefly on sex, the sanctity of marriage, and the honour of women. Mere eccentricity of behaviour (such as the Irish peer Lord Wallscourt's habit of strolling in the nude in the grounds of his ancestral home, wearing, at his wife's suggestion, a cowbell to warn the maidservants of his approach) could be pardoned; but society took seriously enough the outraged father of the real-life girl portrayed as the heroine in H.G. Wells's *New Machiavelli*. Every day he would sit in the Savile Club at a small table in the great bow window overlooking Piccadilly, waiting, with a loaded revolver beside him, for Wells, also a member of the Savile, to approach. "The Committee", according to Compton MacKenzie, "were naturally disturbed by the prospect, and Wells was asked to resign" (*My Life and Times*, Octave 4, p.114).

One of the test cases of Edwardian morality was Lord Russell's bigamy. The Earl, elder brother of Bertrand Russell, succumbed to the flood of contemporary hypocrisy aroused by the state of the law on divorce—and in particular by the King's expressed disapproval of the marital habits of the aristocracy. Russell's first marriage, contracted in 1890, had had a bizarre history: within a year his wife had sued, unsuccessfully, for divorce on the grounds of cruelty; in 1894 she sued again, for restitution of conjugal rights; and in 1895 Russell obtained, but lost on appeal, a judicial separation. Finally, worn out by the cost and frustration of litigation at home, he obtained an American decree, and then married an American divorcee, Mrs Somerville. The divorce was not recognised in England and Russell was sacrificed to public morality, tried for bigamy by his peers, fined £1,500 (on top of costs of at least £5,000) and sentenced to three months' imprisonment.

But the law was merely the expression of public morality as defined by the society those peers and bishops represented; and Russell's later attempts to change the law foundered on the veto of the bishops and Lord Chancellor Halsbury—the same Lord Chancellor who had advised against prosecuting Lord Arthur Somerset fifteen years before.

Russell won in the end, in the sense that a Royal Commission on Divorce was set up in 1909. Yet even then the King (whose private habits might have been expected to have given him wider understanding) opposed the appointment of women to the Commission, divorce being a question "which cannot be discussed openly and in all its aspects with any delicacy or even decency before ladies". It came down to a morbid sensitivity to the intrusion of the "real world" into the province of an idealised womankind, and a more rational fear of what would happen if dissolute habits grew among a previously docile and deferential working class. This is what the Duchess in *The Edwardians* meant when she said "only the vulgar divorce". Woman had to stand on her pedestal; and, when Iris, in Pinero's play of the same name, takes advantage of her lover's insistence, and the facility of his cheque book, to fly with him to Vienna, she finds, not illicit happiness, but an ostracism as all-embracing as it would have been in London—a retribution accurate as a contemporary observation, and appropriate to the preconceptions of Pinero's audience. Equally, while it was quite permissible—even fashionable—for men of position to marry beneath them (after Lord Bruce married the actress Dolly Tester in 1884, eighteen other peers followed his lead, usually with Gibson girls, before 1914), acceptance of the reverse was never admitted. If a gentlewoman married in this way, she simply demeaned herself, as is made clear in *The Edwardians*: "It was manifestly impossible that Margaret [Lady Roehampton's daughter] should be allowed to marry the creature. To begin with he was illegitimate .... 'That's the penalty you see, Margaret darling', she said, 'and we all have to pay it in one form or another. It's a terrible thing to become *declassée*.' "

Sexual, like criminal misdemeanours, posed a challenge to the accepted theory of society and were punished accordingly. The insupportable, rather than the intolerable, were let off more lightly. For the incorrigibly eccentric, the slightly insane, the out-and-out black sheep, there was always (money permitting) a perpetual grand tour of Europe to be organised, or residence, on a monthly remittance, in one of the healthier colonies, like Kenya or the newly acquired Rhodesias. Gentlemen whom England or their families rejected sometimes made good in remoter areas as district commissioners or local magistrates; and if, on the contrary, they "went native" or, worse, committed sins against another code, like Conrad's hero in *Lord Jim*, they were usually too far off, and too long forgotten, to implicate their families in dishonour.

When the code was not so openly broken, the response was less predictable. In that moneyed era, speculation, financial fraud and share manipulation throve, and very few would have agreed with Stanley Baldwin's dictum that "a man who made a million quick ought not to be in the House of Lords but in jail". At the peak of his tarnished eminence, Horatio Bottomley could remain on fraternal terms with high political society, while using his paper *John Bull* in ways which today might have exposed him to criminal charges: thus he made money by campaigning against leading stores, such as Waring and Gillow, with the slogan "Gillow is not wearing well", buying their shares cheaply and at the same time taking bribes to cease his attacks, and taking a further profit when the shares rose.

The most celebrated financial scandal of the day involved several of the Liberal leaders in the 1910 government, and posed, in public, uncomfortable questions about public morality, and the distinction between the exercise of wits and criminal activity.

Early in 1912 the Marconi Company won the contract for the Imperial chain of wireless stations. The government tender was signed in March, but had to be approved (no mere formality) by the House of Commons. The affair became the focus of bitter political infighting between Liberals and Tories, and aroused the most vindictive personal hatreds, to say nothing of the anti-semitism latent in British public life.

In the previous six months, Marconi shares had risen from £2 8s 9d to £9. Rumours began to suggest political as well as private gain. Why had Sir Herbert Samuel, the Liberal Postmaster General, blocked discussion of the tender in the House of Commons? Why had Marconi so easily got the contract? Was there a link between Godfrey Isaacs, the managing director, and his brother Sir Rufus Isaacs, the Attorney General? Could there have been a Jewish conspiracy to defraud? At the same time, it was asked in the City if there had been spectacular share rigging—for the shares dropped again after a large new issue by the American Marconi Company. The press outcry was led by the avowedly anti-semitic Chesterton brothers and Leonard Maxse, and in October 1912 a Select Committee was appointed to look into the affair. At the same time an expert committee examined the contract, which it later confirmed. In front of the Select Committee, the whole case was argued out, and a misinterpretation given to the most damaging allegation—that Samuel and the two Isaacs brothers had actually profited from the boom in share values—gave Sir Rufus the chance to take the London editor of *Le Matin* to court for libel. There, in public, it was revealed that no one had benefited—but that Sir Rufus Isaacs had bought 10,000 shares of the new American issue, and that of these he had sold 1,000 each to Lloyd George and Lord Murray, the Liberal Chief Whip.

Meanwhile Cecil Chesterton had been hammered in criminal libel, having evaded giving evidence to the Select Committee; and the Committee's own report, when it emerged, was obscured by party divisions. There were in fact three reports, on divergent lines: the majority cleared all four Liberal Ministers implicated; but the Tory minority report censured them for "grave impropriety". In the two-day debate which followed, the government carried the day, in defence of its members, by 346 votes to 268. But Lord Murray, censured by a Select Committee of the Lords, found it expedient to resign; and a further court of inquiry took to task the stockbrokers and jobbers who had handled the American issue.

Lloyd George and Rufus Isaacs survived, their reputations more than a little tarnished. But they had at least been vindicated *in public*; and that, by Edwardian standards, was sufficient to preserve them in public political life. That distinction between "sailing close to the wind" and outright scandal can be seen at its clearest in the careers of those two outstanding Edwardian mavericks, Frank Harris and Horatio Bottomley.

Frank (christened James) Harris was born in 1856 in a poor village in Ireland. The son of a ship's steward, he survived a mean, hard and unprepossessing upbringing largely by his own efforts. From his school days in a clinically religious institution in Wales, he exhibited a remarkably virile temperament and an ability to embroider and fantasise on his sexual exploits, qualities which made him, apparently, almost irresistible to women throughout his life. But what gave him an entry to London society at the end of the nineteenth century was his wit and his journalist's capacity to turn his experience of life into vivid prose. The experience, at least in his early days, was picaresque even by the standards of the America he had known as a "little Irish immigrant" in the 1870s. Employed variously as bouncer in a casino, waiter, box-office attendant and butcher, he subsequently made money as a broker in real estate with his brother in Kansas. Then, leaving, by his own account, a trail of deflowered maidens gasping for his return, he came back to England, emerging as an ill-paid tutor of French at Brighton College. A facility for capitalising on great names showed itself, and he made much of a brief acquaintance with the aging Carlyle; but his real assault on the literary world began in the 1880s, when at the age of twenty-seven he was offered the post of editor of the *Evening News*.

Harris the journalist succeeded Harris the small-town Casanova; he campaigned on a radical, often socialist, platform, exposed the seamier side of urban life and crossed swords with W.T. Stead over the latter's revelation of prostitution in London. Soon he was well enough known to be satirised in George and Weedon Grossmith's brilliant little *Diary of a Nobody* as the thrusting Mr Hardfur Huttle (most Englishmen at this time mistook Harris for an American). He left the *Evening News* for the *Fortnightly Review*, married a rich widow fifteen years his senior, and began a rapid climb, using her house in Park Lane to entertain. But his political ambitions failed. Instead of becoming, as he dreamed, "the British Bismark", he lost his first asset, the Liberal candidature at South Hackney—not, perhaps, surprising for a man who openly defended Parnell in the storm over his liaison with Kitty O'Shea.

Max Beerbohm sketched him in the 1890s, when he was running the *Saturday Review*, the best literary periodical of the time: "he had a marvellous speaking voice, like the organ in Westminster Abbey, and with infallible footwork". But Max had no illusions about the *habitué* of the Café Royal: "Frank Harris is going about like a howling cad, seeking whom he may blackmail." When asked if Harris ever told the truth, he replied, "sometimes, don't you know, when his invention flags!" (David Cecil, *Max* (1964), p.164). Yet Harris's life was fiction rather than lies; just as his wildest fantasies grew out of his powerful attraction to women, greater even than that of that other Edwardian womaniser, H.G. Wells. He had a genuinely radical turn of mind; he used both the *Fortnightly* and the *Saturday* as vehicles of his crusade against cant, hypocrisy and humbug, and he was one of the very few who had the courage to defend Oscar Wilde after his conviction.

Harris could never have been counted more than an affiliated member of upper-class society, yet he was entirely characteristic of one facet of it in the 1890s and 1900s. He had come to London with a passionate yearning: "If you have never been intoxicated you have never lived. London made me drunk for years and in memory still the magic of those first years ennobles life for me and the later pains and sufferings, wrongs and insults, disdains and disappointments all vanish and are forgotten .... London when you are twenty-eight and have already won a place in its life; London when your mantlepiece has ten times as many invitations as you can accept, and there are two or three pretty girls that attract you; London when everyone you meet is courteous, kind and people of importance are beginning to speak about you; London with the foretaste of success in your mouth while your eyes are open to a million novelties and wonders; London with its rounds of receptions and court life, its theatre and shows, its amusements for the body, mind and soul: enchanting hours at burlesque prolonged by a boxing match at the sporting club; or an evening in Parliament where world famous men discuss important policies; or a quiet morning spent with a poet who will live in English literature with Keats or Shakespeare; London: who could even give an idea of its varied delights?" (Quoted in Philippa Puller, *Frank Harris* (1975), p.92).

He was a collector of people, who clustered around him at the long lunches at the Café Royal; of the adventurers in modern life who recognised a certain kinship with him, like Lord Randolph Churchill, his son Winston, and, above all, the Prince of Wales (though few of his stories about the Prince's dependence on his wit can be credited). He gathered for the *Saturday Review* a team of contributors brilliant even for those days—among them Shaw, D.S. MacCall, Beerbohm, H.G. Wells and Arthur Symons. Yet, in another sense, Harris could never be acceptable: he was a man for raffish male parties or for women like Princess Alice of Monaco (a typically Jamesian figure, the real-life American girl in Europe), but hardly one to invite for the weekend or introduce to one's daughters. Behind his fantasies lay a mocking stance, sometimes close to hatred of the upper-class view on life, that later on, in his decline, turned into a metaphorical defiling of society and the women who had supposedly given him their favours. After all, as he wrote to Shaw in November 1900, his play *Mr and Mrs Daventry* (which opened at the Royalty in October 1900 with Mrs Patrick Campbell in the title role) was intended to expose the hypocrisies of marriage and their consequence, adultery. "The decay of Christianity and a belief in a future life has had for chief consequences, first the demand of the people for a better life on this earth—socialism—and second the demand by the other oppressed class woman, for its larger satisfaction of her instincts in this world. This new woman wants nothing but love, whatever form she may individually affect, affection or passion. I have taken her to demand affection in this case ...."

Gradually Harris's talk became too long, loud and egoistic for the others of his circle. He drifted towards sheer promiscuity, and his writing deteriorated. Obsessed with money, impatient with the veneer of manners, he showed himself too frank for tolerance. Dining with Shaw in a London club, he replied loudly to his host's inquiry about the wine, "Oh yes, I suppose it is good enough for this collection of seedy prigs". He would as soon describe the luridly erotic drawings of Felicien Rops to a bishop's wife as he would to a colleague on the *Saturday Review*, and eventually even Shaw and Beerbohm began to find him impossible. William Rothenstein told of a dinner at the Café Royal when Wilde, in reply to Harris's boasting talk of all the great houses he had frequented, tartly observed, "Yes dear Frank, we believe you. You have dined in every house in London—*once.*"

His association with the crooked financier Ernest Hooley, and his use of the *Saturday* as a vehicle for advertisement and promotion of crank schemes and puffed-up companies, brought him very close to outright fraud. After driving down the shares of Bovril by running attacks on the company, until Hooley could buy the company cheaply, he turned at once to Bovril's virtues as a beverage. Later Lord Alfred Douglas was to accuse him of blackmail—possibly unjustly. Most often, Harris's schemes lost him money; in particular, a series of libel suits in the 1900s debilitated his fortunes just when he was running two *ménages* for his mistresses.

After the *Saturday Review* came *The Candid Friend*, a sort of poor man's *Tatler*, with the memoirs of fashionable actresses mixed in with muckraking exposures, society gossip and literary advertisements, usually for Harris's own books. By 1907, when he bought *Vanity Fair*, he was running downhill, physically as well as socially. Through the remaining Edwardian years, he dodged his creditors and his private fear of madness; his talk became, in Wells's phrase, "a rich, muddy noise"; his articles began to repeat past phrases and scenes; even his percipient study *The Man Shakespeare* was brilliant more as a portrait of Harris than of his hero. By 1914 he was editing a rather shady periodical, *Modern Society*, steering between bankruptcy and the law of libel. Brought to court in a minor case, he lost his temper with the judge and was committed to Brixton prison for contempt—a light-enough penalty in the end, since he was allowed to have his meals sent in from the Café Royal. For years his friends had supported him—the Duke of Marlborough, Winston Churchill (who used him as a literary agent), Hugh Kingsmill and Enid Bagnold, who loved him greatly; but he could sometimes rat even on these.

Harris's life was never less than public, even when, in a last attempt to salvage his fortunes, he embarked with Lady Warwick on her extraordinary scheme to blackmail £100,000 out of the Palace in 1914, in return for King Edward's letters written to her when she had been his mistress. The affair—"My darling Daisy"— was handled by Arthur du Cros, a Tory MP, and the threat was that Harris would publish the letters if the money was not paid; but the Palace skilfully delayed, and the war put the possibility of scandal, and much else in Harris's life, out of the public mind. He returned to America, and his attacks on the English oligarchy, with accusations that England was fighting only out of jealousy of Germany, branded him in London as a traitor. Final social extinction occurred in 1922 with the publication of the first volume of *My Life and Loves*, with its pornographic—albeit fantastic— descriptions of past conquests. Ironically, he had dictated it, long after he had become impotent, to a series of pretty secretaries, most of whom seem to have been in love with him.

Harris's fall can be set against the changing standards of the time, for the gradual emancipation of taste which took place after about 1912 made him, in a curious way, redundant. His heyday largely corresponded to that of another strange manifestation of Edwardian society: an amazingly persuasive talker, though without Harris's literary talent, a confidence man, more openly fradulent, yet in some ways more socially acceptable, Horatio Bottomley.

Bottomley's origin was mysterious: product of a Victorian orphanage, he may have been the illegitimate son of Charles Bradlaugh, the social reformer and radical MP, whom he grew closely to resemble. Bottomley liked to refer to his upbringing as the "university of life"—it taught him the importance of appearance, self-confidence, and a firm belief in the gullibility of the greater part of mankind. After a career as shorthand writer in the law courts, he moved to newspapers, and in the 1880s founded the *Financial Times*, as a competitor of the *Financial News*. His first experience of conmanship and snowball finance came with his *Hansard Union*, an abortive attempt (its collapse came in 1891) to take over the reporting of Parliamentary debates. His knowledge of the law, acquired in the long days of taking notes in court, enabled him to evade almost certain imprisonment for fraud; he was recognised as the foremost amateur lawyer of the day, when, watched amusedly by Frank Harris, he undermined not only the Crown case, but also the credibility of the Official Liquidator himself.

Bottomley scorned regular practice at the bar and, instead of qualifying, turned to mining finance, operating a whole series of Australian mining companies to keep ahead of creditors and prosecution. Normally his companies paid one dividend (out of capital) and Bottomley's "expenses" and then collapsed, either in liquidation or in "reconstruction" from which only he profited. By the turn of the century, he had paid off his former creditors in the *Hansard Union* bankruptcy, and his *Financial Times* ranked him as one of the "men of millions", together with Barney Banato, the South African diamond king, and Whittaker Wright. It was, of course, a pyramid of paper sustained by the insane credulity of investors brought up on dreams of instant fortunes, made possible only because there *was* gold in the Transvaal and Australia. Unfortunately, it rarely lay in Bottomley's mines. He once wrote to his stock-jobbing partner, "My dear Harry, What on earth have you done with our nugget—the one we used to show to shareholders in the old days? I have got hold of a promising client, all he wants is a sight of the stuff" (Alan Hyman, *The Rise and Fall of Horatio Bottomley* (1972), p.169).

Bottomley's use of his money seems typical of the *parvenu* in Edwardian society. His newly-built red-brick mansion, The Dicker, sprawled out in its ornamental grounds near Eastbourne; the local train stopped regularly at Dicker Halt to collect him; champagne and kippers provided his breakfast; flats in the West End housed his succession of inamorata—minor actresses, none of whom accompanied him on his forages into more elegant fields. But he rose, with undoubted success, and in the 1906 general election became Liberal MP for South Hackney (in the wake of the less fortunate Harris). His appearance, something between a beadle's and a bishop's, was less *outré* than that of the flamboyant Harris, though through drink and over-indulgence it later worsened. Beverley Nicols pictured him, speaking at the Oxford Union after the war, as "a grotesque figure. Short and uncommonly broad, he looked almost gigantic in his thick fur coat. Lack-lustre eyes, heavily pouched, glared from a square, sallow face .... It was not till he began to talk that the colour mottled his cheeks and the chilly hues on his face were lightened" (quoted in Hyman, *Rise and Fall of Horatio Bottomley*, p.123).

To the worldly-wise sophisticates who avoided his share promotions and rarely read his most successful paper, *John Bull*, Bottomley was a transparent rogue; but he had an endearing side, as the brilliant young advocate F.E. Smith, later Lord Birkenhead, admitted. Writing after Bottomley's bankruptcy had forced him to resign from the House of Commons, Smith called him "one of the most attractive speakers to whom I have ever listened .... His House of Commons style was almost ideal." He was fortunate in his opponents, who sued for libel at crucial times in his career, and lost, against Bottomley's plausible self-defence in front of impressionable juries; he was lucky in finding the subtle mind of Julius Elias, later the editor of the *Daily Herald*, to sustain the mechanics of *John Bull*; he was a superb actor, appearing at one moment as the sober, almost sanctimonious, politician, and at the next as a brazen adventurer, drumming up funds for a project as ludicrous as the South Sea Bubble; and he had dreams—rather like Harris, he saw himself as a saviour of his country, as a Chancellor of the Exchequer to rank with Gladstone.

John Bull, and in particular his own column, "The World, the Flesh and the Devil", gave him opportunities not only to attack his *bêtes noires*, publicise his coming men (Churchill among them) and indulge in skilful muckraking, but also to raise cash. The John Bull Investment Trust brought him £100,000 in the lean time after the Australian boom had ended; and the hordes of informers and petty criminals who gave him material for his stories also left information which could be—and was—used for blackmail. Bottomley aroused hatred as well as admiration: he hounded the inoffensive Liberal Minister C.F.G. Masterman, and in the 1911 Woolwich by-election he printed a facsimile of Ramsay MacDonald's birth certificate, showing the Labour leader to have been illegitimate. He lived always close to the edge, spending without thought of income, buying racehorses whose only merit was consistency in failure, and ordering the construction, from his palatial Long Acre offices, of a secret exit by which to escape the bailiffs, who he knew would come in the end.

Most of his firms were simply bucket shops, and his survival to 1912 may be explained by the fear he inspired among the swindled, who had seen him, and F.E. Smith on his behalf, sway case after case in court. But he was brought down by the incorruptible solicitor Edward Bell, at the end of a five-year partnership with Ernest Hooley. The two confidence tricksters had battened on the senile rich and immature heirs to fortunes, and between them had launched such schemes as the revival of the Basingstoke Canal, a waterway long dry, bought with worthless duplicates of shares in their own companies. After years of delaying actions, Bottomley was declared bankrupt in 1912, forced to apply for the Chiltern Hundreds, and denounced by MacDonald as "a man of doubtful parentage who has lived all his life on the threshold of jail".

Yet Bottomley survived. *John Bull's* sales reached 1.25 million in 1913. His horse won the Cesarewitch, and, when the war came, he climbed on the patriotic bandwagon, setting himself up as a civilian Kitchener, England's recruiting sergeant. In the over-heated atmosphere of 1914–15, the virulent anti-German stance of *John Bull*, and Bottomley's own hectic populism, brought him back into the mainstream of political life. Yet he was not chosen, like the press Lords Northcliffe and Beaverbrook, for ministerial office under Lloyd George; and, although he managed, in an orgy of fraudulent prospectuses and stock conversion, to raise the money to pay off his creditors again, and re-enter Parliament in 1919, his War Stock Combination scheme and his final, hasty and ill-prepared swindle, in Victory Bonds, brought him in 1920 to disaster. "I've been sitting on a barrel of gunpowder for thirty years", he told Hooley before the trial, "and it might go up at any minute." Despite the defence put up for him by Edward Marshall Hall, Bottomley was flayed in court, and went down to seven years' penal servitude. More even than that of Harris, his career highlights the contrast between the way up and the way down. The pre-1914 world offered, as F.E. Smith said in 1926, "glittering prizes for those with sharp swords ready to take them". The penalties, however, demolished everything.

PART II

LIVING

CHAPTER FIVE

Public Duty

A public meeting in the 1900s would have regarded as sheer archaism Disraeli's famous address to the electors of Shrewsbury in 1843, with its claim that the landed interest represented all that was valuable and lasting in English society; and it would have seen as almost equally outdated the brilliant polemics of Robert Lowe, in the 1860s, against widening the franchise: for Lowe was defending a body only slightly less oligarchic—the landed interest plus the aristocracy of merit and intelligence. While it might still have been correct to say that a gentleman was someone of no occupation, the great majority of the numerically far larger gentry of Edwardian England pursued occupations either directly or under another name. They managed their estates, took their seats as directors of banks or businesses, became stockbrokers and even accountants, qualified for the Army, or for the civil or foreign service. Very few ignored the duty that had become the consequence of privilege: the performance of some form of public service. There could be no better valediction to the past than the *Times* obituary on the death of Lord St Aldwyn in 1916: "He belonged to the class of country gentlemen who have in the history of modern England devoted themselves to public life …. He always managed his properties himself without the aid of an agent. They were invariably left in excellent order, and the happiest relations existed between landlord and tenant."

A remarkable, yet characteristic, family, the Lyttletons, spanned the whole range of public duties. The fourth Lord Lyttleton married twice and left fifteen children, fourteen of whom survived into and beyond the Edwardian period. Charles, the fifth Lord Lyttleton, managed the ancestral estates; his brothers were, in order of age, an Anglican clergyman, a soldier (Commander-in-Chief Ireland, 1908–12), the private secretary to Prime Minister Gladstone, the Bishop of

Southampton, a solicitor and author, headmaster of Eton, and Colonial Secretary; and his sisters married a bishop, a barrister, an MP, an Irish statesman, the Dean of Durham, and the Keeper of the National Portrait Gallery.

It had been fashionable, thirty years earlier, to decry professional status and affect horror at the idea of a career in business. "My governor is quite savage because I won't accept a stool in old Blank's counting house", says a character in an 1878 tract for schoolboys. "Likely notion isn't it? First brings me up a gentleman, and then expects to set me down to dirty work like that. Why I'd rather go to the diggings at once!" The father then points the moral: "The difficulty there is in these days of finding employment in England for the numbers of young men growing up and wishing to earn their livelihood here as gentlemen. Every profession is overstocked: there are more men (yes and capable well educated young men) than there are places for them to fill" (Anon, *Quite a Gentleman*, p.45).

But the Edwardian youth was more likely to have to contend with training and examinations. Thus the dialogue in a popular boys' adventure story emphasises the need for scholastic qualifications:

"When you are two-and-twenty, your chance of getting any appointment whatever in the public service is at an end."

"Then interest has nothing to do with it?"

"Well, yes. There are a few berths in the Foreign Office, for example, in which a man has to get a nomination before going in for the exam; but of course the age limit tells there as well as in any other."

"And if a man fails altogether what is there open to him?"

The other shrugged his shoulders. "Well, as far as I know, if he hasn't capital he can emigrate, that is what numbers of fellows do. If he has interest he can get a commission in the militia, and from that possibly into the line, or he can enlist as a private for the same object. There is a third alternative, he can hang himself. Of course, if he happens to have a relation in the city he can get a clerkship, but that alternative, I should say, is worse than the third."

"But I suppose he might be a doctor, a clergyman, or a lawyer?"

"I don't know much about those matters, but I do know that it takes about five years' grinding, and what is called 'walking the hospitals', that is, going round the wards with the surgeons, before one is licensed to kill. I think, but I am not sure, that three years at the bar would admit you to practice, and usually another seven or eight years are spent before you earn a penny. As for the Church, you have to go through the university or one of the places we call training colleges; and when at last you are ordained you may reckon, unless you have great family interest, on remaining a curate with perhaps one hundred or one hundred and fifty pounds per annum for eighteen or twenty years."

"And no amount of energy will enable a man of, say four-and-twenty, without a profession, to obtain a post on which he could live with some degree of comfort?"

"I don't think energy would have anything to do with it. You cannot drop into a merchant's office and say 'I want a snug berth out in China', or 'I should like an agency in Mesopotamia'. Of course men of business can take their sons into their own offices and train them to their own profession; but after all, if a man has four or five sons he cannot take them all into his office with a view to partnership. He may take one, but the others have to make their own way somehow." (G.A. Henty, *With Kitchener in the Soudan* (1905), pp.318-19.)

The age of the meritocracy had begun.

Yet no period in history is ever uniform, and it was perfectly understandable, indeed a matter for edification, that a lecturer at Oxford in the summer of 1914 could open his lectures to second-year undergraduates—Harold Macmillan among them—with the homily, "Gentlemen—you are now about to embark upon a course of studies which will occupy you for two years. Together they form a noble adventure. But I would like to remind you of an important point. Some of you, when you go down from the university will go into the Church, or to the Bar, or to the House of Commons, to the Home Civil Service, to the Indian or Colonial Services, or into various professions. Some may go into the Army, some into industry and commerce; some may become country gentlemen. A few—I hope a very few—will become teachers or dons. Let me make this clear to you. Except for the last category, nothing that you will learn in the course of your studies will be of the slightest possible use to you in after life—save only this—that if you work hard and intelligently you should be able to detect *when a man is talking rot*, and that, in my view, is the main, if not the sole purpose of education" (quoted in Harold Macmillan, "Oxford Remembered", *The Times*, 18 October 1975).

If he were fortunate enough to be first-born and to inherit the estate, the prospects for an Edwardian landowner were less gloomy than they had been in the previous generation during the great agricultural depression and the battles over the landlords' remaining in political power. The troubles in Ireland, the boycotts, cattle-maiming and rick-burning had largely ceased with land reforms, and the terrible nineteenth-century clearances in the Highlands of Scotland had almost ended. Though the memory and bitterness lived on in the Celtic fringes, a new image was developing, in towns rather than in the real countryside, of the idealised village, with its squire, rector and rows of model cottages, their inhabitants humble yet contented with their lot.

"The squire's sense of station", according to one view, "was nicely balanced. They remained for the most part exclusive but unassuming, and little different, apart from their greater wealth, in habits and ideals from the yeoman class from which half of them were sprung. In rural districts, the squire's guiding hand was everywhere apparent, and that parish in which there was, for some reason, no squire, was instantly recognisable by its neglected, unkept, unloved appearance, and the reputedly 'bolshie' attitude of its inhabitants" (J. Lees-Milne, "Landed Properties and Proprietors", in *The Landed Gentry*, 1965).

This timeless picture was admitted to have some truth, even by the radical critic C.F.G. Masterman, writing in 1909: "The beauty of English landscape, the beauty of landlords' country—the open woods, the large green fields and wide hedges, the ampleness which signified country given up less to industry than to opulence and dignified ease. The one is a park: the other a source of food supply and the breeding place of men. The typical English countryside is that of great avenues leading to residences which lack no comfort, broad parks, stretches of private land, closely cultivated, but convenient for hunting, shooting and a kind of stately splendour .... The record of the great landowners of this country is of vast accumulations of acres: aggregations of whole counties, or estates dotted over many counties, each organised on the same plan of inherited feudal traditions. Where the money can still be obtained from external sources—the new wealth of the towns, or tribute from new stations abroad—some semblance of that feudal tradition still remains. Cottages are let at less than their market prices, old men and women on the estate are comfortably pensioned, there are alms houses and model villages and church schools, a deferential and grateful population, and all the apparatus of the model village, guided and controlled by the occupant of the great house" (*The Condition of England* (1909), p.157).

Yet Masterman saw that the depression had already forced smaller estates into decay, or into the hands of the new plutocracy—some of whom assumed the paternalistic tradition in promoting rural welfare, while others simply exploited it for their own enjoyment. Steady depopulation, the drift to the towns, formed a sombre backcloth even to Vita Sackville-West's picture of Chevron, the great house in *The Edwardians*. The son of the bailiff is about to leave and go into the motor trade; and the hero, Sebastian, reflects on the relationship between master and man:

> I think we have evolved a good system on the whole, which made for a good understanding between class and class. Nothing will ever persuade me that the relations between the squire and the groundsman, or the squire and the labourer, or the squire and the farmer, don't contain the elements of decency and honesty and mutual respect. I wish only that civilization could have developed along these lines. We have got away now from the day when we underpaid our labourers, cut off their ears for stealing a bit of wood, and we might have looked forward to an era when we could all have lived peacefully together, under a system peculiarly well suited to the English people. But, as you say, there are now too many people. There is too much industry. While idyllic England vanishes.

Yet, when he hands out a rise of five shillings a week to the woodman, he realises how paltry an amount this is.

> Five shillings a week is £13 a year, and—say that he employed a hundred men—that meant £1,300 a year; very little more than his mother would spend on a single ball; a negligible sum in his yearly budget. He felt ashamed ....

Money apart, he felt that his relationship with old Turner was false. What did he really care for old Turner's rheumatism? Or for his age? Or for the fact that he walked three miles at five o'clock every morning to go to his work, winter and summer, and three miles back every evening? Sebastian could stroll into the pumping shed every now and then, and gossip with old Turner, in a friendly way for ten minutes and he knew that old Turner liked it and retailed every word of the conversation to his old woman in the evening; but supposing that on a cold winter's night Sebastian had found his fire unlit, and on ringing the bell, had been told by Vigeon that old Turner had omitted to cut any faggots that day—would not he, Sebastian, have damned with rage, demanded what old Turner thought he was there for, if not to cut faggots? And would have thought himself a lenient master if he did not sack Turner without further enquiry" (*The Edwardians*, p.152).

Not many records survive of what Turner and his like thought of their masters, and of the patriarchal tradition. "If you couldn't do a job, you were reminded that plenty more could", a Suffolk labourer recalled, sixty years later. "So you had to be careful. I had to accept everything my governor said to me. I learnt never to answer a word. I dursn't say nothing. Today you can be a man with men, but not then. That is how it was. It will never be like that again. I lived when other men could do what they liked with me. We feared so much. We even feared the weather! Today a farmer must pay for the week, whatever the weather! But we were always being sent home. We dreaded the rain; it washed our few shillings away" (Blythe, *Akenfield*, p.53).

Sir Henry Rider Haggard, surveying the countryside in the 1900s, heard this from a Suffolk farmer: "The labourers 'back to the land'. That is the cry of the press, and the fancy of the people. Well, I do not think that they will ever come back. Certainly no legislation will ever bring them. Some of the rising generation may be induced to stay, but it will be by training them to the use of machinery and paying them higher wages. It should be remembered that the most intelligent men have gone: these will never come back, but the rising generation may stay, as competition in the town increases, and the young men of the country are better paid. It should be remembered too that as many men as formerly are not required to till the land .... Uniformity of wages should also be discontinued, and the best man must be the best paid; this will help them become farmers themselves better than any other means .... The fashion of the present day is the worship of money, and from this the labourer is no more exempt than the townsman .... It is not a question of rent or labour, or the farm, it is the man and, let me add, his wife."

This is light years away from the sentimental townsman's view of the land. Of course, there were still landowners who took their duties as seriously as Sir William Heathcote, who would not have a Dissenter for a tenant, in case religious differences came between them. But the reality probably lay elsewhere. As the primacy of money came to be openly admitted, and as a flood of new tenants came into occupation during the 1880s and 1890s, owing none of the old ties to particular families and estates, the idea of land as capital, like any other investment, took root. What recovery there was in the 1900s came from good, prudent management, judicious buying and selling to round off holdings, careful economies, or the skilled breeding of cattle and horses. Land, however, returned a poor rate of profit in rents, and expenditure on improvement fell away to half what it had been in the 1860s. Landowners' capacity to provide services—repairs to buildings and cottages, roads, drainage, fences—declined, and the state began to take over their "charitable" functions—provision of a full-time parson, a school, or relief in hard times. Meanwhile, the bargaining power of tenant farmers increased (since no landlord liked to have farms unlet and uncared for). Although the census of 1911 showed something of a return to the land, the very fact that "model farms" of the period were singled out for comment pointed towards the post-war world and the replacement, except on the very large estates, of the landowners by the gentleman farmer and by independent farmers who had bought out their tenancies and retained none of the old paternal attitudes towards the farm labourer.

As they inherited land, so many gentlemen inherited family businesses; and they were faced with a similar conflict between a still-present patriarchal tradition and enormous pressures to modernise in order to survive. British industry lagged behind that of its principal competitors, Germany and the United States, yet Teutonic thoroughness and American business methods became synonyms for describing the hard, uncaring modern world, which drove men out from secure employment and imposed the tyranny of the stopwatch and the production line.

When the ironmaster Alfred Baldwin died in 1908, his son Stanley took on both the managing directorship of the ironfounding firm of Baldwins and his father's seat in the House of Commons—first step on the road to 10 Downing Street. At that time Baldwins was a medium-sized firm, centred on the rolling-mill at Wilden, in Worcestershire, with an associated tin-plate and galvanised-sheet works at Pontypool and an open-hearth furnace at Port Talbot in Wales. Father and son lived in the ironmaster's house, almost in the shadow of the forge, until Stanley Baldwin married; and, looking back from the industrial troubles of 1925, he pictured the atmosphere in nostalgic colours.

"It was a place where I knew and had known from childhood, every man on the ground; a place where I was able to talk with the men not only about the troubles in the works, but troubles at home and their wives. It was a place where strikes and lock-outs were unknown. It was a place where the fathers and grandfathers of the men then working there had worked, and where their sons went automatically to the business. It was a place also where nobody ever 'got the sack' and where we had a natural sympathy for those who were less concerned in efficiency than is this generation, and where a large number of old gentlemen used to spend their days sitting on the handles of wheelbarrows, smoking their pipes" (quoted in Middlemas and Barnes, *Baldwin* (1969), p.9).

Baldwin's talents were administrative rather than managerial, and he followed his father into the business out of convention more than enthusiasm. Nevertheless, he carried on a gradual modernisation and expansion until politics drew him away. More than many employers before 1914, he understood the tension between the old tradition and the conditions of an industry no longer rooted in the local countryside. His inclination was clear: throughout his life, he carried the aura of a country gentleman, seeming to be most happy in the company of farmers and their livestock; and he also had a strong sympathy for industrial workers. During the great strike of 1912, he refused to lay off his own men, who were in no way involved: "A thousand men who had no interest in the dispute that was going on were thrown out of work through no fault of their own, at a time when there was no unemployment benefits. It seemed to me at that time a monstrous injustice to these men because I looked upon them as my own family and it hit me very hard ... and I made an allowance, not a large one, but something, for six weeks to carry them along, because I felt they were being so unfairly treated" (*Baldwin*, p.26).

A generation later, Baldwin was to be accused of buying peace in industry at the price of allowing industry itself to become obsolete. How different his attitude was from those whom Mastermen called "the Conquerors": "Representatives of the rich, from the security and ignorance of the country house and the country house outlook upon society, bring charges against the working man: of loathing and neglecting his labour; of betting, drinking and idling; of organising trade unions as a tyranny on the 'ca-canny' principle, designed to restrain the honest toilers from giving a fair day's labour for a fair wage" (*The Condition of England*, p.214). These could only approve the American managerial methods which were elsewhere blamed for wholesale sackings of workmen and junior management alike, for the introduction of new production norms, and for the growth of a frame of mind caught, in its home-grown environment, by D.H. Lawrence in *Women in Love*. On his father's death, Gerald Crich inherits the family coalmine, and, instead of letting the old inefficiencies continue, adopts the methods of the sorting shed and conveyor belt:

> As soon as Gerald entered the firm, the convulsion of death ran through the old system .... Terrible and inhuman were his examinations into every detail; there was no privacy he would spare, no old sentiment but he would turn it over. The old grey managers, the old grey clerks, the doddering old pensioners, he looked at them, and removed them as so much lumber. The whole concern seemed like a hospital of invalid employees. He had no emotional qualms. He arranged what pensions were necessary, he looked for efficient substitutes, and when these were found, he substituted them for the old hands.

This was not the face that Edwardian industry cared to display in public. If Gerald Crich was obliged by the pressures of economic decline to behave like the Capitalist pilloried in socialist pamphlets, he remained, among his equals, a gentleman. Even in 1920, upper-class society would take quite calmly the astonishing inability of the Duke of Northumberland, when questioned by the

Sankey Commission, to justify in any way his retention of royalties on the coal mined under his land. And "society" still regarded science and technology, the means of Britain's long-term survival, with distaste. The great Edwardian engineer William Armstrong and the scientist Lord Rayleigh were accepted as gifted eccentrics; but the majority of the Fellows of the Royal Society in 1905 had not even attended the "correct" universities. Of those whose educational background is known, twenty-four were Oxford men and sixty-seven Cambridge, as against eighty from London and twenty-nine, from Manchester, sixty-two from Scottish and twenty from Irish universities, and thirty-four self-taught. Hardly any had been to a well-known public school. (A.R. Ubbelohde, "Science", in *Edwardian England*, ed.S. Nowell-Smith (1964), p.227).

Lack of inheritance, in a world ruled strictly by primogeniture, forced many a young man to look to a career. If he were among the minority intelligent enough to have graduated from university, the chances were that he would go on to take the competitive examination for the civil service, or seek to qualify for the legal or some other profession. But, if he had left school at seventeen or eighteen, then, as Edward VII had pointed out in his advice to Winston Churchill, he might profitably spend a few years in the Army. He had probably already served in one of the cadet corps at public school, such as the Eton College Rifle Volunteers, and acquired the basic military disciplines of drill and weapon training. Since the purchase of commissions had been swept away a generation earlier, he would first have to qualify at Sandhurst—attended by many, from schools such as Cheltenham or Wellington, whose studies had been shaped primarily towards a long-term career in the Regular Army. But Britain had no military tradition in the style of Bismarckian Germany or Napoleonic France; and the young recruit of 1900 would have found a considerable gap between the pretensions of the military and their actual capacity in war.

"War is honourable", declared Thorstein Veblen, of "civilised Europe" in 1896; "and warlike prowess is eminently honorific in the eyes of the generality of men; and this admiration of warlike prowess is itself the best voucher of a predatory temperament in the admirer of war. The enthusiasm for war, and the predatory temper of which it is the index, prevail in the largest measure among the upper classes, especially among the hereditary leisure class" (*The Theory of the Leisure Class*, p.165). But that ideal suffered considerably at the hands of Boer farmers in the South African War.

Montagu Norman, the banker, who served during the siege of Mafeking, observed with a sour disdain the mounted aristocrats of Paget's Horse: "they are, I believe, supposed to be recruited from the 'upper classes'. Certainly, the result is not satisfactory. For I have never seen a more hopeless, helpless lot of soldiers. They had forgotten half their cookery pots, could not pack their wagons, saddle their horses, or fold up their greatcoats." Norman's professional mind found it nauseating that such men should treat war as a sport for amateurs; and when,

Dining out became part of courtship among the slightly more emancipated upper class.

"Take Great Care Of Yourself." Throughout the Edwardian era, partially because of the King, the cult of "a certain age" was dominant, as were lengthy attachments between the aristocracy and the dazzling demi-monde.

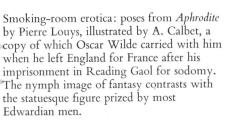

Smoking-room erotica: poses from *Aphrodite*
by Pierre Louys, illustrated by A. Calbet, a
copy of which Oscar Wilde carried with him
when he left England for France after his
imprisonment in Reading Gaol for sodomy.
The nymph image of fantasy contrasts with
the statuesque figure prized by most
Edwardian men.

The King was an habitué of the Paris opera, and like most of the great English visitors was lionized by the French.

The Mandolin Seranade
(drawing by Balliol
Salmon, 1909). (*Mansell
Collection*)

Racing at Longchamps or promenading at Biarritz, the English milord renewed the pleasures of the season abroad, the Continent then being an extension of the British season.

honoured with the Distinguished Service Order, he returned home on sick leave, he said disgustedly of the broadside award of medals, "This to my mind, exaggerated system of rewards is, I fear, a sign of the times for which the newspapers, learning in turn from the Americans, are much to blame. Everything is to be sacrificed to sensation; without sensation nothing is popular. How many fights have not during all these months been called the stiffest of the campaign? How many commonplace individuals have not been held up to newspaper readers as nothing short of heroic?" And he quoted a colleague, "who was candid enough to say the other day that his DSO was for continual and regular attendance at the Mafeking Hotel" (Andrew Boyle, *Montagu Norman* (1967), p.59).

There is truth in the jibe that the distinction between real and ornamental soldiers corresponded to the line between, on the one hand, the cavalry and the Brigade of Guards, and, on the other, the infantry, gunners, engineers and the rest. Yet some of the reformers of the 1900s were cavalrymen, like Colonel Douglas Haig; not all resembled Colonel Brabazon of the Tenth Hussars, epitome of the dashing cavalry officer—friend of the Prince of Wales, "distinguished at court, in the club, on the race-course, in the hunting field ... one of the brightest military stars in London society" (Winston Churchill, *My Early Life*, p.67)—who, even five years after the disasters of the Boer War, could be found testifying to the Committee of Imperial Defence on the value of sabre and lance in modern warfare.

The superiority affected by the cavalry extended to all the "fashionable" regiments, which to their officers were something between a finishing school and an extension of London's clubland. These distinctions long survived the reforms instituted by Haldane; and it was only with the outbreak of war that the cavalry became less insufferable to gunners and engineers, who finally saw themselves confirmed as the architects of success in modern battles. The reforms, aimed at creating a more flexible, unfettered Army took a long time to filter down. The Army lacked a single figurehead like the ebullient Admiral Fisher: old, famous, tired men—Roberts, Wolseley, and Redvers Buller—retained their posts, and a massive promotion-block kept at relatively junior ranks a new generation of commanders like Allenby and Plumer, whose talents were not to be recognised until after 1914.

In that organisation, there was a place for the officers whose regular career lasted only a few years. They represented no threat to the promotion of career colleagues, and, after retirement, could assume a more decorative, part-time appointment with the militia or the yeomanry. (In 1905 the Regular Army numbered 250,000, the militia 100,000 and yeomanry and volunteers 280,000.) But how slow promotion might be, and how frustrating, can be seen from the career of Stanley Maude, private secretary to the Secretary of State for War, H.O. Arnold-Foster, in 1904–5. Emerging from Eton, after heavy financial sacrifice by his father, he had been commissioned in the Coldstream Guards, and went on to emerge from the Boer War as a brigade-major. Twelve years later, despite his undoubted ability, he had progressed only as far as colonel—at the age of fifty. War made him a full general within two years.

Lack of a private income may have been as serious a handicap to Maude as the cluster of elderly brigadiers and generals above him. Few regiments maintained the mundane level of entertainment which would have allowed an officer actually to live on his pay. In any of the fashionable quarters, a private income was essential; and even in India it was not uncommon to find junior officers in straitened circumstances, living virtually in isolation. For the fortunate, on the other hand, peacetime had sweet rewards. Light duties, usually over by midday, would be followed by long afternoons of sport, hunting, steeplechasing, shooting, fishing, and, in India, polo and pig-sticking, with many an uproarious party in the mess, or the normal evening social round in London. This, as Ponsonby had found, was all highly expensive: in particular, cavalry regiments lavished money on horse and polo ponies, and carried to inordinate lengths rivalry with the United States for the Westchester Cup. (Yet, in the three years before the Great War, the Durham Light Infantry, mounted on cheap ponies but brilliantly trained by Beauvoir de Lisle, swept the world stage in polo competition.)

The most internecine rivalries and the worst of rather brutal ragging in the mess were dying out (despite a minor scandal in the Scots Greys in 1906, on which the popular press capitalised), and with the reforms of 1906-9 the Army took on a more professional appearance. Army officers had never formed a caste as in Germany or France, and, despite some resistance, Haldane was able to improve both the chain of command and the appalling conditions of the private soldier. The concept of an Expeditionary Force had been created, in theory at least, by 1910; reorganisation had affected the Indian Army as much as the War Office; and, as the Regular Army, better equipped and trained, prepared at last to face up to the vast conscript forces in Europe, the part-timers were faced with the choice of more intensive regular service or withdrawal—not to the militia, which, in the face of strong protests, had been converted into a fighting reserve, but to the new Territorial Army, created by Haldane out of the volunteers and yeomanry, and handed over, as a sop to local interests, to the county associations.

Edward VII put his energy and prestige behind these reforms, and the effect can be seen in the enormous enthusiasm of local gentry, which helped buoy up the Territorial Army and, associated with it, the new Officer Training Corps, in schools and universities. As a popular image, the dashing cavalry officer survived; but by 1914 he had in fact been replaced by very different stereotypes: the infantry officer schooled in tactical warfare at Sandhurst and Staff College, and the gunner trained in mathematics at Woolwich.

The Navy offered space only for the career officer. In 1900 he would have found many similarities with the world of Nelson: a service vastly underpaid (for a midshipman, 1s 9d daily; for a lieutenant, 10s; for a captain, £1 2s 6d; and for an admiral, £1,200 a year), and promotion bound rigidly by the rules of seniority. In spite of the presence of Prince George (later George V), the Navy was hardly counted fashionable, and the conditions of life on board—food and accommodation being little better for officers than for men—discouraged the uncommitted. Fisher himself, chief architect of reform and naval splendour after 1904, used to claim, "I entered the Navy penniless, friendless and forlorn. I have had to fight like hell, and fighting like hell has made me what I am." However, his own flamboyant, volatile personality, and the quarrels it inspired with the "Blue Funk" school and Lord Charles Beresford, gave the Navy a new appearance in the public mind. During the successive invasion scares after 1906, in which Germany figured as the (often terrifying) enemy, the Navy was cast in the role of island defence. In Erskine Childer's enormously popular thriller *The Riddle of the Sands* (1903), two Englishmen explore the North Sea Coast of Germany by boat and discover a plot to invade Britain. One is a sailor, a simple patriot, set to restore England's decline:

> We've grown by the sea and live by it; if we lose command of it we starve. We are unique in that way, just as our huge empire, only linked by the sea is unique. And yet, my God! read Brassey, Dilke and other "naval annuals", and see what mountains of apathy and conceit have had to be tackled. It's not the people's fault. We have been safe so long, and grown so rich, that we have forgotten what we owe it to. But there is no excuse for those blockheads of statesmen, as they call themselves, who are paid to see things as they are.

In the anxious questioning about England's decadence, the Navy—even before the war, the rise of Jellicoe and Beatty, and the long disparagement of the generals for their supposed failure in trench warfare—figured as regenerator, as *the* fighting service. But despite the Fisher–Selbourne reforms of 1902, which gave engineer officers the same status as others, and despite Fisher's long crusade to widen and democratise the recruiting ground, the Naval high command remained a narrow preserve. "There are not more than $1^1/_2$ million people in all England from whom officers for the Navy can be taken," Fisher wrote in 1906. "The remainder of the population is $41^1/_2$ million and of these no single one can ever hope to become an officer in the Navy." As late as 1912 the authoritative *Naval and Military Review* could state flatly: "The British Navy has long obtained an ample supply of capable officers, also a fair proportion of the most able admirals and captains in the world, without recruiting from the Democracy to any visible extent. ... We should view with grave apprehension any attempt to officer the Fleet at all largely with men of humble births."

The Church still stood as it had done in the nineteenth century, and the black-clad maids still walked in procession from great houses like Montacute and Eaton Hall on Sunday morning. But the heat had gone out of ecclesiastical debates: John Henry Newman's conversion to Rome had ceased to shock, and even Nonconformity seemed less reprehensible to an increasingly tolerant upper class. Lacking fervour, the Church had lost some of its attractions. Many members of the upper-class had lost real faith (as opposed to social conformity) as early as the eighteenth century, and, despite the revival of religion in the mid-nineteenth century, the advent of Darwin and the "higher criticism" of the Bible had emphasised the trend. "From the record of a good many personal histories, it seems to have been from the late 1860s increasingly more unlikely that a really highly educated man would be a Christian" (Kitson Clark, *The Making of Victorian England*, p.286). The 1900s brought rapid changes in fashion, and, as the satirical attack built up against what was seen as Victorian hypocrisy and humbug, organised religion, in all its forms, suffered deeply. Agnostic and indifferent attitudes quickly filtered down: Masterman noticed how, by 1909, the middle classes had assimilated upper-class scepticism: "It is the middle-class which is losing its religion, which is slowly or suddenly discovering that it no longer believes in the existence of the God of its fathers, or a life beyond the grave" (*The Condition of England*, p.211).

The Nonconformist chapels continued to recruit ministers, while the Church of England faltered and the social class of its clergy began to alter. Even if a gentleman were not deterred by a stipend which had not kept pace with the twentieth century, he might find it hard to have to undergo training when he could no longer guarantee that his connections would give him early and easy preferment. The world of Archdeacon Grantly was gone; the parson's freehold, which had too often been the last recourse of "sloth, incapacity, eccentricity to the point of madness, immoderate addiction to fox-hunting or to liquor, in fact almost anything except open immorality, complete neglect of duty, or absence without leave" (Kitson Clark, *The Making of Victorian England*, p.154) had been reformed. The Church of England, like the civil service, had been handed over to the sober graduates of the theological colleges.

Edwardians, if they aspired to professional life, would look to the bar, to consultant medicine or new professions like accountancy, to the diplomatic or colonial service or to the enormously expanded Home Civil Service, which, in line with the increasing complexity of government, had increased its complement of staff from 20,000 in 1832 and 85,000 in 1900 to 280,000 by 1914. Holders of the senior posts were relatively well off in terms of remuneration, pension rights and security of employment, and this attracted vast numbers of applicants every year. Recruitment was by competitive examination, but the emphasis was on the liberal-arts curriculum, and graduates of Oxford and Cambridge enjoyed an advantage. Within government departments a strict hierarchy existed, in fact if not in theory. The knowledgeable aspirant would apply for the Treasury rather than the Local Government Board; and he would probably prefer the Foreign Office to either.

In 1898, after tedious months of cramming from a mathematics tutor, Maurice Baring found himself launched into the African Department and spending half his day in minor clerical work, until suddenly the Fashoda crisis brought the country near to war. The most anguished debate took place on whether despatches should be kept folded or stored flat, and the high point of the week was the sending off of the diplomatic bag. "Someone nearly always out of excitement used to drop the sealing wax on the hand of the clerk who was holding the bag, and sometimes the bag used to be sent to the wrong place. One day both Lord Sanderson and Sir Frank

Bertie came into one of the departments to make sure the bag should go to the right place. The excess of cooks had a fatal result and the bag which was destined for some not remote spot, was sent to Guatemala by mistake, whence it could not be retrieved for several months."

In Paris, in the finest embassy building in Europe, a great 18th century country house only yards away from the Champs Elysées, Sir Francis Bertie held sway, exuding a Rabelaisian sense of humour; but lower down the neophyte had to fit himself into a vast postal system, to keep informed—or misinformed—the nerve centre of a world and imperial power. The fun lay elsewhere: "People of all nationalities used to call at the Embassy and have to be interviewed by someone. A lady would arrive and say she would like to paint a miniature of Queen Victoria; a soldier would arrive from India who thought he had been bitten by a mad dog, and ask to see Pasteur; a man would call who was the only legitimate king of France, Henry V, with his title and dynasty printed on his visiting card, and asked for the intervention of the British government; or someone would come to say that he had found the real solution of the Irish problem, or the Eastern question; or a way of introducing conscription into England without incurring any expense and without English people being aware of it. Besides this, British subjects of every kind would come and ask for facilities to see museums, to write books, to learn how to cure snake bites, to paddle in canoes on the Oise or the Loire, to take their pet dogs back to England without muzzles (this was always refused), or to take a book from the Bibliothèque Nationale, or a missal from some remote museum. All these people had to be interviewed" (*The Puppet Show of Memory*, pp.177–80).

But then the third secretaries would have a fight, hurling inkpots down the Chancery stairs and along the Faubourg St Honoré; or would find themselves invited to ascend in a hot-air balloon, flying from St Denis as far as the forest of Creçy. Baring's own career soon widened to give him coverage, as a correspondent, of Russia, Manchuria, the Russo-Japanese War, and the Balkan War of 1912. Given a brief apprenticeship, a sparkling wit, and well-distributed connections, there was no need for an enterprising mind to moulder among the files.

For the large number who neither needed nor aspired to a permanent career, public service offered the supreme occupation. At Westminster, on local councils, as a justice of the peace or as chairman of some voluntary body, the Edwardian gentleman could contribute as much of his time and energy as suited him, unpaid and thus untrammelled, in the full assurance that he was thereby repaying his debt of privilege to society.

The idea of public service is something quintessentially late Victorian, with its intermingling of social values and moral standards, educational training and dispassionate execution. It is obvious that gentlemen had for centuries, at least since the institution, under Elizabeth, of justices of the peace, functioned on behalf of central government, while retaining the leadership of local communities. As late as the mid-nineteenth century, these positions had been important strongpoints in the battles over a political system underpinned by nepotism, patronage and corruption. Whatever the morality expounded from Westminster, the gentry had never scrupled to dirty its hands in Eatanswill elections, in order to get into the House of Commons or win the centres of local influence and power. But before 1900 all this had gone, swept away by reform of the franchise, the growth of national political parties, the enforcement of the Corrupt Practices Act of 1888, and, above all, a hardening of opinion that only "fit and proper persons" were acceptable in public life. The change had a practical as well as a moral element: great municipal corporations and county boroughs at their peak of administrative excellence simply would not put up with government or representation by the incompetent or the absentee.

At the same time, the manner of reform tended to perpetuate the entry of suitably qualified gentlemen and the exclusion in many country areas of the products of grammar schools or provincial universities. Lord Salisbury had rebutted his more diehard Conservative colleagues' fears of the Local Government Act of 1888 (which transferred to county councils most of the functions of justices of the peace) with the reflection that the gentry would still rule—legitimised by having had to seek election. In defence of continued oligarchy, it was said that it was no small advantage to have in public life men who did not need to stoop to corruption or the pressures of interest groups (what Salisbury called "the taint of greed") and whose broad, traditional approach avoided both the arrogance of the "expert" and the insolence of the new rich.

Political theorists of the Edwardian period elevated this into a philosophy. No one could ignore the problems of poverty, nor the need to harness the energy of the upper-class, preferably through the medium of Christianity, in coming to terms with the challenge of socialism (see, for instance, "Zero", *A Gentleman of the Nineteenth Century*, 1896). One American observer saw it as a valuable deterrent to class warfare: "The enormous amount of unpaid voluntary service to the State, and to one's neighbours, in England, resulted in the solution of one of the most harrassing problems in every wealthy nation: it asked the leisured class to do something worthy, something important to do....When a man has made wealth and leisure for himself, or inherited them from others, he is indeed the renegade if he does not properly offer them as the willing sacrifice upon the altar of his country's welfare" (Price Collier, *England and the English*, 1909). James Bryce, then serving as ambassador in Washington, noted "the diffusion among the richer educated classes and a warmer feeling of sympathy and a stronger feeling of responsibility to the less fortunate sectors of the community: the altruistic spirit, now everywhere visible in the field of private, philanthropic work seems likely to spread into the field of civic action" (*Hindrances to Good Citizenship*, 1909).

Before the Liberal landslide at the 1906 election, the House of Commons still seemed to many an assembly of the English gentry. Yet even by 1895, when it was calculated that 420 out of 670 MPs were gentlemen, a substantial middle-class intrusion had occurred. Among prominent Liberal leaders in the 1900s were David Lloyd George, from a humble if not actually poverty-stricken Welsh background,

Henry Herbert Asquith, a stolid Yorkshire Nonconformist, married to a wife of equally humble birth, and the Jewish lawyers Herbert Samuel and Rufus Isaacs; while on the opposite benches sat Joseph Chamberlain, epitome of the self-made man, and the business cohorts. Social distinctions scarcely affected party strategy; and expediency proved a more important rule than exclusiveness: in 1903 the Liberal Chief Whip, Herbert Gladstone, inheritor of his father's great estate at Hawarden, had no scruples about making an electoral pact with Ramsay MacDonald (then Secretary of the Labour Representation Committee) through which a number of Labour and Liberal candidates could each fight their seats uncontested by the other.

In place of the previously tiny group of Lib–Lab and trade union MPs, the 1906 election returned fifty-three Lib–Lab and straight Labour men, while the Liberals won an overwhelming majority (377 seats, as against the Tories' 157). The composition of the House changed abruptly: Balfour, his father, and two other Cabinet Ministers lost their seats, and Henry Chaplin fell after thirty-nine years as an MP. The defeated prophesied disaster, and blamed not the tariff, nor even Balfour's indolence, but "the conviction for the first time born in the working classes, that their social salvation is in their own hands" (Sir Almeric Fitzroy, *Memories* (1925), p.172).

The exclusive, clubbable gentlemanly atmosphere at Westminster did not, however, vanish at the first trumpet of Labour. Dr Montagu Butler, headmaster of Harrow, had hit a very old-fashioned note when he advised the young Baldwin not to try for the House of Commons: "I doubt whether it will be worth entering." An autumn session was still a rarity, and Sir Edward Grey, the Foreign Secretary, could still count on spending his weekends fishing in the Itchen near his Hampshire cottage, and the long summer holidays at Falloden in Northumberland, almost undisturbed by the red boxes of government documents. On the other hand, Sir Henry Lucy, veteran of the lobbies, writing for *Punch* in 1906, thought the House of Commons had been "revolutionised"; and in the "unprecedently cantankerous and uncomfortable" years 1909–11 something very ancient does seem to have died away.

Among the majority of backbenchers and Ministers, the numerous ties of blood, marriage and friendship cut across party divisions, giving no clear guidance on class distinction. A man of Churchill's background could cross the floor and become a Liberal without suffering much worse than cries of "rat"; seven years later, having learned the language of radicalism from Lloyd George, he had reached the Cabinet. If high politics had been a respector of status, Lord Salisbury would hardly have bothered to wean Chamberlain away from Gladstone; but, however much he might deplore the plutocratic aspect of the Tory Party, it was a price he knew had to be paid for electoral survival. He believed in "natural" leaders—"the aristocracy of a country in the original and best sense of the word"; yet, nine years after he retired, his party chose as leader (in preference to the country squire Walter Long, and Austen Chamberlain) Andrew Bonar Law, a Canadian-born Glasgow steel manufacturer—austere, unsympathetic to working-class aspirations, and backed by, of all people, the Canadian press magnate Max Aitken. As for the Liberals, Campbell-Bannerman, son of a new-generation Scottish laird, was replaced in 1908 by Asquith, now a well-known lawyer, unconnected with the land, but rising rapidly in the social scale after his second marriage—to Margot, daughter of Sir Charles Tennant and sister-in-law to Lord Ribblesdale. "Asquith *qua* Asquith," Campbell-Bannerman once said, "is a fine fellow, an honest man and a sincere Liberal. But Asquith *cum* Margot is a lost soul." How lost can be gauged from his style of life; the Yorkshire background had dissolved, given his income of £10,000 a year from the Bar, into a house in Cavendish Square with fourteen indoor servants. "Here we are", lamented Lord Esher, looking at the Liberal Cabinet, "overwhelmed by the middle-classes!" Yet the Speaker of the House from 1905 to 1921 was James Lowther, later Lord Ullswater, whose family had held Westmorland seats almost continuously for 600 years.

Conflicting trends could exist side by side, as they did with new and old peers in the Lords. Only about a tenth of the 560 hereditary peers attended regularly what Lord Newton once called "the most good-natured assembly that exists". Lord Salisbury dominated it until his death, while on the Woolsack sat Lord Chancellor Halsbury, already old, soon to be diehard leader of the backwoods peers against Lloyd George's budget and the Parliament Act of 1911. Halsbury was then seventy-two; he lived until 1920; and his experience stretched back to the politics of Dickens and Trollope. (A story was told of an occasion when, as Lord Chancellor, he was considering candidates for a legal appointment. "*Ceteris paribus*", began one of his advisers. "*Ceteris paribus* be damned," he interrupted. "I'm appointing my nephew.") Lord Lansdowne and the Duke of Devonshire, both secessionists from Gladstone, may serve as the archetypes of Edwardian Tory peers. Yet the belief which Balfour held, that the Lords was simply the Tory Party under another name, led to irreconcilable conflict between the two Houses, and irretrievable damage to the prestige and power of the Lords. Although the conflicts over the 1909 budget and the Parliament Act may not have sustained public excitement for the full two and a half years over which they extended, Lloyd George's stinging sarcasm ("a fully equipped Duke costs as much to keep up as two Dreadnoughts ... is just as great a terror and lasts longer", he told a Limehouse audience) and the bathetic response (Rosebery actually claimed that the Lords were "a poor but honest class") introduced a new tone of disillusioned rancour which the King, in particular, deplored.

Old deferential attitudes, and the assumptions based on them, were dying long before Asquith and his Cabinet put the Lords on the wrong footing by appealing to the effective rather than to the formal constitution. Two new MPs who joined the House in these years point the contrast: Baldwin, who remained a quiet, unambitious backbencher, content to represent the electors of Bewdley, and to speak, rarely and diffidently, on questions of industrial relations; and F.E. Smith, a lawyer of dazzling and cruel wit, whose maiden speech in 1906 broke all the conventions with its brilliant invective against the Liberal front bench.

The veteran Irish parliamentarian Tim Healey passed Smith a note on that occasion: "I am old, and you are young, but you have beaten me at my own game." Thereafter, from the age of thirty-three, Smith was marked out for a political career as outstanding as his future as a barrister. To the Tory party managers, he was a coming man, and Baldwin a mere back-bencher, the cannon-fodder of the lobbies; if Smith came too close to the "adventurer" disliked by Balfour, few could have forecast then that in twenty years he would be a burnt-out wreck, doomed by his own buccaneering outlook, a Cabinet Minister, but serving under the once-despised Baldwin, now Prime Minister.

It would have been hard by 1910 to have found an MP, like Trollope's, who regarded a seat as a useful means to dodge the pursuits of his creditors. Weetman Pearson (later Lord Cowdray) found it necessary to explain to his constituents that public works all over the world would demand most of his attention—and was dubbed the "Member for Mexico" as a result. True, Smith, by then Lord Birkenhead, and a law unto himself, could send a telegram in 1925 apologising for his non-attendance at a Cabinet meeting because his yacht was becalmed in the Solent; but, in general, MPs' conduct had declined from the outrageous to the merely indolent, and constituencies could usually reckon on seeing their Member at least a dozen times in the year.

The House of Commons reflected the flux of society and values, and its hallowed conventions suffered not only from the spleen of Irish members—habitual since the 1880s—but also from the political violence sparked off by Ulster's fight against Home Rule, and by the great strikes after 1911. The greatest change, observers noticed, was that professionalism had crept in. The debate over payment to MPs, inevitable after the Osborn judgement in 1908 had cut off trade union funds for the Labour Party, reflected the change. Ironically it was Austen Chamberlain, son of the most professional of caucus manipulators, who complained that salaries would attract an "intolerable type of professional politician", while it fell to *The Times*, owned by the brash adventurer Lord Northcliffe, to revive Salisbury's old argument that public service was best fulfilled "by men who can afford to be disinterested".

So the memories survive of amateur politicians such as the genial Lord Buxton, squire turned Liberal Cabinet Minister, whose conversation was of natural history and travel, not politics, and who one summer morning set out, dressed in morning coat, from his Sussex house, to attend a Cabinet meeting.

"He decided to walk to the station and, having time in hand, he sat by the way at the foot of a tree listening to the birds. But no sooner was he in his first class compartment than trouble began. He had sat on a nest of red ants, and the ants were beginning to eat him. He pulled down the blinds, took off his pinstriped trousers, shook them out of the window. At that moment an express train passed in the reverse direction, and the blast it caused snatched the trousers from his hands. At each stop he pulled down the blinds and clung to the door-handle. The Postmaster General arrived at Waterloo, wearing a silk hat and tail coat, but trouserless. A guard was beckoned, and a pair of oily blue overalls from the tap room must have shocked Lulu Harcourt and even startled the Prime Minister when their colleague entered the Cabinet room" (Jones, *An Edwardian Youth*, p.223).

Power in high politics was slipping away from the ranks of "natural leaders", even if the ancient alliance of squirearchy and Anglican clergy survived the establishment of parish councils and other assaults on their local power. Yet change took much more than a generation to achieve: the gentry still served as chairmen of most of the new county councils; and the theory of "natural leadership" was scarcely dented among those who, as Sir George Trevelyan wrote, "scorned a peerage but made it a point of honour to stand for their county at the first general election after they came of age".

A sublime confidence suffused the county families in the shires. Charles Mogridge Hudson, writing, for private publication in 1901, the history of a Worcestershire family, summed it up with a lack of inhibition which would have been impossible in the 1920s. "To remember that one is a gentleman by birth, and to act up to it, is a valuable asset in helping one through the world. If your lesson is learnt properly you realise that it is manners and not clothes or money that make the man: it teaches you that you can do any kind of work that is necessitated at the time without feeling false shame; and above all it causes, or should cause you to have a delicate respect for the feelings of those whom accident or duty have placed under you, and which in fact is the explanation why the English gentleman is admitted by all nations to be the most perfect leader of men."

The Empire afforded a field of public service for men who had neither the temperament to serve nor the means to live as a gentleman at home. Yet for them the Empire represented something vastly more complicated than the "enormous system of outdoor relief for the upper-classes" derided by the cynics. Quite apart from the crude propaganda of G.A. Henty, or the bastardised versions of Kipling purveyed by Northcliffe's *Daily Mail*, or Bottomley's *John Bull*, imperial government posed a challenge to the finest administrators of the age. What was to occur in later decades for the French, Dutch and Portuguese empires happened to the British in the period before 1914: as criticism of imperialism mounted, so the standards of government and its future ideals were set on a steadily rising moral plane. Campbell-Bannerman's "true imperialism" meant the eventual transfer of responsibility, and the decade which was stirred by J.A. Hobson's classic onslaught *Imperialism* also witnessed the first significant steps towards eventual self-government in India (in 1909), the creation of the Union of South Africa (in 1910), and the Irish Home Rule Bill of 1912. Canada, Australia and New Zealand enjoyed Dominion status (self-government under the British Crown).

A public school education, followed by a liberal-arts degree, naturally led to the Colonial Service; and something of the familiar distinction between the administrative grade and the specialists—in this case the engineers and the commercial sections—survived overseas. The contribution of the 1900s to modern India, in law and administration, was prodigious, but unmatched by a serious attempt to raise the level of Indian science, technology or industry. Precisely because the emphasis lay on an imperial conception of trade, rather than on a commercial conception of empire, it was possible to prefer administration to industry and, in public propaganda and through the network of imperial societies, to instil the view that empire was "a personal as well as a national duty, a note more inspiring than had ever before been sounded in the ears of a dominant people" (G.N. Curzon, *Subjects of the Day*, 1918).

Public splendour made flesh of this ideal. To the monumental designs of Lutyens, New Delhi rose as administrative capital of India, utterly divorced from Indian history and geography, a monument to the pure will-power of empire-builders, as Madrid was to the early Catholic Kings. At the new capital in 1911, in a ceremony derived partly from the Westminster coronation and partly from Mogul tradition, George V was confirmed as Emperor of India, with all the princes and maharajahs in attendance. Yet there were two sides to imperialism, as one example will suffice to make clear: 1897, year of the Diamond Jubilee and symbolic opening of the Imperial Age, had also been the year of the Jameson Raid, the most outrageous attempt to seize Boer territory to secure the gold mines of the Rand. The same paradox, the stain within the jewel, lies behind the men who governed the colonies.

To begin with, they were not simply, nor even in the majority, gentlemen by the old standards. Blunt used to fulminate against the Empire that it was "a poor cockney affair invented hardly twenty years ago—to the ruin of our position as an honest Kingdom at home" (*Diaries*, p.290); and Masterman claimed in 1909, "It is not from the 'Conquerors', but from a rather harrassed and limited middle-class that the empire builders are now drawn: a Lord Macdonnell from the home of a peasant farmer in Ireland, a Cecil Rhodes from an English country parsonage. The men who are administering with various success, British East Africa and Northern Nigeria, and the huge machine of government in India, are mainly the children of the professional families, drawn abroad by love of adventure or absence of opportunity at home" (*The Condition of England*, p.51).

The brashest of them, like Cecil Rhodes himself, made reputations and fortunes far enough away from their origins not to be too closely analysed. A commission of inquiry failed to pin responsibility for Jameson's Raid on either Rhodes or Joseph Chamberlain; but the full story of the British South African Company, and of the acquisition of what was to become Southern Rhodesia, after Rhodes's treaty with King Lobengula in 1896, did nothing to enhance their reputations.

A whole generation of millionaires leapt, fully accoutred, from Kimberley and the Rand, men like Werner Beit, Barny Barnato, Joseph Robinson, and the Oppenheimer dynasty, and gave a new meaning to the term "colonial gentleman". Rhodes settled in the palatial house of Groote Schuur on the side of Table Mountain; Sir Lewis Oppenheimer ordered that the headquarters for the Anglo-American Corporation, at 44 Main Street, Johannesburg, should be "something between a cathedral and a bank"; and Robinson bought his English peerage from the Liberal Party.

Of the same stamp was Sir John Norton-Griffiths, public-works contractor,

MP for Wednesbury, sometimes known as Empire Jack. Born in 1871 in Wales, educated in the strict Methodist tradition, he began his career sheep-farming in South Africa, drifted to the Transvaal in 1891, took part in the Rhodesian and South African wars, and between 1904 and 1907 built the Benguella railway in Portuguese Angola. Later he constructed the Longitudinal railway in Chile, developed a model colony for emigrants at Calgary in Canada, as a solution to industrial unemployment, and founded his own society, the Imperial League. His election banner was always "the Empire and Tariff Reform." He passionately believed in Imperial Preference and an Imperial Senate to bind together Dominions and colonies; he habitually spent large sums on imperial causes, entertaining the various Dominion statesmen at Temple House on the Thames during the Imperial Conference of 1911; and in July 1914 he raised his own regiment, the Second King Edward's Horse, from ex-colonial soldiers. His advertisement in the *Pall Mall Gazette* read, "*If Duty Calls: MP's invitation to old fighters.* With a view to working in unity, if duty calls, all Africans, Australians, Canadians and other Britishers who have served in either Matabele land, Mashonaland or the South African war ... should apply to Mr John Norton-Griffiths MP."

The fictional siblings of his officers are to be found in novels of the period: Allan Quatermain, the creation of H. Rider Haggard, himself a colonial administrator and advocate of agricultural reform, and Richard Hannay, hero of John Buchan's *Thirty-Nine Steps* and *Greenmantle*. Quatermain, the gnarled white hunter, veteran of a hundred adventures, the best known being *King Solomon's Mines*, was finally allowed to die after an epic battle in a lost country beyond the known frontiers of Kenya Colony. Haggard dedicated this last book (written in 1917) to his son, "in the hope that he, and many other boys whom I shall never know, may find something to help him and them to reach to what I hold to be the highest rank whereto we can attain—the state and dignity of an English gentleman".

Beside the brash and flamboyant adventurers, the administrators make a duller showing, although the Consular Service attracted a number of eccentrics and originals. Yet their choices and duties were as complicated as the others' were simple. It is easy to enumerate the great proconsuls: Lord Milner, British High Commissioner to South Africa from 1897 to 1905, Lord Curzon, Viceroy of India, and Lord Cromer, Consul-General in Egypt from 1883 to 1907; and the host of lesser lights, Milner's so-called Kindergarten, the brilliant group including Leo Amery, Lionel Curtis, Geoffrey Dawson, Philip Kerr (Lord Lothian) and Robert Brand, all influential in imperial politics in the inter-war years; or the gifted but less famous administrative aristocracy of India, such as the Cotton family, for nearly a century the source of engineers, lawyers, soldiers and provincial governors. Yet did all these men serve, as Milner claimed, because "in Empire we have found not merely the key to glory and wealth, but the call to duty and the means of service to Mankind"?

Masterman gave a sardonic answer by attributing to imperialism "the lust for domination, the stir of battle, the pride in magnitude of Empire", the decay of the bright hopes for change which socialists had observed in the 1880s. "All these efforts, hopes and visions have vanished as if wiped out with a sponge." On the other hand, the questioning of imperialism, during and after the Boer War, Campbell-Bannerman's denunciation of concentration camps as "methods of barbarism", Hobson's penetrating critique, and the scandal over indentured Chinese labour on the Transvaal, to say nothing of E.D. Morel's revelations of Belgian atrocities in the Congo, and the exposure of the "pacification" of Algeria by the French commander, Lyautey, went far to discredit territorial aggrandisement in Edwardian eyes. "The truth is", Campbell-Bannerman wrote to a friend in 1903, "we cannot provide for a fighting Empire and nothing will give us the power. But a peaceful Empire of the old type we are quite fit for."

Thus a gentleman's duty in the colonies came to be seen as that of wise judge and far-sighted legislator; he stood only a mental step away from the path leading to self-government. Those who attacked the Morley-Minto reforms in India (which introduced a limited area of election to legislative councils in 1909) were to be found ranged on the same side against the Government of India Act twenty years later, led on that occasion by Winston Churchill (in Baldwin's phrase "once more the subaltern of the Hussars of '94"), whose only knowledge of India dated from his service with the Malakand Field Force. In its enjoyment of the sweetness of power, laced with a certain bitterness of guilt, Edwardian thinking had outgrown the straightforward commercial inspiration of Victorians like Thomas Brassey, the greatest of railway builders, who wrote in 1870, of his work in the Argentine: "We go into the heart of a country abounding in wealth, possessing a soil and climate unsurpassed .... The European element of population will in a few years exceed the natives; these are the best tests, for who would go if prosperity were insecure?" Yet there was still a blandness behind assumptions implicit in the Duke of York's remark after an East African tour in 1925: "There is a very good type of settler out here, and most of them are gentlemen in the true sense of the word. Everything is so new and utterly different to other parts of the Empire. Being so young it should be made gradually by the best people we can produce from home."

Something of the dilemma can be seen in E.M. Foster's *A Passage to India*, written in 1910. Ronny Moore, the district officer, dispenses justice without too much introspection: " 'We're not out here for the purpose of behaving pleasantly ... we're out here to do justice and keep the peace. I'm not a missionary or a Labour member or a vague sentimental sympathetic literary man. I'm just a servant of the government.' ... That morning he had convicted a railway clerk of overcharging pilgrims for their tickets, and a Pathan of attempted rape. He expected no gratitude, no recognition for this ... it was his duty." In contrast, Fielding—a "seasoned Anglo-Indian"—thinks too much and comes to be regarded as a disruptive force. Implicitly, McBryde, the doyen of the British community, rebukes him for deviance: "If you leave the line, you leave a gap in the line."

But the harshest conflict between the values set in the gentlemanly ideal and reality in outlandish places is to be found in Conrad, in *Lord Jim* and *Heart of Darkness*, and later in the novels of Joyce Cary, the stories of Somerset Maughan and of Graham Greene. After the great imperial war had finished, fewer and fewer voices could be heard defending imperial values. Nevertheless, in Edwardian England they still shone brightly, and nowhere more than at home, where the problems of empire succumbed more easily to the logic of wishful thinking. They could be set against the pervasive fear of Old England's moral decline which infected books like Douglas Newton's *War* and Saki (H.H. Munro)'s *When William Came*—a bleak picture of a country already under the German heel; where only among the young was there scope for resistance or revival. The Boy Scouts (symbols of empire) refuse to parade in front of the German Emperor in Hyde Park; they would not join "the ranks of the hopelessly subservient; in thousands of English homes throughout the land there were young hearts that had not forgotten, had not compounded, and would not yield".

For all the training in administration and the enthusiasm for a mission, the home-grown plant flourished best in congenial air, free of the acid secretions of nationalism and commercial gain, whether in Ireland or India, South Africa or the West Indies. In the last resort, the Empire for which Britain fought, supposedly, in 1914 was devalued by the most imperious of Edwardian mandarins, Field-Marshal Lord Kitchener, who valued so little the Dominion and colonial military contingents that he gave all priorities instead to bringing to Europe the British army in India, and until his death reckoned the capabilities of the Anzac contingents well below those of the despised Territorial Army. At Gallipoli the Empire came of age; but the Dominions' future leaders were to be Canadians, South Africans or Australians, not honorary Englishmen; only in India, for a decade, and in parts of Africa did the imperial missionary survive the Great War.

CHAPTER SIX

Private Pleasures

"We eat, drink and rise up to play, and this is to live like
gentlemen", wrote Lord Conway in the 1660s; "For what
is a gentleman but his pleasures?" 250 years later, such
simplicity must often have seemed forgotten, given the cloying perfection and gilded
magnificence of Edwardian entertainment. Dining with the Sassoons, in their
mansion in Park Lane in 1913, Max Beerbohm became aware of an odd feeling of
boredom.

"I suppose the rooms of the house through which one passes into the dining
room are too many and too perfect. Also the dining room itself is too big for less
than a thousand diners. One little perfect porphyry table without a table-cloth; and
a crystal bowl with a lid, and with pink carnations floating inside it in the middle;
and Voisin cuisine—and two automobiles without—take the heart out of one—and
one only wants to say 'I am glad I am not rich', and one can't say that, and so one
is rather at a loss"(Cecil, *Max*, p.333).

The boredom of the jaded palate lay on one side, like hell in a mediaeval fresco,
confronted with the heaven of enjoyment, won not by simply luxuriating in idleness,
but by competitive effort. Desmond MacCarthy, remembering his friend Roger
Fry, the finest art critic of his day, wrote, "it was the strenuous pleasure he took in
things that stands out in retrospect. The strenuousness of his delight in works of art
is clearly seen in his criticism; it animated also his enjoyment of food, talk, travel
and the way he set about practical projects ... he was a hedonist, but a hedonist of a
peculiar kind .... There was not a touch of grossness, either of the over-fastidious
or the over-greedy kind, in his love of pleasure" (*Memories*, p.177).

What gifted Bloomsbury could achieve by mental exercise had to be won
otherwise by the majority. Thorstein Veblen observed the extraordinary range of

competitiveness produced in contemporary America by the possession of inordinate wealth—the struggle for status, to show tangible proof by investing every aspect of leisure—sport, fashion, dress or art collecting—with conspicuous spending.

What was true of the brash American new rich—the denizens of Newport and Saratoga Springs, the Goulds, Vanderbilts and Harrisons, those who, like Henry Frick and Henry Huntington, competed obsessively for the latest Gainsborough discreetly offered for sale by the grandest dealer in eighteenth-century taste, Joseph Duveen—applied to few of the upper class in England. Nevertheless, to enjoy the private pleasures of life before 1914, it was necessary to possess money; and money, combined with greater leisure and freedom from drudgery and pain than at any previous time in history, enhanced and formalised a competitiveness which had not previously existed, at least since the late Middle Ages. Masterman castigated the "insane competition" which accompanied the rising standard of living: "Where one house sufficed, now two are demanded; where a dinner of a certain quality, now a dinner of superior quality; where clothes or dresses or flowers, now more clothes, more dresses, more flowers." The contagion spread upwards to affect all social groups except the "Incorruptibles" and those outside fashionable society altogether, and sharpened the old distinction between London and the provinces, between the smart set and the country bumpkins.

Thus an illusion grew, fostered equally by public demand for sensation and by the gossip columns of the cheaper papers which met it, like Lord Northcliffe's *Daily Mail* or Frank Harris's *Vanity Fair*, that society consisted *only* of the smart set, its pleasures and sports. The novels of Elinor Glyn might criticise the smart set, but they served to increase the illusion. The great mass of the gentry families were ignored, and in turn alienated themselves from behaviour they could neither afford nor emulate. Consider this passage from the description in *The Edwardians* of a country family arriving at Belgrave Square for the season:

Of impeccable respectability and historic lineage, they had long looked forward with dread to this year when it would be necessary to transport themselves, their household, their carriages, and their plate up to London in May and devote themselves for three months to the task of taking their Alice "out", involving not only weariness for them, but also a constant irritating anxiety as to possible contact with things and people of whom they would disapprove.

This contrast of style showed itself in the world of leisure as in everything else: in the contrast between the pleasures of small rough shoots and the formal precision of pheasant drives organised to entertain the King; between the amusements of a country family like the Margessons at Findon Place in Sussex and the Duke of Devonshire's elaborate weekends at Chatsworth. At no other time has so much money been poured into the building of great yachts, as men like Lipton contended (unsuccessfully) for the America's Cup; or into polo teams, pheasant coverts, or deer preservation in the Highlands. It served no purpose to deplore unrestrained competition; King Edward himself indulged it, as in setting the cutter *Britannia* against Kaiser Wilhelm's *Meteor*.

In *The Ivory Child* H. Rider Haggard used the twin themes of competitiveness and tension between new wealth and old family to depict an epic battle between his hero, Alan Quatermain (based on the famous white hunter Captain Francis Selous), and the jumped-up swindler Sir Junius Fortescue (alias Van Koop). The men wager £250 to settle an old debt on who could kill the most head of game in a single day. As the owner of the shoot, Lord Ragnall, points out, excusing Fortescue's presence, "Shooting has become a kind of fetish in these parts. For instance, it is a tradition on this estate that we must shoot more pheasants than on any other in the county, and therefore I have to ask the best guns, who are not always the best fellows." In the end, after a wild day of gales and some incredible shooting, Quatermain wins his bet by a single pheasant—and donates the cheque to the local cottage hospital. Fortescue vanishes and is not heard of again, and Quatermain is left ruefully adding up the cost of his day's shoot:

Cartridges	£5 0s 0d
Game licence	£3 0s 0d
Tip to keeper	£2 0s 0d
Tip to underkeeper	10s 0d
Tips to collectors of pheasants	15s 0d
Total	£10 5s 0d
	(equivalent to £100 today)

"Truly pheasant shooting in England is, or was, a sport for the rich!"

Even if sport did not conceal such social or racial conflict (British sporting superiority was frequently invoked in answer to the prophecies of national decadence and German invasion that were then fashionable), it remained highly competitive. The mid-Victorian view of organised sport as a means to build character and inculcate a sense of honour and correct behaviour was rapidly giving way to a new cult of team games for their own sake: an extension of public school and university into adult life. In place of individual haphazard forms of play came meticulous organisation, sporting associations, rules and definitions. Standard pitches, balls and bats had been creations of the late nineteenth century; sport in Britain in the Edwardian decade was marked by a degree of expertise, training and technical innovation which has never been surpassed in a single country. In that golden age, British sportsmen dominated the competitive sports of the whole world, from the first modern Olympiad in 1896 to the last Test Match before war broke out. Britain topped the United States at the Olympic Games of 1908 with fifty-six firsts to twenty-two. Gentlemen amateurs with leisure and single-minded ambition to pursue the sports they had learned at school turned from the old aristocratic preserves of real tennis or rackets to the team games—rugby, football, hockey and, above all, cricket. Their names and those of the famous professionals echo even after three generations: Ranjitsinhji, Hobbs and Rhodes at cricket; Taylor, Braid and Varden at golf; Applegarth and Shrubb at athletics; John Daniell and Poulton at rugby; G.S. Smith and Morgan-Owen of the Corinthians football club. A handful reached a pitch of all-round success which in the specialised modern world can never be re-created: C.B. Fry, England cricket captain, soccer international, world record holder for long jump, boxer and gifted at every other sport; R.E. Foster, a soccer international who scored 287 against Australia in the Test Match of 1903; J.W.H.T. Douglas, international cricketer, footballer and perhaps the finest amateur boxer in the country; and R.P. Keigwin, hockey international, county tennis player, with Blues for cricket, soccer and rackets.

The amateur code became more rigid, reflecting the profound social rule that indulgence in sport remained the prerogative of the gentleman; until the 1920s, the rules of the Amateur Rowing Association specifically debarred any "menial or manual worker" from competition—even if he *were* an amateur. But, as the newspaper reports show, even in highly competitive fields like championship tennis the ideals survived; new techniques and new equipment, and the dimension of the partisan audience, seemed to have enhanced the competitive spirit without introducing more modern extremes of temperament and vindictiveness. For example, at Henley in 1908, the Leander Team actually waited while their Dutch opponents, who had run into the boom, started again.

The University Boat Race drew crowds of thousands along the Thames towpath: "Every cab and bus driver in London tied a dark or light blue bow to his whip, every child wore a favour" (Jones, *An Edwardian Youth*, p. 76). Soccer had long been established at some of the leading schools, and the one great amateur club, the Corinthians, drew in an astonishing volume of talent. The English side which played Scotland in 1895 contained no fewer than nine Corinthians, and these patricians, in their white cricket shirts and dark blue shorts, beat Aston Villa, probably the best side in England, in 1900, and the Cup winners, Bury, in 1904. At Rugby Union, the Harlequins maintained a scarcely lower standard against the long dominance of Welsh professional sides, although their work was made easier by the secession of the Northern clubs to the Rugby League.

But, while a young gentleman might prolong his school days into his thirties as an amateur footballer, cricket took pride of place from the end of April to the beginning of October. No amount of critical analysis can deprive the Edwardian years of a certain supremacy here. It is not mere nostalgia to recall the village greens, the country-house cricket weekends, the county championships, avidly supported by enthusiastic crowds, the perfect surfaces of the Oval and Old Trafford, and the great culminating experiences of the Test Match series. W.G. Grace, epitome of Victorian cricket, retired, appropriately, in 1900, and was followed by a glittering array of stroke players: C.B. Fry, A.C. MacLaren, Spooner, Tyldesley, Hobbs, Palairet, the Gunn brothers, Jessop and R.E. Foster. The elegance of the off-stump game, with its driving and cutting, delighted the crowds, and the era of high scoring ended only with a new generation of bowlers—Bosanquet with the "googly", and the in-swingers Griswell and Jacques.

Yet, for all the memories of the greatest players, it was the village game which truly characterised the Edwardian love of sport. A.G. Macdonnell, in *England their*

England, described the start of an epic game: "There stood the Vicar, beaming absent-mindedly at everyone. There was the forge, with the blacksmith, his hammer discarded, tightening his snake-buckled belt for the fray and loosening his braces to enable his terrific bowling-arm to swing freely in its socket. There on a long bench outside the Three Horseshoes sat a row of elderly men, facing a row of pint tankards, and wearing either long beards or clean-shaven chins and long whiskers. Near them, holding pint tankards in their hands, was another group of men, clustered together and talking with intense animation. All round the cricket field small parties of villagers were patiently waiting for the great match to begin — a match against gentlemen from London is an event in a village—and some of them looked as if they had been waiting for a good long time. But they were not impatient. Village folk are seldom impatient. Those whose lives are occupied in combating the eccentricities of God regard as very small beer the eccentricities of Man.

"Blue-and-green dragonflies played at hide-and-seek among the thistle-down and a pair of swans flew overhead. An ancient man leaned against a scythe, his sharpening-stone sticking out of a pocket in his velveteen waistcoat. A magpie flapped lazily across the meadows. The parson shook hands with the squire. Doves cooed. The haze flickered. The world stood still."

If he wanted simple recreation, or the satisfaction of individual play, the gentleman might turn to tennis or golf, two relatively new sports, rapidly increasing in popularity. The Doherty brothers revolutionised tennis after the 1897 Wimbledon matches, and the introduction of the Davis Cup in 1903 opened up the game to American and Empire teams. Tennis clubs proliferated, and great numbers of private courts were built. Badminton, too, became fashionable, its techniques following the example of Sir George Thomas, twenty-eight times All-England Champion. Golf could be played either as a most exacting championship game or as a relaxation, following the elegant model of the Prime Minister himself, Arthur Balfour. Beginning with the construction of the Sunningdale course in 1900, a new range of courses sprang up on sandy heathlands; and the introduction of the rubber-cored ball brought to the game a consistency impossible in the old days of gutta-percha. Among the enduring images of the time are those of the King as he drove off at Sandringham, and the pioneers of the Ladies Golf Union, whose long tweed skirts complemented the Norfolk jackets and breeches of their male colleagues.

Meanwhile, on quiet college lawns, in country rectories or cathedral closes, croquet engaged the rivalries of the upper class—so long, that is, as they did not defeat the King, as the Duchess of Sermoneta found out when a lucky shot chanced to knock his ball out of play and into the rose beds. "By the icy stillness that prevailed", she wrote, "I realised that never, never was such a thing to happen again." For those who travelled widely, the fashionable Swiss resorts of Zermatt and Wengen offered skiing and skating in conditions quite different from the austere lodgings frequented by pioneer Victorian mountaineers like Edward Whymper. The motor car and the luxurious sleeping cars of the Compagnie Internationale des

Wagons-Lits had between them removed the problems of geography.

Car ownership rose rapidly, among those who could afford it. A French friend of Blunt paid £800 for a Peugeot in 1900 and he doubted "whether they will become popular in England until the mechanism has been simplified and cheapened very considerably"; in 1908 a Darracq with Paris coachwork might have come to £850, and a year later Compton Mackenzie's father paid £2,000 for a large Mercedes with its body hand-tailored to his requirements. In 1904 the number of cars licensed in the United Kingdom stood at a mere 8,465; but, with the introduction of a range of cheaper models, this rose to 132,015 by 1914. The King was an avid amateur, having acquired the taste when driving with Lord Montagu in a Daimler as early as 1899. Shortly after the coronation he began to buy his own cars, including a Mercedes and a Renault, both painted a rich claret and distinguished by their lack of number plates. Royal patronage was granted to the automobile exhibitions in 1903 and 1906, and the title Royal to the Automobile Club. All the King's travelling in Ireland in 1907 was done by car and there were always limousines in attendance at Marienbad and Biarritz; but, despite his love of motoring, the King remained lamentably ignorant of the workings of the internal combustion engine, and once found himself unable to tell the Kaiser what fuel the royal cars used. A mechanic regularly accompanied the royal chauffeur and the King's efforts were limited to urging his driver to overtake all the cars in front of him. Desregarding the absurd speed limits of the day, they reached a maximum of sixty miles an hour on the Brighton road in 1906. The sense of adventure was what Edward relished, and he was courageous enough on one occasion to take his car right to to the top of the mountains in Majorca, when others in the royal party had abandoned their vehicles after the mountain track had grown too steep, twisting and dangerous.

When his friends George Wyndham and the Duchess of Westminster arrived one day in August 1908, Blunt, now the crusty country squire, deplored what he called the "perpetual gallop". "They had been at the manoeuvres all the morning, had then motored over here, some thirty miles, stopped an hour for tea, and were to motor back and go out for dinner. This is a good example of the life at high pressure of our ladies of fashion. She has with her in camp, a lady's maid, a footman, a chauffeur, and a cook. The Duke in the meanwhile is motoring in Ireland with another chauffeur, another cook, and more servants, besides a motor boat, the one he races" (*Diaries*, p.625).

Worse still, for him, was the intrusion of weekend joy-riders on the dusty secluded lanes of his beloved Sussex countryside; but the gentlemen's world slowly adapted to the decline of the horse. The 7,500 hansom cabs of London dropped to a mere 2,000 and were replaced by motor cabs, known at first as "Clarences". Magnificent as were the coach-built bodies which suceeded the landaus and victorias, their noise and speed changed the aspect of cities and the countryside. Coachmen and footmen became chauffeurs and mechanics, and straw was no longer laid in the streets outside houses where the inmates lay sick. Only a handful of eccentrics, like Lord Rosebery, resisted the changing fashion, and the mews where horses had been kept sat empty, awaiting the chic conversions of the 1920s.

If the horse as a means of transport was on the way out, at least hunting and racing had never seen better days. Again, the King set the tone, at Ascot and Longchamps, and caught the public's fancy. As an owner he was not noticeably successful before 1909, failing to recapture the brilliant performances of Persimmon and Diamond Jubilee, his Derby winners in 1896 and 1900, in spite of the talents of his manager, Marcus Beresford, and trainer, Richard Marsh. But in 1909 he had twenty-three horses in his string, including Minoru. Entered for the Derby that year, Minoru was a fancied runner and he came home at 4 to 1. The scenes that followed were remarkable for the enthusiasm of the crowds. The King was mobbed as he led in the winner, and the crowd roared "Good old Teddy" and sang "God Save The King". Edward was most moved by the reception. In this one year he came second in the order of winning owners, with a total of £20,000—a fitting climax to a long career and involvement in the affairs of the turf.

The rewards could be high, but the costs were prohibitive to all but the rich. Led by its first steward, the uncompromising Earl of Durham, the Jockey Club established total and autocratic control of the sport, regulating everything from starting gates to the exclusion or readmission of offenders. Inordinate competition for the classic races set in train long-term improvements in horse-breeding, and Colonel Hall Walker founded the Tully Stud (at the Curragh), which he later gave in 1915 as the National Stud. But it was the colourful personalities—Lord Lonsdale, known as the Yellow Earl from the colour of his carriages, the Aga Khan, Lord Londesborough, president of the Four in Hand Club, Lord Rosebery (three times a Derby winner), or Lord Derby, who won twenty classic races with the descendants of a stable of eight brood mares in the 1890s—who set the tone on Epsom Downs or Newmarket Heath. The gallery at Tattersalls on Sunday nights, when owners met to look over horses for the following day's sale, was as fashionable a setting as the opera, and Ascot week or Newmarket races formed a staging post in the season like Cowes Week or the "glorious Twelfth".

In the hunting-field, as on the racecourse, all classes could meet and mix; and for many immured behind the barriers of gentility this may have been one of its attractions. Hunting had changed somewhat since the days of Surtees, when it attracted the interest of all sections of rural society; yet something of what Sir Christopher Sykes had written at the end of the eighteenth century was still true: "When the pleasures of the chase can be made the means of calling the gentlemen of the country together, they become really useful and beneficial to society. They give opportunities of wearing off shynesses, dispelling temporary differences, forming new friendships, cementing old, and draw the gentlemen of the country into one closer bond of society." Most landowners still regarded it as an obligation to provide a pack of hounds for the entertainment of the entire community. Edwardian England—or Ireland—knew no higher distinction than that of Master of Foxhounds, and a great Master was as much a hero of society as the captain of a successful Test Match team—a fact which lent poignance to the lament of the then Duke of Northumberland, the hereditary Master of the Percy Hunt, who could never manage to blow a horn nor tell one hound from another. Foxes were, of course, jealously preserved, and a tenant farmer might well be at risk if he dared to shoot one, whatever damage had been done to his crops or poultry. "Vulpicide" was in fact a social crime, to be denounced by all levels of society; and when foxes became scarce, as they sometimes did, there arose grave ethical choices between preservation and destruction. The old landed interest held together—a handful of great magnates, like the Fitzwilliams at Milton, still prepared to pay £3,000–£5,000 to maintain their own packs; but the majority of hunts after 1900 were financed by subscription, opening up to difficult argument the questions of which outsiders were acceptable, and which were not. Many hunts by the 1900s had reached a pitch of organisation and fashionable eminence which debarred all but the richest followers; yet among small hunts, and especially in Ireland, the old spirit survived.

> Today, all day I rode upon the down,
> With hounds and horsemen, a brave company;
> On this side in its glory lay the sea,
> On that the Sussex weald, a sea of brown ...
> My horse a thing of wings, myself a god.

So Blunt saw himself, in the poem *St Valentine's Day*.

After the war, the poet Siegfried Sassoon happily recalled his youth as a fox-hunting man: "Cubbing days are among my happiest memories. Those mornings now reappear in my mind, lively and freshly painted by the sunshine of an autumn that made amends for the rainy weeks which had washed away the summer. Four days a week we were up before daylight .... In the kennels the two packs were baying at one another from their separate yards, and as soon as Dennis (the Master) had got his horse from the gruff white-coated head groom, a gate released the hounds—twenty-five or thirty of them, and all very much on their toes. Out they streamed like a flood of water, throwing their tongues and spreading away in all directions with waving sterns, as though they had never been out in the world before .... The mornings I remember most zestfully were those which took us up onto the chalk downs. To watch the day breaking from turquoise to dazzling gold while we trotted up a deep rutted lane; to inhale the early freshness when we were on the sheep-cropped uplands; to stare back at the low country with its cock-crowing farms and mist-coiled waterways; thus to be riding out with a sense of spacious discovery—was it not something stolen from the lieabed world and the luckless city workers—even though it ended in nothing more than the killing of a leash of fox cubs; (for whom, to tell the truth, I felt an unconfessed sympathy). Up on the downs in fine September weather sixteen years ago ..." (*Memoirs of a Foxhunting Man*, pp. 177–8).

Traditional pursuits like shooting and fishing underwent changes, either for commercial reasons (with the renting of some of the deer forests and many miles of the best salmon rivers in Scotland), or from the search for perfection which competitiveness inspired. It was not merely a question of comparing the bag with that of other neighbouring estates, nor even of individual owners planting pheasant coverts, or constructing jetties and weirs for a generation of fishermen to come. Blunt was an exception in seeking "to justify the expense of game preserving. My logic about shooting here in England is that it is the only way of preventing the destruction of wild animals. If there was no shooting, no-one would be at the expense of paying game-keepers, nor would it be possible to prevent the rag-tag and bob-tail of the towns from snaring and netting" (*Diaries*, p.237). Those who took their shooting seriously expected to be offered sport on a scale which has never since been surpassed. Gone were the days of nineteenth-century rough shooting when a great shot like Captain Peter Hawker could record in his diary "a right and a left at a bat and a stag beetle". To satisfy ten Edwardian guns might take the labours of 150 keepers, underkeepers, loaders and beaters. At Chatsworth, the house might feed 400 extra mouths, as long as the party lasted. Predictably the cost rose rapidly in the late nineteenth century. Most large houses had their own separate game department, and in the 1890s the cost of this was £3,000 a year at Longleat, and £1,5000 at Savernake, seat of the Marquis of Ailesbury. Unlike hunting, shooting remained a class preserve. Farmers and tenant farmers were rarely invited, except to the occasional end-of-season battue, and generally showed themselves hostile to the game laws and preservation. (After the 1881 Act, they were allowed to shoot ground game—rabbits and hares; but many of them, and most agricultural labourers, saw poaching as a legitimate supplement to income or diet. Feuds with gamekeepers survived well into the twentieth century and sporadic violence sometimes brought back memories of the open warfare of poaching gangs in the hungry years after Waterloo.)

The immense bags of the Edwardian era came after a century of strict legal protection, preservation and the trend towards root crops and more rapid cycles of corn sowing. These conditions, a run of predominately warm and dry springs and early summers, and the skilled attention given to breeding and stocking, brought pheasant and partridge shooting to a climax. At Gorhambury, for example, the game books of the Earls of Verulam give 1900 as the best year between 1821 and 1923, with 2,319 pheasants. Most of the all-time game records date from Edwardian days, the largest bags of snipe (1,108 to two guns at Tiree in the Hebrides, in two days in 1906), woodcock (228 to six guns in County Galway in 1910), grouse (2,929 to eight guns in Lancashire, 13 August 1915), rabbits (6,943 to five guns at Blenheim in 1898) and pheasants (the near incredible total of 3,937 to seven guns at Hall Barn, Beaconsfield, on 18 December 1913) all dating to within about five years either side of Edward's reign. The Marquis of Ripon, born in 1867, and probably the finest shot of the period, recorded the greatest total of game ever shot by a single man: 556,000 birds, including 241,000 pheasants; and he died, appropriately, in his butt on the grouse moor, taking his fifty-second bird on the morning of 22 September 1923.

Such sportsmen ranged far beyond the conventional circuit: Chatsworth, Sandringham and Balmoral. The heirs of pioneer big-game hunters like Captain

Francis Selous roamed East Africa or India in the 1900s equipped with the latest double-barrelled magnum rifles, seeking the finest trophies. Rare antelopes in Arabia, chamois in the Alps, tigers in Bengal fell to the remorseless barrage; while in stations where the British gathered for any length of time, particularly in India, there grew up strange local hunts, riding after imported foxes with enthusiasm and a bewilderingly mongrel assortment of hounds.

Fear of boredom—the unpaid price of money and leisure—lay behind the frenzied pursuit of amusement and the elaborate formality which shaped and divided up the Edwardian day. However inventive or engrossing, sport could not fill all the hours of leisure; and, since women could share in few of these male-dominated preserves, their deprivation needed to be compensated by other diversions, if it were not to be channelled into something so outrageous as the emancipation movement. All the ingenuity of mind of the upper classes concentrated on the ordering of life to prevent that confrontation. For the intellectuals it raised few problems, but then not everyone could share the views of Balfour, who, when asked by his sister, Lady Rayleigh, what he would like for entertainment, replied "Oh something amusing; get some people from Cambridge to talk Science."

Edwardian society was many-faceted, and to distinguish the "smart set" from the rest of the upper class is not simply to distinguish between town and country life. A house party at Chatsworth might be simply a stage in the essentially London season; while in London itself existed circles far removed from the smart set. Nevertheless, the geographical distinction contains sufficient truth to make it viable as a basis for description.

So much has been written of London high life in the 1900s that the reader is left with the impression of an endless round of parties, theatre-going and dances of an almost unrelenting self-indulgence. "Never had there been such a display of flowers .... A profusion of full-blooded blossoms, of lolling roses and malmaisons, of gilded, musical comedy baskets with carnations and sweetpeas, while huge bunches of orchids, bowls of gardenias and flat trays of stephonotis, lent some houses an air of exoticism. Never had Europe seen such mounds of peaches, figs, nectarines, strawberries, at all seasons, brought from their steamy tents of glass; champagne bottles stood stacked on the sideboards ... and to the rich, the show was free" (Osbert Sitwell, *Great Morning*, p.21).

The young bachelor in London could live very well on £550 a year, paying no more than ten guineas for the best suit from Savile Row, £1 10s for his handmade boots, or £1 for his glossy top hat. He could ride in the morning in Hyde Park, to watch the most eligible young ladies and see fashionable hostesses drive their phaetons; or perhaps, like Compton MacKenzie, he would walk down the Open Arcade, to a barber's shop like Burgesses.

"Here not a brush was made the bristles of which had not come from a Siberian hog. Here one could still buy a pot of bear's grease. Here one walked upstairs to be shaved and sat for the operation in a Regency chair with one's legs on a Regency stool. Here on the walls were framed prints of Gillray and Rowlandson. Here when one waited one's turn one read the *Times*, the *Morning Post*, the *Illustrated London News*, the *Graphic* or *Punch*. If a customer had brought with him a *Daily Mail* or a *Daily Express* or even a *Tatler*, he would probably have been asked to take his beard elsewhere" (*My Life and Times*, Octave 4, p.130)

Later he would probably retire to his club in Pall Mall or Piccadilly—the Bath, the Turf, Brooks, Boodles, Whites, or, if he were politically minded, the Reform or the Carlton—to talk over matters with his contemporaries. After a prodigious lunch, he might pay a few calls, thus ensuring an ample supply of invitations for the remainder of the season. Still later he would change from morning dress (or suit, if he had not been in the smarter parts of the capital) into evening dress for the culmination of his day. What a world lay ready for him to sample as, dressed in white waistcoat, tails, hat and gloves, sporting a gardenia as buttonhole and carrying a stick, he set out on his way. As Mrs Patrick Campbell once remarked, "You can do anything you please here, so long as you don't do it in the streets and frighten the horses!"

If he dined at home, then the family evening would be enlivened by playing the piano, or listening to the phonograph, or perhaps the newly invented gramophone, with recordings of Fritz Kreisler on the violin or Patti and Caruso singing arias, or of the new music pouring in from America (*Alexander's Ragtime Band*, *Waiting for the Robert E. Lee*, *Row, Row, Row*, and so on). But no young gentleman needed to dine at home: he would be on the "list" of the eligible and his room would be crowded with invitations to balls, small dinners, supper parties, theatre parties—all of them stages of the most elaborate and formal marriage market. A series of young women presented that year at court would pass before him, carefully chaperoned, eager to enter on their programmes for waltzes, polkas, and two-steps the names of the aristocracy and gentry. And there, on the tide of music, to the heavy scent of tuberoses, and the seemingly endless supply of champagne, he would stay till the last lancers and the final galop, blown on hunting horns.

The season did not last for ever; and he would soon become a little jaded, like Edward Marsh and Winston Churchill, who used to stand near the ballroom door, watching the ladies come in; and on the basis of Marlowe's line "Was this the face that launched a thousand ships?" would assess the beauty of each newcomer. " '200 ships or perhaps 250?' the one might remark tentatively, gazing ahead as he made his reckoning. 'By no means' the other might reply. 'A covered sampan, or a small gunboat at most.' Among the very few who scored the full thousand in the opinion of both assessors were Lady Diana Manners and Miss Clementine Hosier, who Mr. Churchill was to marry" (Hassall, *Edward Marsh*, p.131). Later still, he might turn against the new music and the new dances, like Marsh himself, who found the season of 1913 too much: "It got bloodier and bloodier—the one-step—the turkey trot—the bunny hug or fish walk—or whatever you choose to call it—carried all before it, and my general dislike of its vulgarity, combined with my particular dislike of being on the shelf as a non-trotter—hugger—or walker, works me up into a frying frenzy of disgust and socialism." Similarly, the aging Blunt

deplored the introduction from Paris, at Stafford House in the sweltering summer of
1911, of the Apache dance: "the same which used to be called the can-can, with
other gymnastic eccentricities formerly confined to the Jardin Mabille, for our
amusement; an astonishing display, which would have shocked us, I think, even at
Mabille in the days of the Second Empire and would certainly have been impossible
in London in my young days at a public dancing hall, let alone in a drawing room."

Still, single or married, the gentleman in London need never lack for
somewhere to go or something to do. There was always the club: and, even if his
friends were not in, there would be the evening papers and the wine lists to read, the
suggestion book to write in. What long evenings must have inspired the requests for
the *Calcutta Daily News* and the *Allahabad Pioneer*, for Bengalese hash or Vienna
steaks to be served, for more cigar rests in the lavatories, an extra curry cook to be
appointed, for the wind indicator to be repaired, and "noisy tea-drinkers to be
spoken to"!

In the less fashionable months, there would be fewer parties at those modest
houses rented by country families; no grand balls at Londonderry or Devonshire
House; and none of the select parties that the Duchess of Northumberland gave
during the season, and to which young men were "nominated" by her friends. But
the theatre and the opera, the music hall and the concert hall remained. It was the
great age of actor-managers, of Bancroft, Wyndham, Hare and Tree, of the new
generation of playwrights, Pinero, Galsworthy and Shaw, of the "incomparable
Max" Beerbohm. At the beginning of the reign, there was Henry Irving in *The
Bells* at the Lyceum, and at the Haymarket were the French frolics so dear to the
King's heart; later came such intellectually testing plays as Shaw's *Man and
Superman* (1903), Pinero's *His House in Order* (1906) and Galsworthy's acute
comment on industrial politics, *Strife* (1909). An intense realism pervaded the
English stage: for Sullivan's operetta *Ivanhoe*, Sir Thomas Beecham remembered,
"tons of timber were ordered for the scenes of the tournament and the burning of
the castle of Torquilstone. In those days we had not yet escaped from the cycle of
ultra-realism in stage decoration and everything had to be as life-like as possible. If
there was a house on the stage it must be a real house; trees and waterfalls must be
the things themselves; and artists as well as the public took a childish delight in
going further than merely holding the mirror up to nature" (*A Mingled Chime*
(1973), p.89). One actor-manager loosed a brood of tame rabbits during Oberon's
great speech in *A Midsummer Night's Dream*, and Beecham himself was once
offered a live bull to accompany the sacrificial lambs at Clytemnestra's first entrance
in *Elektra*.

The range of concerts and opera was amazing to all who remembered the later
nineteenth century. On a warm summer evening in Piccadilly, a stroller might hear
the voice of Caruso or Dame Nellie Melba amusing a late night party after the
Opera, while the bill at Covent Garden itself, fulfilling a vociferous demand, ranged
from Wagner's *Ring* to *opéra comique*. Nothing was ever the same after Sir
Thomas Beecham brought over the Russian ballet with Karsavina and Nijinsky
dancing the *Spectre de la Rose* in June 1911; stage decoration and women's

fashions responded equally to the Russian stimulus and to the even more successful visit by Diaghilev in 1912. In 1913 Beecham was able to introduce *Boris Godunov* sung in Russian, with Chaliapin. Eddie Marsh watched the Diaghilev company dancing *Scheherazade*: "All the papers and most people hate it, but don't you believe them, it is delicious, I went thoroughly meaning to dislike it, so it isn't snobbism on my part. I was enraptured from the moment the curtain went up. It's a post-impressionist picture put in motion. It has almost brought me round to Matisse's pictures!" (Hassall, *Edward Marsh*, p.231).

Patrons and patronesses abounded: an Aird might summon an orchestra to play in his London house, but Beecham gave a curt answer to a country clergyman who, unable to spend the night in London, blithely suggested that the singers of the *Tales of Hoffman* might assemble for his exclusive benefit for a quiet hour one afternoon. Yet Beecham acknowledged the power and value of patronage; it was the rich who appreciated his introduction of unfamiliar master works: "In the case of our first Russian season it was only when it began to be known that the stalls and boxes were filled nightly with an audience of persons famous in politics, society and art, that the man in the street also came to applaud and approve." The rest preferred *opéra comique*: "the audience [at Johann Strauss's *Die Fledermaus*] which had yawned over the anguished frenzies of Werther and the tender sentimentality of Muguette, or had politely endured the sublime raptures of Mozart, demonstrated unmistakeable joy at seeing this popular favourite trotting out all time honoured devices for securing a laugh, such as falling over sofas, squirting soda water syphons in someone's face, or being carried off to bed in a complete state of intoxication" (*A Mingled Chime*, p.96). So it was that Franz Lehar's *Merry Widow* and Edward German's *Merrie England* ran for month after month.

For a more florid audience, Pelissier's *Follies* or the music hall offered a rich and usually ribald assortment of talent—Marie Lloyd's salacious wit, Albert Chevalier, Henry Tate and George Robey, the Gibson girls, Vesta Tilley, and the great comedienne Edna May. Champagne cost no more than sixpence in the bar—a curious contrast to what were then real extravagances, like the Gondola Dinner given one night by the management of the Savoy. For this the back courtyard was sealed, and filled with water, and the diners, attended by mock Venetian waiters and waterborne minstrels, sat in gondolas.

Not everything was confined to London: Brighton, Bath and Harrogate all had their "season" in miniature, where the jaded or, in the case of Brighton, lustful taste might be cultivated in changed surroundings. Irving brought his plays to the provinces, as did the Carl Rosa or Moody Manners opera companies. Granville Barker and Forbes Robertson played on most provincial repertory stages. Thus, unless a man were wholly inured to the pleasures of life, he could barely have avoided them; and, looking back from the bleak wastes of 1919, John Maynard Keynes, least sentimental of analysts, was constrained to admit the uniqueness of the era that had ended in August 1914.

"The inhabitant of London could order by telephone, sipping his morning tea in bed, the various products of the whole earth, in such quantity as he might see fit, and reasonably expect their daily delivery upon his doorstep. He could at the same moment and by the same means adventure his wealth in the natural resources and new enterprises of any quarter of the world, and share, without exertion or even trouble, in their prospective fruits and advantages; or he could decide to couple the security of his fortunes with the good faith of the townspeople of any substantial municipality in any continent that fancy or information might recommend. He could secure forthwith, if he wished it, cheap and comfortable means of transit to any country or climate without passport or other formality, could dispatch himself to the neighbouring office of a bank for a fresh supply of precious metals as might seem convenient, and could then proceed abroad to foreign quarters, without knowledge of their religion, language or customs, bearing coined wealth upon his person, and would consider himself greatly aggrieved and much surprised at the least interference. But, most important of all, he regarded this state of affairs as normal, certain and permanent, except in the direction of further improvement, and any deviation from it as aberrant, scandalous and avoidable" (*The Economic Consequences of the Peace*, pp. 9–10.)

However, a gentleman's tastes would extend far beyond mere frivolity and entertainment. Unless he wished to be taken for a boor, he would be a judge of painting and architecture. He would be, probably, not well, but correctly, versed in these things—for, as Masterman saw, much of his life was talk: "It is talk, talk, talk, usually commonplace, sometimes clever, occasionally sincere; of a society desirous of being interested, more often finding itself bored, held with a resolute conviction that it must play the game; that this is the game to be played, but it must be played resolutely to the end" (*The Condition of England*, p.38).

It was a period of collecting rather than of patronage of gifted living artists, of good taste rather than individual flair, in which the canons of the early eighteenth century extended from architecture to the domestic arts. "Sir Hugh Lane", observed Sickert waspishly, "has been knighted for admiring Manet. Would he have been knighted for merely *being* Manet?" Lane stood out, however, as the originator of a unique collection, and a more typical figure was Lord Swaythling (formerly the financier Moses Samuel), a member of the Burlington Fine Art Club and a collector of silver—not of the work of contemporary masters like Omar Ramsden, but of the "safe" period of Queen Anne. Soames Forsyte, in Galsworthy's *Forsyte Saga*, expresses accurately enough the conception of art as an investment, as well as a field for conspicuous spending:

He stood before his Gauguin—sorest point in his collection. He had bought the ugly great thing with two early Matisses before the war, because there was such a fuss about those post-Impressionist chaps .... On the other hand, he knew very well that "aesthetics and good taste" are necessary. The appreciation of enough persons of good taste was what gave a work of art its permanent market value, or in other words, made it "a work of art".

The Academy and the institutions were dominated by a clique of accepted (and acceptable) painters: the aging Alma-Tadema (two of whose "narrative machines" were sold in 1903 for £6,000 apiece), Orpen, Steer and Sargent, whom clients, like Sir George Sitwell, thought "good enough for anyone". (The artists themselves, however, often distained this fulsome admiration. Sargent used to be so bored by the society women he painted that he would retire behind a screen to refresh himself by sticking his tongue out at them, and he preferred Jewesses "as they have more life and movement than our English women".)

The derision which greeted Durand-Ruel's exhibition in 1905 and the famous Post-Impressionist exhibition in 1910 indicated the limits of conventional taste. E.M. Forster, despite his Bloomsbury training, found Gauguin and Van Gogh too much; Wilfred Blunt, what had shown himself a fine collector of illustrated manuscripts and oriental miniatures, was appalled: "The exhibition is either an extremely bad joke or a swindle. I am inclined to think the latter, for there is no trace of humour in it. Still less is there a trace of sense or skill or taste, good or bad, or art or cleverness. Nothing but that gross puerility which scrawls indecencies on the walls of a privy .... In all the three or four hundred pictures, there is not one worthy of attention even by its singularity, or appealing to any feeling but of disgust. I am wrong. There was one picture signed Gauguin which at a distance had a pleasing effect of colour" (*Diaries*, p.143).

It is true that well-known figures—Lionel Cust, Keeper of the King's pictures, Lord Henry Bentinck and Lady Ottoline Morrell—were among the organisers; but too many of the viewers succumbed to the same inhibition that afflicted Sir George Sitwell when asked to admire his son's Modigliani: "Being at the lowest a man of imagination and aesthetic perception, and, in some branches, of a liking for new ideas, he treated the picture seriously, and listened to all I had to say, until it seemed clear that he would at last fall in with one of our plans, and that in consequence it would reach fruition." But then he was interrupted by a guest "inspired by Good Taste". "Something in the painting before him clashed with the ideals upheld by the Queen Anne Coffee Pot; wherefore this was not and could not be Art", and Sir George "was frightened out of it, by the force of conventional opinion". (*Great Morning*, p.125).

For the conventional collector, however, galleries multiplied, and at Colnaghi's and Agnew's gentlemen bought eighteenth-century portraits and drawings, and paid higher prices (in real terms) for the British school than have ever been paid since. Lord Michelham, for example, presented the National Gallery with a portrait of Lady Pole, which had been sold by Christies in June 1913 for £41,000; and in the same year Henry Frick (an American, however) paid £82,700 for Gainsborough's portrait of the Hon. Frances Duncombe.

The galleries might display the latest sketches or cartoons by Max Beerbohm, but only the adventurous would look for the controversial products of the Camden school for an Epstein or Muirhead Bone or Augustus John. Edward Marsh was decidedly unusual in combining an expert taste for early English watercolours (he paid £2,400 for 200 or so paintings in the Horne collection, which included several Gainsboroughs, Blakes, Turners and Wilsons) with the acquisition of paintings by

Matthew Smith, Bone, John and Duncan Grant.

The total lack of confidence in individual judgement, rather than the lack of money, seems to have afflicted architecture. The vast country houses of Victorian England, Gothic extravaganzas like Eaton Hall, no longer suited—for reasons of comfort and warmth and because of the rising cost of domestic service. But the will to build was also absent. Owners turned to modernisation and improvements such as draining, and central heating or interior decoration, rather than follow the example of men like Sir William Armstrong, who created at Cragside in Northumberland a monument to his own genius with private electricity plant and hydraulically operated lift. Lutyens, decorous practitioner of classical styles, built smaller country houses, traditional in every way; and architecture (with the exception of C.R. Mackintosh's work in Scotland) dropped out of the mainstream of European history, away from the vivid energies of art nouveau and modernism.

The duality of Edwardian taste, especially in the field of interior design, can be seen in the type of furniture on sale at Maples, Harrods and Liberty's: Maples and Harrods both offered furniture in older styles (Maples, Georgian; Harrods, Italianate and Second Empire), rendered in a peculiarly heavy, ornate Edwardian fashion; while Liberty's, catering to a more discerning palate, offered the later furniture of William Morris's factory, and modern pieces designed by C.F. Voysey and Ernest Gimson (the protagonists of art nouveau in the 1890s) and Ambrose Heal and Gordon Russell (developers of new themes from English rural traditions). To shop at Liberty's in the 1900s was to belong to the intellectual set, to have fast—and possibly subversive—opinions; and there is much truth in the view that the division between conventional and modern taste also corresponded to the gulf between conservative and radical politics, intellectual achievements and the goals of *l'homme moyen sensuel*. Thus Knowsley, seat of the intensely traditional Earl of Derby, was compared by one guest to "a large tasteless hotel"; another said of his host that he had eight houses and no home. In complete contrast, Thorpe Lodge, on Camden Hill, as renovated by Montagu Norman, seemed to Janet Ashbee (wife of the famous designer), who visited it in 1907, like a miniature from the Arabian Nights.

"I am sitting by a great beech fire—for it is wintry cold still—which smoulders orange under a heavy Italian stone mantle with the *palle* of the Medici upon it, grey and velvety like mole skin. The room is vaulted in white plaster and gives you the spacious ease of soul that you express in a contented sigh. The floor is mottled and shining elm, overlaid partly by rose and plum-coloured Persian rugs. The electric light glows unseen above a cornice, or glints through mother-of-pearl shutters. A scarlet lacquered screen and the dark bluish discs of old Worcester plates are the only decorations. But the beauty of the room is in its panelling, carried high up to the spring of the vaulting, in unpolished wood. It is impossible to describe the warm, gentle, caressing feeling given by this wood, or definitely to say what its colour is: the nearest I can get is smooth, sunburnt flesh" (Boyle, *Montagu Norman*, p.80).

The numerous literary coteries and societies that flourished in the 1900s produced a wide range of weeklies, monthlies and quarterlies—many short-lived, but some highly influential. There were A.R. Orage's *New Age*, Ford Madox Ford's *English Review*, the *Poetry Review* and the *Blue Review* (with contributors like Katherine Mansfield, James Elroy Flecker and Hugh Walpole) and, of course, less self-consciously literary magazines, like Frank Harris's *Vanity Fair*. At the same time, Ezra Pound, T.S. Eliot and D.H. Lawrence made their first appearance in print; James Joyce, Virginia Woolf and E.M. Forster were in full flight; and the Bloomsbury group, the period's most notable coterie, fascinated, attracted (and sometimes repelled by its eccentric morality) the rest of literary London. One way of highlighting the change in tone is to set the "Souls" (among others, Balfour, Baring, George Curzon, Lord Ribblesdale, St John Broderick, Harry Cust, George Wyndham, Lady Desborough, Margot Asquith and Mrs Grenfell)—the brightest stars of the 1890s, become by 1914 pillars of the establishment—against the members of Bloomsbury: Lytton Strachey, author of the piercing and destructive *Eminent Victorians*, Virginia and Leonard Woolf, Thoby and Adrian Stephens, Vanessa and Clive Bell, John Maynard Keynes, Duncan Grant, E.M. Forster and the rest; who were, in due course, to become the intellectual eminences of the 1920s.

The English literary scene was as divided as the artistic between the modernists and traditionalists. Fine presses turned out elegantly bound volumes to grace a gentleman's library, while poor Alfred Austin, made Poet Laureate by Lord Salisbury for no discernible reason, attempted to set the florid essence of the period to verse. But what did gentlemen *read*? Some seem to have been almost illiterate: George Cornwallis-West, second husband of Lady Randolph Churchill, liked the story of an Eton contemporary who, in writing to his old tutor, asked to be remembered to his *yph* (wife); and Frank Harris claimed to have heard a millionaire, newly enobled, boast that he possessed only two books— the "Guid Book" (the Bible, which he never opened) and his cheque book. The romantic era had vanished by the 1900s, and with it the "impossible dream" of the Pre-Raphaelites. Nothing that was not "smart" or "realistic" could become fashionable. A new biography might arouse discussion, and H.G. Wells was widely read. Essays and short stories reached a peak of popularity, as men read *Blackwood's Magazine* in their clubs or turned to the exquisitely damaging satire of Beerbohm or the pointed vignettes of Saki (H.H. Munro). In the shadows lurked the great sombre figure of Conrad, and D.H. Lawrence; but, according to Lawrence Jones, his contemporaries were unaware of Henry James, ignorant of Conrad, and knowledgeable only about Hardy and Kipling. Even then, their tastes were not widely shared: "It was a Balliol Prime Minister whose Balliol Private Secretary rang up Buckingham Palace, on the occasion of Hardy's seventieth birthday and suggested that a Royal telegram to 'old Hardy' might be appreciated. 'Jolly good idea', was the reply, 'it shall be done', and Mr. Hardy of Alnwick, renowned maker of fishing rods, was astonished to receive Royal congratulations on attaining an age he had not attained, on a day which was the anniversary of nothing" (*An Edwardian Youth*, p.97).

Most popular were Elinor Glyn, Ouida (Marie Louise de la Ramée), Marie Corelli, and the writers of thrillers—E. Philips Oppenheim, William le Queux, Edgar Wallace and A.E.W. Mason—who set up mirror images of the gentlemen's style. Possibly the best-seller of the period was H. de Vere Stacpool's *Blue Lagoon*—the saccharin-sweet story of two shipwrecked children, on a lonely island, growing up into maturity and discovering—in the most innocently salacious way—the facts of life. All these were darlings of the circulating libraries, Mudie's, Smith's and Boots, which could make or break a new novel, as Compton Mackenzie found with Smith's quasi-censorship of *Sinister Street*. As for the Press, it is a sad comment on standards that one of the most distinguished dailies, the *Westminister Gazette*, lapsed into bankruptcy and had to be sustained by Lord Cowdray; circulation of the *Telegraph* and *Manchester Guardian* steadily declined; only the Northcliffe papers (which after 1908 included *The Times*) actually made money.

The lack of educated appreciation of modern art and literature may be explained partly by the most baffling diversity of calls on a gentleman's leisure—not only in London. Even when he left for the country, his time would be allocated with a formal precision, most obvious at a great house, but still evident in the smaller establishments which formed the heart of English rural society. With cricket and croquet, shooting and hunting by day, party games, charades, music or whist at night, the weekend unrolled. If the host was literate and lively, and his guests chosen with care, the talk might be memorable. Max Beerbohm might be there, asking quizzically, "Why do Englishmen, when offered a glass of port, always say 'Yes I would like a *little* port'—never 'I would like a lot of port' or even 'I would like some port'—though one of the two is generally what they mean"; or writing, in contributing to a shilling fund, to pay for a presentation to W.G. Grace, "I send you this shilling, not because I am a great admirer of cricket, but as an earnest protest against golf" (Cecil, *Max*, p.268). At Newtimber, in Blunt's day, there might be Asquith himself, or Churchill "going on energetically about prison reform, making most amusing little House of Commons speeches". In Lawrence Jones's words, "all was friendliness and gaiety and 'sun-burnt mirth'; no sound or rumour from the neighbouring countryside, where men and women were presumably living laborious lives, ever penetrated that self-sufficient enclave". But there were other notes struck, and not all the talk was as witty or pleasing. Princess Daisy of Pless left a sardonic memoir of a stay at Chatsworth in January 1903, when the party included the Dukes and Duchesses of Connaught and Teck, A.J. Balfour, Lord and Lady Desborough, Count Mensdorff, the Marques de Soveral, Lord and Lady de Grey, and of course the Devonshire family. The male guests all shot or played golf, while the women were left to rehearse a play. Chatsworth, she thought "was not a happy house ... it breathes society and nothing else".

Frances, Countess of Warwick, found the same: "We had mountains of

trunks—roofed trunks. Whenever I see men or women to-day going off for a
week-end carrying their own neat suit-cases, I remember with amusement the
mountains of luggage that were landed at a railway country station when one of our
parties broke up. I wonder how the good-tempered porters dealt with it. The whole
platform from end to end seemed to be piled with luggage, with any number of
gentlemen's gentlemen and ladies' maids in attendance. The maid always carried
her lady's jewel-case and put it down on the seat of the third-class carriage where
she sat, no doubt making eyes at some valet meanwhile .... The large coronets and
conspicuous letters on our mountainous trunks made interesting reading for the
country crowd. Rubbing shoulders with their luggage was the nearest they got to
rubbing shoulders with the aristocracy .... We began the day by breakfasting at ten
o'clock. This meal consisted of many courses in silver dishes on the side-table.
There was enough food to last a group of well-regulated digestions for the whole
day. The men went out shooting after breakfast and then came the emptiness of the
long morning from which I suffered silently. I can remember the groups of women
sitting discussing their neighbours or writing letters at impossible little ornamental
tables. I could never enjoy writing at spindly-legged tables. I like plenty of elbow
room and a broad expanse. We were not all women. There were a few unsporting
men asked—"darlings." These men of witty and amusing conversation were
always asked as extras everywhere to help to entertain the women; otherwise we
should have been left high and dry. The "ladies" then were not like the women of
to-day. They rarely took part in the shoot, not even going out to join the shooters
until luncheon time. Then, dressed in tweeds and trying to look as sportsman-like
as the clothes of the day allowed, we went out together to some rendezvous of the
shooters. A woman who was very bloodthirsty and sporting might go and cower
behind some man and watch his prowess among the pheasants. But there were very
few even of these brave ones. After a large luncheon, finishing up with coffee and
liqueurs, the women preferred to wend their way back to the house. They would
spend the intervening time until the men returned for tea once more, changing their
clothes. This time they got into lovely tea-gowns. The tea-gowns of that day were
far more beautiful than the evening gowns worn for dinner. We changed our clothes
four times a day at least. This kept our maids and ourselves extraordinarily busy. I
remember one tea-gown that was thought to be beautiful. It was of *eau de Nil* satin,
draped with gold-spangled *mousseline de soie*—the georgette of the day—with gold
waist belt and bands of fur at the hem and at the neck, and with large angel sleeves;
the whole effect of green and gold and white looked very fine. Imagine a woman of
the present day descending to five o'clock tea in such a garment! When I think of
all these gorgeous gowns round a tea-table I fancy we must have looked like a group
of enormous dolls. Conversation at tea was slumberous. Nobody woke up to be
witty until dinner time with its accompanying good wines. The men discussed the
bags of the day and the women did the admiring. With the coming of bridge in later
years the hours between tea and dinner were relieved of their tedium. It used often
to be sheer boredom until seven when we went off to dress for dinner" (*Life's Ebb
and Flow* (1929), pp. 190–1).

Princess Daisy (an Irishwoman by birth) was honest enough to admit that she used to try and avoid such invitations and let her husband go alone. "So often 'il faut souffrir pour etre poli'. I always had to place our most exalted guest next to me at dinner, and I was bored so often." At the height of the shooting season, in her own house, she "never had time to rest", and, when she tried out a stratagem of the French Empress Eugenie, of drawing lots for places at dinner, she found she had to cheat by following the wishes of the men.

In the male-dominated world, boredom afflicted the women most. Men, after all, could vent their ill-temper on the golf course, or with the gun, or, if wet, on the billiards table; and men could visit the far places charted out by nineteenth-century explorers, or, like Captain Scott, venture further. The most heroic story of the age is that of Scott's second Antarctic expedition (1910–12), in which Scott and four others reached the Pole, only to find that they had been beaten to it by Amundsen, and then died on the way back. The heroism of Captain Oates in walking off into the night to give his companions a chance of life is unforgettable.

Exotic travels formed part of the unbringing of most Edwardian gentlemen, who, like Lord Curzon, later Foreign Secretary, could talk and move "with majestic omniscience over the continents, rolling out one sweeping generalisation after another, and suddenly revealing minute knowledge of a path over a small hill in the Caucasus" (Thomas Jones, *Whitehall Diary*, vol. 1 (1969), p.164). The decade abounded in memoirs with titles like *Eighteen Years in the Khyber* and *Journeys in the Pamirs*, and archetypal figures like Buchan's Richard Hannay were credited with the ability to speak half a dozen outlandish dialects. In real life, Wilfrid Blunt actually did travel widely in four of the five continents, and became personally involved in the political storms of Egypt, the Sudan and India; Conrad himself watched Roger Casement "swinging off into the unspeakable wilderness [of West Africa] carrying nothing but a crook-handled stick and two bull-dogs for weapons"—and return two months later, "serene as though he had been for a walk in the park"; John Hope-Johnstone and Gerald Brenan set out as schoolboys, with £16 between them, to walk through France, Italy and Yugoslavia to India (and, true to the public-school code, never called each other by name, despite their misfortunes in jails and doss-houses all across southern Europe); Maurice Baring came to know intimately Russia and Manchuria as well as Turkey and the Balkans; and the eccentric Auberon Herbert walked the Egyptian desert like the streets of London, "clad in grey flannels, without a coat, and carrying a lantern in one hand and a staff in the other, with a wallet full of stones strapped to his back, like the picture of Christian with his bundle of sins in *The Pilgrim's Progress* .... He stopped to dine with us and set-to like a famished man, which he was, for he had been wandering in the valleys since 11 and had brought nothing with him but some coffee and milk in a bottle" (Blunt, *Diaries*, p.497).

More sedately, Edwardian families followed the example of the King in visits to Europe. Most well-to-do families crossed the Channel on holiday at least once a year—not yet, as in the 1920s, to lie on sunburnt beaches, but to see the cathedrals of France, the castles of the Rhine valley, the sights of Switzerland, Vienna and

Venice, or to gamble in the casinos of Deauville or Cannes. Some would use the facilities of an agent like Thomas Cook, flourishing after his thirty years in business, or rent houses in fashionable spas and resorts; and most would take seriously the advice given in Murray's *Guidebook*. "Any Englishman having the usual knowledge of Ancient Greek will be able to read the Athenian papers with ease." There would be more select pilgrimages of the *cognoscenti*, to visit Bernard Berenson, master of Italian Renaissance studies (and associate of Duveen in certain rather dubious attributions of Old Masters aimed at the American market) at I Tatti, outside Florence, or Max Beerbohm at the Vilino Chiaro, on the road between Genoa and Rome. Younger men, like Edward Marsh, might discover Spain and test their stamina watching bullfights in the gory days before horses were protected. Masterman noticed how the old Grand Tour had been modified by his "Conquerors": "they stamp their life upon invaded cities; demanding and in consequence obtaining those things which they judge indispensable to the discipline of their existence. These include especially *l'installation hygiénique* and *l'installation sportive*. At Biarritz today [1909], the villas which are not entirely sanitary do not let." But they spread far beyond the Victorian bounds, wintering in Madeira, or in Cairo, at the famous Shepheards Hotel, of which it was said that if a man sat long enough on the terrace he would see everyone he had ever known pass by. Raffles Hotel in Singapore, where, according to local legend, a tiger had once been shot under the billiard table, was only slightly further from the beaten track, and began in the 1900s to provide rooms for visitors from passing liners and from the rubber plantations up country.

Violet Asquith remembered a cruise on the Admiralty yacht *Enchantress* in the summer of 1912, when Churchill was First Lord of the Admiralty: "We had a wonderful picnic yesterday among the ruins of an old Greek fortress [in Sicily]. We lunched among its fallen walls, great blocks of stone all overgrown with rosemary, wild lavender and candy tuft. Admiral Beatty's eyes gleamed when he saw a pot of fois gras in the basket .... We went up to the Greek theatre towards sunset and lay there among the wild thyme and humming bees and watched the sea changing from blue to flame and then to cool jade green as the sun dropped into it and the stars came out. The theatre is a vast stand-up theatre .... W and F were interested to test its acoustics and Eddie [Marsh] was (appropriately) selected to speak to us from the stage. There to our delight he recited A.E. Housman's parody of a Greek tragedy beginning:

> Oh suitably surmounted with a hat
> Head of a traveller...

in his highest falsetto and every word was clearly audible. He said afterwards that he was afraid lest 'the offended shade of Aeschylus should despatch an eagle to drop a tortoise on his head' " (Violet Bonham Carter, *Winston Churchill As I Knew Him*, pp.264–5).

At home, in the last few years before the war, the car at last began to rival the railway as the means of travel, and opened up great stretches of Ireland and Scotland to short holidays. Some even used the bicycle, though few gentlemen were so persistent as the young Bertrand Russell, who would ride off with Bernard Shaw for twenty miles at a time, or a friend of R.D. Blumenfeld's who took his bicycle across the Channel, and cycled to Paris, Provence, Marseilles, Genoa and Venice.

As might have been expected, the social vices of the upper class had become more extravagant and highly formalised. By 1910 those with long memories could see that in many ways Edwardian England had reached an extraordinary pitch of civilisation in which the wilder, grosser elements of eighteenth-century behaviour had first been tempered by Victorian high-mindedness, and had finally been resolved in elaborate ritual. A parallel might be drawn with court behaviour in Versailles in the days of Louis XIV—the distinction being that in England imitation flourished in the remotest areas. Dress, design and decoration reflected the slightest shifts of fashion in London; all three were turned into arts in themselves, bound by a code of rules all the more rigid because they lacked any obvious sanction. The same applied to food and drink; gross drunkenness, still habitual in the nineteenth century, had ceased to be socially acceptable, declining in any case as the scope for diversion increased. Drinking, of course, remained: a staple in whiling away tedium; as Wilde observed caustically, "work is the curse of the drinking-classes". The gentleman's cellar would still contain heavy clarets and racks of vintage port, but the popularity of American cocktails was rising: recipes for such concoctions as the Martini, Manhattan, Yankie Invigorator and Brain Duster were widely circulated. The medical profession had begun its slow, insidious attack on the evils of alcohol, reinforcing the teetotal lobby; though few evaded their prescription with the nicety of the Vice-President of Trinity College, who, instructed by his doctor never to drink wine unless it was watered, had his servant stand behind him with a glass of water and a toothpick on a silver salver. He would then dip the toothpick in the water and let a drop or two fall gently into his glass of port (Sir John Masterman, *On the Chariot Wheel, an autobiography*, p.65).

Eating still provided occasion for vast indulgence. Frank Harris remarked on the grossness of table manners and the appalling stench at City banquets and at many English houses; and the (fictional) Sebastian was similarly disgusted: "Those meals! Those endless extravagant meals in which they indulged all the year round! He wondered how their constitutions and figures could stand it—then he remembered that in the summer they went as a matter of course to Homburg or Marienbad .... " But in the age of Escoffier, the grand master of sauces, formality and decoration ruled the day; whatever the King might do, it is doubtful that many of the guests at banquets of a dozen or so courses would indulge in every course. Meals were elaborately ceremonial not only in the serving and eating, but also in the arrangement of places, the ebb and flow of conversation, and the way, quite simply, that they divided the day and determined changes of dress.

Since the eighteenth century, the pursuit of chance had been a dominating

pastime among the upper classes of English society, and the late Victorian and
Edwardian periods brought little change except in making gambling more
organised. The gentleman's club continued to be a major focus of gambling activity,
as it always had been—the "wagers books" continued to list the various contests
that took place among members. But now gambling activity moved out of the clubs,
and became a formal part of any large gathering of the nobility and gentlefolk. Race
meetings, country-house weekends, military manoeuvres, "health" visits to the
Continent—all were associated with the flow of cash between gamblers. The
bookmaker was already an established figure in London life—the rivalry between
John Gully and William Crockford had been a major talking point in fashionable
society during the nineteenth century, and Gully combined his interest in horses
with the ownership of a coalmine and the duties of an MP.

Despite rising Nonconformist hostility during the nineteenth century, horse-
racing held its ground as an acceptable pursuit. Scandals such as that surrounding
the 1844 Derby did little to discourage its devotees, and the patronage of the Prince
of Wales and Lord Rosebery gave racing a distinct social "cachet" around the turn
of the century. But perhaps the most colourful figure of this period was Bob Siever,
the owner of the famous filly Sceptre. Siever won and lost several fortunes during his
lifetime—in 1888 he went to Epsom with £25 in his pocket, and left three days
later with £16,000. In 1900 he won over £60,000 at four meetings (£33,000
coming from one victory alone). Along with his gambling activities went scandal and
legal action. He was nearly ruined when he lost a libel action against Richard
Wootton, and won a spectacular victory when charged with blackmailing the mining
king Jack Joel.

Actually to own a racehorse required large sums of money, and the annual
dinners that the Prince of Wales gave to the members of the Jockey Club attracted
only the most wealthy of the sporting classes; but the later decades of Victoria's
reign saw the expansion of sporting journals catering to less elevated tastes. The
situation led to a classic swindle in 1880, when the editor of *Bell's Life* received a
letter from the Secretary of the Trodmore Hunt, asking him to publish the enclosed
Easter Monday racing programme and promising to send the results by telegram.
The results arrived in due course, and were published in the Journal. The illegal
betting shop establishments that flourished in London paid out several thousand
pounds to lucky backers. However, a query about quoted odds led to an inquiry and
disclosed the disturbing fact that no such place as Trodmore existed!

Gambling was technically illegal, but the nobility need pay little attention to
such restrictions. One guest at a party at Sandringham in 1890 was displeased on
finding baccarat being played in the small hours: "I think it is a shocking affair for
the Royal Family to play an illegal game every night. They have a real table, and
rakes, and everything like the rooms at Monte Carlo." The Prince of Wales carried
around with him his own set of counters (in denominations varying from five
shillings to £10), engraved with his feathered crest; and in this he was doing no
more than keep himself ready for what had become *the* aristocratic pastime. Even
the circumstances surrounding the Tranby Croft scandal did little to diminish the

enthusiasm of the English gentleman for risking his capital; although in the 1900s
the gambling mania diversified into the more sophisticated network of the City and
the share market. But, even after the law became more strictly enforced in England
(notably during the 1914–18 war), the English gentleman could still travel to
continental casinos—most of which owed their origin to the demands of indulgent
and wealthy Edwardian visitors seeking recuperation from the excesses of their
everyday routine. As late as the 1920s it was possible for Gordon Selfridge to lose
about £2 million at the tables, and there were other British gentlemen eager to take
up the challenge laid down by Zographos's Syndicate.

Churchill was one of those to be found at Monte Carlo. He wrote to Edward
Marsh in 1910, "We have had a pleasant journey so far [to Naples] though we had
one rough night and I was very seasick. I am now better and am, I think, getting
accustomed to the less devilish forms of motion attendant upon marine adventure.
You will be glad to hear that I visited the Monte Carlo gambling hall on four
occasions and took away from them altogether upwards of £160" (Hassall,
Edward Marsh, p.167).

Marsh was an excellent bridge player, and found Winston's erratic partnership
hard to bear. "I can still hear Eddie's cry of pain", wrote Violet Asquith, "when
Winston, having 'led up to' and sacrificed his partner's King, declared 'Nothing is
here for the tears. The King cannot fall unworthily if he falls to the sword of the
ace'—a dictum which left Eddie's tears over his fallen King undried" (Violet
Bonham Carter, *Winston Churchill As I Knew Him*, p.224).

Of course gambling could prove a heavy drain on the pockets of those who
could ill afford such losses. The social nature of the activity often concealed its
potential danger, as is illustrated by Ponsonby's account of a baccarat game played
at a country-house party in 1907: "The game began very well with no one staking
more than one pound as a maximum, but as is inevitable at baccarat, the stakes got
higher and higher. Poklewski, who took the Bank, steadily won every coup,
although he wanted to lose as it was chicken's feed to him. I had played steadily,
but lost continually, when Lady Elcho came and asked me to play bridge as they
wanted a fourth. I had lost about £30 and did not at all like leaving the game and
missing the chance of getting home .... I played very bad bridge with Mrs. Willy
Grenfell, Arthur Balfour and Lady Elcho, and won eight shillings" (*Recollections of
Three Reigns* p.175).

The Edwardian taste for hoaxes proved less dangerous to the pocket—provided
that the police and authorities (where involved) exercised their traditional
indulgence towards the upper classes. Max Beerbohm perpetrated an elaborate joke
against Shaw, by carefully altering many of his photographs from the *Bookman*,
exaggerating his peculiarities into distortions more hideous than caricature; these
were then photographed and tinted so that they looked like old family portraits, and
posted to Max's friends in England and America, with a request to send them to
Shaw himself, accompanied by a letter announcing their discovery in peculiar places
round the globe, and asking for Shaw to autograph and return them. What Shaw
thought is not recorded. Most of the recipients of Beerbohm's parodies (with the

exception of A.C. Benson) were amused rather than hurt. But the solemn—and minor—poet Herbert Trench was, as Max put it, "a little offended" when he received a copy of his portentous narrative poem *Apollo and the Seaman* with all the aitches cut out and replaced by apostrophes, so that the Seaman appeared to speak with a cockney accent.

The most inventive of Edwardian hoaxers was Horace de Vere Cole, a brother-in-law of the Chamberlains and a favourite of the Bloomsbury group, who could not resist, for example, slipping his gold watch into a MP's pocket, daring him to a race in a London street, and then crying "Stop thief!" That episode led both to Vine Street police station, and to court. Cole's finest hour came at Weymouth in 1910, when he arranged by telegraph for a review of HMS *Dreadnought* on behalf of, ostensibly, the Emperor of Abyssinia. The Admiral's pinnance embarked a party of swarthy princes and princesses—Cole, Virginia Woolf, Adrian Stephen, Duncan Grant and Anthony Buxton among them—with Leonard Woolf cast in the role of interpreter; the "Abyssinians" conversed in a garbled nonsense-language, with the recurrent phrase "Bonga-bonga", and for more than an hour the Admiral commanding the Navy's newest and most powerful ship guided his guests and entertained them, until twenty-one guns saluted their departure. Undone by the photographer of the occasion, Cole was finally exposed, and the First Lord of the Admiralty had to answer embarrassing questions in the House of Commons. "The Hon. and gallant gentlemen will not ask me to go further into the matter which is obviously the work of foolish persons."

CHAPTER SEVEN

Priapus in the Shrubbery

In no aspect of Edwardian life was there stronger tension between the dignified tones of officialdom and the complex variety of private living than in sexual morality; but the lines of battle have since been overlaid by writers' concentration on, first, the "golden age" aspect, and, second, the farther reaches of behaviour—lurid, scatological or merely pathetic—which disfigured the period. The intricate relationship between the outward and the "double" standards, and their necessary congruence have only recently been explored (in particular by Steven Marcus in *The Other Victorians*, and by Samuel Hynes in *The Edwardian Turn of Mind*).

Thus an almost standardised picture of Edwardian sexual life exists, in which arranged marriages followed the annual London season (with its display of newly-presented girls, ready for their admiring suitors, like fillies displayed in the ring at Tattersalls), marriages remarkable chiefly for almost total sexual ignorance on the part of women, and the wide licence given by society to extramarital affairs— provided, that is, no breath of scandal reached the prurient Edwardian public. This is not wholly a caricature: the "manual of instruction" most widely available at the end of the nineteenth century, William Acton's *The Functions and Disorders of the Reproductive Organs*, represented the sexual drive both as something fearful and as an uncontrollable scourge. Written almost entirely from a male point of view, it gave expression to what seems to have been a very widespread interpretation of the contrast between illicit and married sex: "It is a delusion under which many a previously incontinent man suffers, to suppose that in newly married life he will be required to treat his wife as he used to treat his mistresses. It is not so in the case of any modest English woman. He need not fear that his wife will require the excitement, or in any respect the ways of a courtesan." This sort of assumption was

The initiation into social manhood: learning how to tie a dress tie.

Lord Loreburn   H. H Asquith   Herbert Gladstone

Members of the Liberal Cabinet as children

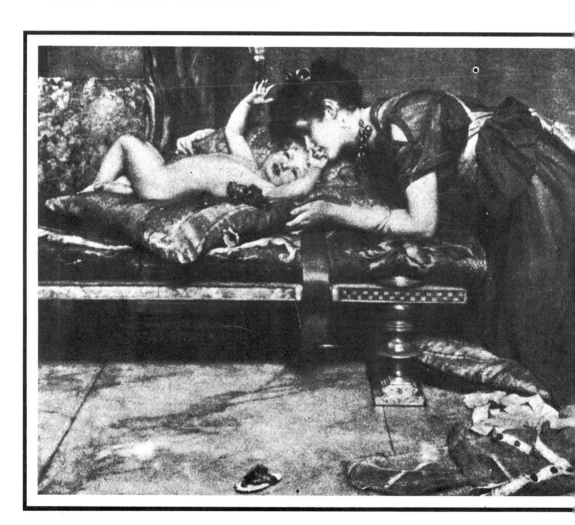

The Edwardian cult of mother-and-child relations: "An Earthly Paradise" by Sir Lawrence Alma-Tadema.

R. B. Haldane

David Lloyd George

Winston Churchill

The child as idol—in his velvet suit with his hoop.

The progress of the sporting gentleman: (BELOW RIGHT) Robin, 8th Lord Londonderry on his Shetland pony at their family estate; (ABOVE RIGHT) Charles, Lord Castlereagh before a day's shoot (*both by kind permission of the Marquess of Londonderry*); the famous pigeon shoot held outside the Casino at Monte Carlo mecca for Edwardian gamblers (LEFT)

Joseph Chamberlain   Lord Curzon   Lord Haldane
Arthur Balfour   Lord Redesdale   Rudyard Kipling
H. H. Asquith   Lord Kitchener   H. Campbell-Bannerman

Alma-Tadema H. Granville-Barker Max Beerbohm
Thomas Hardy   Sir Henry Irving   Sir E. Lutyens
Stanley Baldwin   Lord Baden-Powell Augustus John

A hint of stocking.

still current in the 1900s, as one Edwardian undergraduate found, listening to a well-meaning but unperceptive Oxford doctor: "It was a party of undergraduates, and over the port one of our number boldy asked A.P. whether women enjoyed sexual intercourse. 'Speaking as a doctor,' said A.P., 'I can tell you that nine out of ten women are indifferent to or actively dislike it; the tenth, who enjoys it, will always be a harlot'. It is hard to imagine a more mischievous message to young men, or one more calculated to worry and to disconcert them."

Male boredom (which must have been common enough—if the above were true) was made an explanation, and often an excuse, for sexual aberrations, brothels male and female, child prostitution and pornography, and even organised sadism and masochism. Such things were, among men, known to exist, but were rarely referred to in public and never in front of women, whose supposed ignorance might have been roughly shaken. Occasionally, as with W.T. Stead's crusade against child prostitution in 1884, and the Cleveland scandal in 1889, and Oscar Wilde's trial in 1895, they were exposed; but they continued, and indeed flourished, in the London of the 1900s. A measure of how widely they were *believed* to be indulged in by the Edwardian upper class came in January 1918 with the publication in the magazine *The Vigilante* of an article by the MP Pemberton Billing. Billing alleged that the German secret service had compiled a Black Book, a thousand pages long, with a mass of scabrous details of sexual malpractices and deviations among leading members of British society. "There are the names of 47,000 English men and women ... the names of Privy Councillors, youths of the chorus, wives of cabinet ministers, dancing girls, even Cabinet Ministers themselves, whilst diplomats, poets, bankers, editors, newspaper proprietors and members of His Majesty's Household follow each other with no order of precedence." Billing was prosecuted for criminal libel, and enlivened the case by alleging that the judge and a member of the jury were themselves in the Black Book. Yet, despite the lack of any real proof of his charges, the jury found him not guilty. Even in 1918, the existence of such a shabby world seemed only too credible.

In contrast, the personal histories of many Edwardians suggest the existence not merely of conventional happiness in marriage, but of enlightenment, frankness and delight in sexual life. It is, however, almost as if there had been a tacit conspiracy to play down the existence of pleasure and mutual love, in favour of the fashionable view that marriage was a mere convention. Thus Edward Marsh recorded a "very interesting discussion" at Winston Churchill's house, "as to whether it was better for a husband to be in love with his wife or vice versa", and added, unquestioningly, *"assuming that reciprocity was so rare as not to be worth considering"*. This is on a par with the stereotyped view of Jones's Oxford doctor; and it followed naturally enough that most of Churchill's luncheon company considered that "the wife should always be the one in love" (Hassall, *Edward Marsh*, p.125).

There are few means of measuring truth here: autobiographies are either evasive or silent, or occasionally full of fantasy (like Frank Harris's), and fictional treatments of sexuality (like E.M. Forster's posthumously published novel about homosexuality, *Maurice*) leave much in shadow. In spite of the availability of Freud and Havelock Ellis to the knowledgeable reader, there is very little of the rationalised tolerance achieved, after many years of experience, by the late Victorian gentleman who wrote *My Secret Life*:

"Why, for instance, is it permissible for a man and a woman to enjoy themselves lasciviously, but improper for two men and two women to do the same things all together in the same room....Is copulation an improper thing to do; if not, why is it disgraceful to look at its being done?...Why should not any society indulge in these innocent though sensual amusements if they like, in private? What is there in their doing so that is disgraceful? It is the prejudice of education alone which teaches that it is ... though I still have prejudices, yet for the most part I can see no harm in gratifying my lust in the ways which the world would say is highly improper, but which appear to me that men and women are intended by instinct as well as by reflection to gratify."

The obsessions with secrecy, shame, scandal, and with men's desires at the expense of women, are understandable in the context of profound social change, the transfer to urban life, and the growing dominance of middle-class values. Sexual habits, even sexual roles, were changing rapidly in the 1900s, imposing a new tension over and above the Victorian division between sex and the rest of life. The "new woman", whether as caricature in the openly chauvinistic *Daily Mail* and *Morning Post* or as a real-life suffragette, was making demands which could not easily be met. Habitual attitudes had developed which paid outward service to high ideals about womanhood while permitting the existence of their reverse—romantic love coupled with pornography, normality with every form of sexual deviance. Underneath, deep channels of anxiety opened up. It was the next generation which would benefit from the liberating ideas contained in Freudian analysis, in Havelock Ellis's clinical discussion of sexual phenomena, and in the assault on bourgeois morality of a whole range of European and English artists and writers. In Edwardian England these ideas were officially repelled: the standard work on erotic art (Eduard Fuchs, *Illustriete Sittengeschichte*, Munich 1909) remained safely in the original German; Ellis's *Studies in the Psychology of Sex* (published in six volumes, 1897–1910) was at first suppressed; while Freud's methods were received in an atmosphere of bleak hostility by the medical establishment until their value was proved in the treatment of wartime shell-shock cases. (The 1913 edition of *An Interpretation of Dreams* contained the following publisher's note: "The sale of this book is limited to the Members of the Medical, Scholastic, Legal and Clerical professions.")

Instead, a counter-revolution developed, in publications designed to teach a more "socially acceptable" view of sex. Baden-Powell's *Scouting for Boys* (1908) advised duty and abstinence, and its counterpart, *The Handbook for Girl Guides* (1912), was, curiously enough, more outspoken in its warnings: "All secret habits are evil and dangerous, lead to hysteria and lunatic asylums, and serious illness is the result....Evil practices dare not face an honest person; they lead you on to blindness, paralysis, and loss of memory." What the practices were was not specified; but cold baths and healthy exercise were the antidote.

The decade witnessed an International Moral Education Congress, a Parliamentary Report on Indecent Advertisements, and a National Purity Crusade; James Marchant, director of the National Council of Public Morals, published in 1909 his *Aids to Purity*, a series of letters for young men to read, and the Council itself issued a series of "New Tracts for the Times", which made it quite clear that the Council believed society as a whole to be in a state of decadence, having declined in recent times from a golden age of innocence. "We do not share the mood of extreme toleration which is sometimes cultivated today ... such excessive leniency, which is afraid to stamp down, or it may be to stamp out, what is evidently bringing man nearer to the beast, betokens a slackening of intellectual and moral fibre" (*Problems of Sex* (1909), p.28).

With its reliance on the myth of a golden age, and its conservative view of national decadence, this is a long way from the earnest inquiry after moral truth characteristic of the best Victorian thinkers. To see why the moral crusade erupted towards the end of the Edwardian period, and why the artists, writers and scientists who tried to break through the thick skin of prejudice were rejected, one needs to come back to the slow change in roles of men and women, itself the product of late industrial society. The "new woman" derided by conventional dramatists (even by Shaw and Pinero, who took it for granted that women's lives were bound up in marriage) looked beyond the partial emancipation won in the late nineteenth century by such measures as the Married Woman's Property Act. Her desire for freedom to chose her own profession, the number of her children and her place in society lay behind the emancipation movement in the 1900s, and, if the Women's Social and Political Union claimed the vote as its prize, that was partly because contraception was not exactly a suitable slogan to use in public. The excesses on both sides, the suffragettes' violence and shocking tactics, the repression and forcible feeding ordered by a Liberal government led by the peaceable Asquith, in fact the whole of what contemporaries called "the sex war", can be explained by the profound threat which these demands made to established patterns of life.

Hence the opposition to divorce reform; anxiety about the falling birth rate; and, conversely, the vindictiveness of many women campaigners against stubborn male dominance: "No woman begins that way," says Vida Levering in Elizabeth Robins's play *Votes for Women* (1907). "Every woman's in a state of natural subjection—no, I'd rather say allegiance to her idea of romance and her hope of motherhood. They're embodied for her in man. They're the strongest things in life—*till man kills them* .... "

That sort of feeling produced outrage, or at best, a sort of condescending pity among men. Sir George Sitwell's view of "woman's position in the world was that she should be out of it", a thought heartily endorsed by the King and Asquith in their response to the suffragettes.

With this mental background, a young man was launched on a society which offered an unparalleled range of sexual opportunity and temptation. His upbringing would have given him that mixture of emphasis on male superiority, uneasiness expressed in vanity, and outright impatience which Spaniards call *machismo*; but it would also have overlaid it with an awareness of at least the existence of homosexuality, with the wealth of adolescent fantasy common to all public schools, and an acquired view of woman remote from his knowledge of the real women around him. During his schooldays, he would have been inculcated with the sort of views expressed by the Reverend Edward Lyttleton, headmaster of Eton from 1905 to 1916, that sexuality was a matter of voluntary choice between moral and immoral acts, culminating in decorous and monogamous marriage. Yet outside school these precepts might mean very little. Probably most young men of the upper class had had their first experience of sex either in the bullocking homosexuality of school itself, or at the hands of a servant or field girl. The author of *My Secret Life* describes with some feeling his first awkward pursuit of one of his mother's maids; later on he talks of servants in the same language he might use about horses: "a nice fresh servant ... clean, well-fed, full-blooded"—scarcely a preparation for the delicately bred girls, encased in billowing skirts, whom he would meet and be expected to entertain at formal parties as he grew up.

As early as 1869 John Stuart Mill remarked (in *The Subjection of Women*) on the contrast between woman on her pedestal of man's imagination, and women in the Victorian stews. Veblen pointed out how in both American and British society the lavish extravagance of women's clothes was in some sense an index of the spending power of their husbands, who might invest not merely in half a dozen elaborate dresses for a weekend, but in a bewildering range of gloves, hats, bonnets, shoes and underwear as well. Yet the idea that women might want to be financially independent—beyond their dress allowances—was rarely welcomed. Only a few could follow Daisy Warwick, Mrs Cyril Drummond or Lady Rachael Byng and open respectable and fashionable shops, selling millinery, haute couture or artistic needlework. Fewer still could find a satisfactory career in journalism or authorship; and the wealth of private and amateur artistic and dramatic talent indicates what a loss to the world at large these conventions imposed. Those of intellectual ability who braved the strongholds of male dominance at the ancient universities had to contend with the publicly expressed views of the great economist Alfred Marshall that women's intellect was inferior to men's, and had to submit to a lifetime of dedication as the price of admission to women's colleges. (In 1897, 2,000 undergraduates petitioned the Cambridge Senate to refuse the admission of women to degrees, and the MAs of that university voted resoundingly against.) Laurence Jones remembered that his father had had no hesitation in spending the lion's share of capital on the education of the first-born son, while the others had had to live on their pay, in the Navy and the Church; "next to nothing was ever spent upon the two girls—they were neither educated to support themselves nor given opportunities of meeting young men who might have worked to support them" (*An Edwardian Youth*, p.158). Sir Thomas Beecham tells a story of a beautiful European woman who escaped from her unhappy marriage to grace the London stage in Tchaikovsky's *Pique Dame*, and then, meeting her husband in Paris, was reconciled. "The little flutter in theatrical life was something that had to be hushed up, and the only effective way of achieving this was that a veil of oblivion should descend and hide it" (*A Mingled Chime*, p.101).

Meanwhile, in the company of (or at least vaguely attached to) their husbands, the doyennes of the London salons—Lady Desborough, Margot Asquith, Lady Elcho, Lady de Grey—commanded the wit and intelligence, if not the adoration of every man who passed through their doors. "The goddess" was elevated to her pedestal, the "professional beauties" moved like queens. The letters directed by a host of "lovers" to Ettie Grenfell (quoted in Nicholas Mosley, *Julian Grenfell*, 1976) were entirely in character with the mood of romantic adoration. "The dog-like affection which binds me to your feet" inspired a youth half her age, while Curzon, then Viceroy of India, wrote, "For a whole night I have dreamed of you— no hope of reciprocity"—sentiments as remote from real passion as the songs of mediaeval troubadours.

Behind the screens, the other face of sexuality showed itself. After Wilde's trial and imprisonment, homosexuality was driven even further than in the nineteenth century from any shadow of condonement; not yet the 1920s' Oxford of Evelyn Waugh's diaries, with its cheerful and almost regular sodomising. Edward Carpenter, a relapsed cleric, disciple of the Christian socialist F.D. Maurice, and notable exponent of communal life, dared to defend homosexuality and sexual emancipation in *Love's Coming of Age* (published in 1896, and reissued in 1906) and won the admiration of the Bloomsbury group, especially of the equally homosexual E.M. Forster. Similar views were often advocated by Frank Harris— who had had the courage to visit and help Wilde in prison. W.T. Stead had written in *The Review of Reviews* of June 1895, "Should everyone found guilty of Oscar Wilde's crime be imprisoned, there would be a very surprising emigration from Eton, Harrow, Rugby and Winchester to the jails of Pentonville and Holloway. Until then, boys are free to pick up tendencies and habits in public schools for which they may be sentenced to hard labour later on." But sexual deviations (after schooldays) were relegated to the shadows (not least because of the operations of the law—the "blackmailer's charter") to the establishments around Leicester Square, or to visits to the Middle East, where tastes were less circumscribed. As E.J. Hobsbawm has pointed out, the passion for climbing the Alps shown by Anglo-Saxon intellectuals in general, and by Cambridge academics in particular, may have had something to do with "the close company of tough and handsome native guides" (*The Age of Capital*, p.231).

The enjoyment of pornography, prostitution, and a peculiarly English taste for flagellation inhabited the same twilight world—as adolescent fantasies survived into immature middle-age. By the end of the nineteenth century a distinction had been made between acceptable forms of eroticism, in the category of high "art", usually in classical disguise, and low and vulgar pornography. In Edwardian days, this distinction was taken to its hypocritical limit, and endorsed by a form of official censorship which, clearly, was designed more to prevent subversive material reaching the less educated than to protect society as a whole from corruption. Thus, whereas expensive reprints of salacious eighteenth-century classics like John Cleland's *Fanny Hill*, or apparently learned works on Indian eroticism and ancient Greek rites could be brought easily enough, overt pornography skulked in the bookshops in Charing Cross Road and Soho—as it does today. There the prying gentleman might have found *Randiana*, *The Amatory Experiences of a Surgeon*, and *The Story of Dildo, a Tale in Five Tableaux*, published by the enterprising, fly-by-night firm of William Dugdale. If he wanted something better, then he would probably have to look abroad, purchasing on his next visit to Paris something like de Maupassant's classic story of the brothel, *Le Maison Tellier*, with its sardonic illustrations by Degas. More likely, though, he would return with the volumes of frankly repetitive stuff printed there in the 1900s by the Englishman Charles Cunningham—or perhaps that favourite of the 1890s (extolled by Oscar Wilde), Louys's *Aphrodite*, full of etchings of nude maidens endlessly (and rather naïvely) disporting themselves against improbable backgrounds. It would be a decade or more before he could find anything as literate as *Ulysses*, also printed in Paris, with its rich sexual imagery and Molly Bloom's famous soliloquy, or even hear of Lawrence's *Lady Chatterley's Lover*.

High art, of course, excused a great deal: public galleries were prepared to show nineteenth-century classics like Delacroix's famous *Odalisque with a Slave*, with its passive nude, waiting, a mere plaything for whatever man would possess her; or the "Love for Sale" genre made respectable by the studio masters themselves. Alma-Tadema showed *A Favourite Custom* at the Academy in 1909— a view of two chaste nudes bathing in suitably remote Roman surroundings; but Edwardian taste was distinctly shocked by the twist given to the "Slave Market" vogue by painters such as Max Slevogt, whose *Victor—Prizes of War* (1912) showed a tall, cool, black hunter with three white maidens bound, ready to deflower. England produced, of course, its own native tradition of erotic art. Aubrey Beardsley's illustrations of *Messalina* show the all-devouring female, while the *Lysistrata* series, frankly salacious, disguised most outrageous symbols. There, for example, is Lysistrata herself, bosom uncovered, almost demurely holding an olive branch—yet she rests on a pillar which, on closer examination, turns out to be a giant phallus. The etchings of Felicien Rops could be found circulating discreetly among the *cognoscenti* to whom *Les Sataniques* brought an authentic vision of sexual energy as degradation, turning religious imagery into erotic nightmare and transforming the world of the Creation into a world of phallic creatures growing in primeval slime.

French artists of the 1880s and 1890s had been frank enough about sexual behaviour. Forain, Toulouse-Lautrec and Constantin Guys had painted brothel scenes and Paris whores with a blend of voyeurism and sympathy. In the 1900s, love in its most explicit forms could be found in the paintings of the Vienna Secession—Gustav Klimt and Egon Schiele—or in Paris, where Picasso, Roualt and Matisse were working. It was, however, impossible to imagine anything like this happening in London; and one of the longest-lasting European jokes at the

Englishman's expense was that he was the greatest prude at home, but the most lustful satyr abroad.

Mayhew (in his *Outcast London*) computed that there were 80,000 prostitutes in the many assorted brothels in existence in the 1860s. The most fashionable were centred in the West End, around the Haymarket, Regent Street and Bond Street, Piccadilly and Leicester Square; but well before 1914 the traditional houses had been forced to compete with all sorts of "massage institutions", catering for a variety of tastes, and advertising hypnotism, magneto-therapy, sexual friction baths, and even manicure. A typical advertisement (in *Society* in July 1900) read,

Manicure and Treatment for Rheumatism

Miss Desmond

39 George Street, Baker Street W (side door)
Hours 2–8. Late of 11a Air Street, Regent Street, W.

Other establishments catered to the seemingly inexhaustible demand for flagellation, and supplied, before the First World War, the first electrically operated machines—imported from America. How popular this was can be gauged from a long—and faintly surprised—article in the *Berliner Tageblatt* in 1900, and from the mass of cheap books with titles like *Maison de Flagellation* and *Le Tour du Monde d'un Flagellant*. A low theatre, the Standard, even put on a play, for large audiences, that included a scene of a man being whipped by a woman.

The wide variety of purely erotic sexual enjoyment available in Edwardian London can be seen as a measure of the sterile confusion of many of its inhabitants. Against it, and the outward veil of secrecy and ignorance, D.H. Lawrence was to crusade, making his Lady Chatterley chose between the alternatives of an impotent aristocrat and the natural virile game-keeper. In the process he stamped on what he found futile in the repressed, impoverished world around him. Yet few Edwardians would have found more than pornography in Lawrence's novel, or understood how the sterility of English society might be redeemed. Even in 1929 no one in the Conservative government had heard of him: "Who was D.H. Lawrence, whose filthy poems had been intercepted in the post? Nobody had heard of his books except Winston [Churchill]" (Thomas Jones, *Whitehall Diary*, vol. 2, p.175).

The Bloomsbury group achieved a sort of emancipation (although their varied, slightly incestuous, liaisons led to the remark that "all the couples were triangles and lived in Squares"); and by 1911 or 1912 a very much more relaxed standard obtained, at least in London. Censorship, as manifested in the Lord Chamberlain's often ludicrous objections to books (such as Zola's novels or Joyce's *Dubliners*) and plays (Could the *Merry Widow* really be immoral? Could *Salome* be shown with— or even without—the head of John the Baptist?), began to fall away, largely because of the influx of European ways of thinking. But this was a public withdrawal which seems barely to have touched private lives. Behind what E.M. Forster called the "glass door" of marriage, habits seem to have remained much as they had been at the turn of the century. For very many women of the upper class, marriage had been a managed affair, resulting from the attentions of respectable and acceptable suitors after their coming-out. As Esme Wingfield-Stratford wrote, "The London season, from May to mid-July, was like the mating-time of animals, one of feverish courtships in which the young of both sexes were brought into contact under circumstances best calculated to provoke the sexual urge. Every mother knew that the ballroom served but as a court of approach to that inner sanctuary, the bedroom ... it was an American enterprise that rendered heiresses as marketable a commodity as canned meat." Not many upper-class Edwardian women had enjoyed, like the middle-class heroine of H.G. Wells's *Ann Veronica*, the freedom to choose a husband freely from among a range of acquaintances; and, for those that had, love may not always (or, indeed, may not often) have blossomed afterwards.

Thus an intricate pattern of liaisons developed, with a correspondingly elaborate framework of custom and understanding. Certain things were "done", other things were not. In real life, the Prime Minister, Asquith, could be found writing endless and most indiscreet letters to his mistress Venetia Stanley (later the wife of one of his ministers, Edwin Montagu); and, even more indiscreetly, General Sir John French used to correspond from the front with his mistress Winifred Bennett, the wife of a stolid British diplomat, giving here advance details of his war strategy, and information about the arrivals of the King, Asquith, Kitchener, Churchill or Lloyd George, which would have exposed them to great danger and him to court martial if the information had fallen into enemy hands. But neither he nor Asquith can have reflected on the implications of passing on secrets of state; such letters formed part of the private life which bore no relation to public duty—misfortunes arose only when the two were mixed.

Most clearly this happened when scandals broke: when men committed the unforgivable sin of suing their wives for divorce or blaming them in public. As Daisy Warwick wrote, "A scandal was a romance until it was found out .... " In *The Edwardians*, Vita Sackville-West clothed the Blandford scandal with fictitious names, and made Lord Roehampton follow the same example when he discovered his wife's infidelity: "At first I thought I must divorce you, but that would mean a terrible scandal. I don't think I could face that. Besides, I dislike the idea of exposing these things to publicity. It gives such a shocking example." So, instead, he banished her to the solitude of their country estate; and she went, meekly enough, lamenting to her lover, "people like me must not be found out".

For those who wished to respect the Eleventh Commandment, a subtle knowledge was needed: "Everyone knew that when a discreet one-horse brougham waited outside a certain door, one must not ring the bell, for the lady was otherwise engaged." De Soveral, deriding the English attitude, said, "for a young man to start his career with a love affair was quite 'de rigueur' ". The bedrooms at a country-house party might be arranged to accommodate the liaison of the moment. Princess

Daisy of Pless recorded her husband's reaction when they had to spend nights in separate rooms at their house at Newlands once in 1903. He had to creep along the corridor to visit her, and, as he left, remarked, "I shall see you tomorrow—Oh—I forgot you were my wife!"

Seduction seems to have been an almost casual way for many gentlemen to pass the time. Lady Warwick, for some years the King's mistress, recalled, "During my first season, a certain Lord X professed love for me. I was very much attracted, and not a little inclined to listen to his plea, but one night at a party I happened to overhear him call Lily Langtry 'my darling', as he helped her into her cloak. Then I heard him make an assignation with her." The King himself could excuse a visit to Princess Daisy's bedroom in the South of France, because he was there *en docteur*; he might require the presence of Mrs Keppel at parties to which he was invited; and the gossips christened the fair attendants at his Coronation "the King's loose box". Lesser socialites might avail themselves of the façade provided by Rosa Lewis at the Cavendish Hotel, where the most respectable residents lived, yet where the stable provided a discreet alternative entrance, to comfortable suites in neighbouring houses.

But whatever might be familiar to the initiates was foreign to the outside world—another, and most significant, barrier against an encroaching middle class. When Sebastian set out to seduce Teresa, the doctor's wife, in *The Edwardians*, he enticed her as far as the bedroom at Chevron before she realised what was happening. When he attacked her for hypocrisy (since her husband must, he assumed, have consented, by bringing her to the house party), she stormed, "I suppose it is as difficult for you to understand our ideas as it is for us to understand yours."

Yet a far deeper, more poignant gulf existed, inhibiting married love and encouraging this half-world of liaisons and secret assignations. The real nature of women and of the sexual life, touched on by Shaw and Pinero and the "shocking" plays of Ibsen, coloured the whole of Galsworthy's *Forsyte Saga*. In old age, Jolyon, confronted with the intolerable problem of his—and Irene's—son's love for Fleur, Irene's daughter by Soames Forsyte, writes a long letter to explain what happened to Irene's first marriage:

You see, Jon, in those days and even to this day—indeed, I don't see, for all the talk of enlightenment, how it can well be otherwise, most girls are married ignorant of the sexual side of life. Even if they know what it means they have not *experienced* it. That's the crux. It is this actual lack of experience, whatever verbal knowledge they have, which makes all the difference and all the trouble. In a vast number of marriages—and your mother's was one—girls are not and cannot be certain whether they love the man they marry or not; they do not know until after the act of union which makes the reality of marriage. Now, in many, perhaps in most doubtful cases, this act cements and strengthens the attachment, but in other cases, and you mother's was one, it is a revelation of mistake, a destruction of such attraction as there was. There is nothing more tragic in a woman's life than such a revelation, growing daily, nightly clearer. Coarse-grained and unthinking people are apt to laugh at such a mistake, and say, "What a fuss about nothing!" Narrow and self-righteous people, only capable of judging the lives of others by their own, are apt to condemn those who make this tragic error, to condemn them for life to the dungeons they have made for themselves. You know the expression: "She has made her bed, she must lie on it!" It is a hard-mouthed saying, quite unworthy of a gentleman or lady in the best sense of those words; and I can use no stronger condemnation.

To explain Soames's final rape of his wife, Jolyon goes on:

I don't think harshly of him. I have long been sorry for him; perhaps I was sorry even then. As the world judges she was in error, he within his rights. He loved her—in his way. *She was his property*. That is the view he holds of life—of human feelings and hearts—property. It's not his fault—so was he born. To me it is a view that has always been abhorrent—so was I born!"

CHAPTER EIGHT

The Critics

Men living a life of ease and privilege could hardly expect to be exempted from radical criticism. Although the main flood of bitterness and anger against class differences and inequalities of wealth broke through in the political battles after the Parliament Act debacle and over Ulster and the great strikes of 1911–15, the instigators began much earlier to bring the Edwardian upper class under a devastating fire: for their failure to perform the functions of an élite; for their monopoly of wealth, property and privilege; and for the fundamental sterility of their mode of life. It was no coincidence that the critics mounted their case just at the moment when the upper class seemed to have succumbed to the new plutocracy and when their values seemed least relevant to the needs of the nation at large.

The contention which hurt most—and which won acceptance from many liberal and radical Tories among the upper class—was that the system of birth, breeding and education no longer provided adequate recruits to the political élite. The country was badly led, badly governed, badly educated; and, as Churchill—then a Liberal—said bluntly, the real differences in society were "increasingly becoming the lines of cleavage between the rich and the poor". *The Queen* might declare "the English aristocrat has always been willing to give service in return for privilege", but for many this dictum no longer corresponded to reality, and the service itself too often turned out to be second-rate.

Pretensions to providing a class of leaders appeared out of date when, for the young and articulate, the Liberal inheritance seemed to have passed from Grey and Asquith to Lloyd George; and when Balfour (who viewed the Labour Party with thinly veiled contempt) and his colleagues in the Lords seemed dedicated to the defence of an archaic system of injustice. The leader in modern society, they felt, should come from a more virile background, and rise by his own efforts—like George Ponderevo in H.G. Wells's *Tono-Bungay*, a man of enormous and inventive energy, a tycoon and speculator, whose lifestyle repelled the hierarchical framework of the great house, Bladesover, into which, as a servant, he had been born. Bladesover was itself in decay (unlike Sackville-West's Chevron); and Ponderevo, the symbol of disquieting change, stood out among "the spectacle of forces running to waste, of people who use and do not replace; the country hectic with a wasting, aimless fever of trade and money-making and pleasure-seeking".

George Bernard Shaw considered that the upper class had, like the Russian family in Chekhov's *Cherry Orchard*, simply abdicated. The "new people" in their country houses "were the only repositories of culture who had social opportunities of contact with our politicians, administrators, and newspaper proprietors, or any chance of sharing or influencing their activities. But they shrank from that contact. They hated politics. They did not wish to realise Utopia for the common people ... and when they could, they lived without scruple on incomes which they did nothing to earn" (Shaw, Preface to *Heartbreak House*). The only alternative to Heartbreak House was "Horseback Hall, consisting of a prison for horses with an annex for the ladies and gentlemen who rode them, hunted them, talked about them, bought them and sold them, and gave nine-tenths of their lives to them, dividing the other tenth between charity, churchgoing (as a substitute for religion) and Conservative electioneering (as a substitute for politics)".

Not everyone drew the same conclusions, though even the conservative critics would have agreed with Shaw's castigation of the hypochondria of the society of Heartbreak House, its superstition, addiction to clairvoyance, palmistry. crystal-gazing and the occult, its gullibility in the face of soothsayers, astrologers and practitioners of curious brands of unregistered medicine. An educated class which gave prominence in its evening entertainment to *planchette*, and sat at the feet of mediums like the celebrated Russian charlatan Madame Blavatsky, could easily be cast as exponents of national decline. Max Nordau had set a tone in his book *Degeneration* (published in 1895) which recurred throughout the Edwardian period. Deep concern about the standard of national physique, reinforced by the dismal figures of volunteers rejected, on medical grounds, for the Boer War, turned soon enough into jeremiads about decadence. Well-meaning reports like that on mental illness were used to "prove" a sharp increase in the numbers of idiots; ideas of Social Darwinism caught root, not only among minority groups like the National Social Purity Crusade of 1908, but also among leading politicians. Churchill, at the time Home Secretary in the Liberal government, showed himself strongly in favour of eugenics. He told Wilfrid Blunt, in 1912, that "he had himself drafted the Bill which is to give power of shutting up people of weak intellect, and so prevent their breeding. He thought it might be arranged to sterilize them" (Blunt, *Diaries*, p.813).

The right-wing critics of society seem to have been obsessed with the theme of decadence: Balfour, lecturing on the subject at Cambridge in 1908, compared Britain to Rome and drew attention to "the sense of impending doom, by which man's spirits were oppressed long before the Imperial power began visibly to wane". His remedy was scientific advance, and a withdrawal from further dangerous experiments with democracy; others looked to healthy training with Baden-Powell's Boy Scouts, or the introduction of compulsory military service, on the German or French model. A letter in *The Times*, in November 1913, declared, "one of the surest signs of a nation's decline is indicated as soon as it begins to see its political and social leaders among the masses, and to recruit its naval and military leaders from the rank and file." Saki (H.H. Munro) abandoned the delicate touch of his satirical short stories for a harsh attack on the bourgeois sickness of the England he saw in 1913, and attempted to refurbish what he took to be the true virtues of duty and self-sacrifice; and the President of the Royal Academy, Sir William Richmond, castigated the paintings displayed at the Post-Impressionist exhibition in 1910 as if they were hanging in Sodom and Gomorrah rather than at the Grafton Gallery: "For a moment there came a fierce feeling of terror lest the youth of England, promising fellows, might be contaminated there. On reflection, I was reassured that the youth of England, being healthy, mind and body, is far too virile to be moved save in resentment against the providers of this unmanly show" (*Morning Post*, 16 November 1910).

If conservative critics could show leadership only through rancorous assaults on the classes below them, and in sterile defence of an insupportable status quo—especially obvious in the House of Lords and Ulster crises—many liberals foundered in ambiguity. Although fully able to diagnose the evils of society, they were outflanked by right and left, by extremists seeking only to destroy what they themselves wished to reform. Thus many critiques, like Masterman's *Condition of England*, claimed that the ruling class had failed—yet were reluctant to overturn it completely. Masterman wrote, "The present extravagance of England is associated with a strange mediocrity, a strange stability of characters of supreme power in Church and State. This is accompanied, as all ages of security and luxury are accompanied, by a waning of the power of inspiration, a multiplying of the power of criticism. The more comfortable and opulent society becomes, the more cynicism proclaims the futility of it all, and the mind turns in despair from a vision of vanities. It gives little leadership to the classes below it: no visible and intelligent feudal concentration which, taught in the traditions of government and inheriting strength and responsibility, can reveal an aristocratic order adequate to the immense political and economic necessities of the people. Never, especially during the reaction of the past twenty years, were fuller opportunities offered to the children of wealthy families for the elaboration of a new aristocratic government of a new England; and never were those opportunities more completely flung away."

Galsworthy specifically attacked the governing class in *Fraternity*, and even Hilaire Belloc, a perceptive if indulgent critic, depicted (in *Mr Clutterbuck's Election*, 1908) a political world eaten away with moral corruption and given over to the dominance of moneyed oligarchy—an introduction, as it were, to his later attack on modern evolution, *The Servile State*.

Sterility and mediocrity struck home all the more sharply as intelligent critics looked abroad and compared the state of British commerce, and of British education and technology, with that of their counterparts in America and Germany, respectively. The 1869 Royal Commission's able defence of public schools no longer stood up to reality, particularly as so few of Britain's scientific and business leaders, men of real power and influence, were from the upper class, or had benefited from the classical curriculum. Yet in political life the traditionally-shaped élite still ruled: of 101 Liberal and Conservative Cabinet Ministers in the period 1886–1916, thirty-five had been to Eton, thirteen to Harrow, six to Rugby, twelve to other public schools, and a mere seventeen to grammar schools. The same group of men followed the classical pattern of occupation: forty-one landowners, nine rentiers, nine diplomats, thirty-one from the professions, and only thirteen from commerce and industry. Critics obsessed with the achievements of Germany were not prepared to acknowledge the alternative argument that an élite trained in semi-military style might be an even more dangerous liability.

The defence—foremost among whom was W.H. Mallock—contended that it was not necessary to have experienced other forms of life in order to lead. Conservatives still looked back to Disraeli's claims that their party represented the common people as well as the great institutions and the Empire; while in the constituencies something survived of the dreams of radical Toryism once associated with Lord Randolph Churchill. Yet the way the Lords and Commons voted on the Parliament Bill of 1911 argued the opposite. On one side (with few exceptions) ranged the landed interest and the traditionalists; on the other, the Liberals and their recently created peers. "For the first time in the advance of political democracy in this country, there was hardly a patrician who would aid the process" (Roy Jenkins, *Mr Balfour's Poodle*, p.123). George Orwell, looking back from the year 1940, wrote, not unfairly, "probably the battle of Waterloo *was* won on the playing fields of Eton but the opening battles of all subsequent wars have been lost there. One of the dominant facts in English life during the past three-quarters of a century has been the decay of ability in the ruling class."

If they had failed to lead in the political world, so the upper class seemed unable to appreciate even the nature of the challenge to their ideas (or preconceptions) of the just society. Faced with the divergent paths of socialism and totalitarianism, they preferred to ignore both. Yet the message was pinned high enough on the wall for them to read: in the classic best-seller of the period, Robert Blatchford's *Merrie England*; in that anarchic tract, Robert Tressel's *Ragged-Trousered Philanthropists*; in Hobson's *Imperialism*, or the Fabian pamphlets; while the dilemma facing the comfortable philosophy of paternalism was ruthlessly exposed by Shaw in *Major Barbara*; where, to the detriment of philanthropy, Andrew Undershaft chooses the path of efficiency and autocracy, and wins. Those in the front line of Edwardian conflict—mine-owners, steelmakers, railway and port employers—opted for the latter course (not the least reason for the growing industrial strife), but few of them ranked as gentlemen or "leaders of society". Through the eyes of an imaginary visitor, Galsworthy chose to portray a coterie of "island Pharisees": "the complacency of it all, its satisfaction, its docility of purpose, haunt him like a nightmare".

Even the former claims for the ruling class, in its administration of a great empire, sounded differently in the 1900s. It had been possible to claim in the 1870s that "quite savage nations find out that English people are on the whole truthful, and they like us for that. I hope we shall go on being thought truthful and honourable by other nations. I should not like to belong to a mean, sneaky nation" (Anon, *Quite a Gentleman*, p.68); but many of the next generation, brought up on the undignified and frequently shameful "scramble for Africa", on Fashoda and Rhodes's manoeuvres in Rhodesia, on concentration camps in South Africa and indentured Chinese labour on the Rand, looked sceptically on such ideals. As Joseph Conrad wrote in *Heart of Darkness*, "the conquest of the earth, which mostly means the taking away from those with a different complexion or slightly flatter nose than ourselves, is not a pretty thing when you look into it".

Some observers of Edwardian society confessed to a sense of hopelessness, confronted, in Masterman's brilliant phrase, with "the appearance of a complicated machine which has escaped the control of all human volition and is progressing towards no intelligible goal; of some black windmill, with gigantic sails, rotating untended under the huge span of night". But the majority of critics knew precisely what they wanted: to erode or destroy the basis of privilege and wealth and to redeem the condition of the poor. Whether they argued from a crudely Marxist standpoint, like H.M. Hyndman, leader of the Social Democratic Federation, or from a gradualist conception of progress, like the Fabians and many middle-class members of Keir Hardie's rapidly growing Independent Labour Party, or from radical Liberal principles, like L.T. Hobhouse (in *Democracy and Reaction*, 1904), the targets were the same. And these targets had been exposed more mercilessly than ever by the harsh light of contemporary social surveys of poverty and deprivation: Charles Booth's researches covering nearly 4 million Londoners (seventeen volumes of the second edition appeared in 1902–3) and Rowntree's first statistical survey of York. (Brutally but effectively, in the quite different context of sudden disaster, the *Daily Herald* of 22 April 1915 could publish the figures of the survivors of the *Titanic* disaster, in 1912, on a class basis: first-class passengers saved, 61 per cent; second-class, 36 per cent; third-class, 23 per cent; crew, 22 per cent.)

Equality—if not of status and wealth, then at least of opportunity—was the minimum acceptable to that optimistic generation of radicals; and the class system, the clearest formulation of Edwardian society, came to be seen as the *fons et origo* of inequality, bolstered by the educational system, and proliferating in property, wealth, privilege and ignorance of the world outside. Shaw wished to sweep the whole monstrous edifice away and start again: "We have to confess it: capitalist mankind in the main is detestable ... both rich and poor are really hateful to themselves. For my part I hate the poor and look forward eagerly to their extermination. I pity the rich a little, but am equally bent on their extermination. The working classes, the business classes, the professional classes, the propertied classes, the ruling classes, are each more odious than the other: they have no right to live: I should despair if I did not know that they would all die presently, and that there is no need on earth why they should be replaced by people like themselves"

(The Intelligent Woman's Guide to Socialism and Capitalism (1910), p.219).

Richard Tawney, a pioneer socialist and a founder member of the Workers' Educational Association, saw education as the clearest means to regenerate society, the public schools as the greatest single anomaly standing in the way. In a mordant essay, "Keep the Workers' Children in Their Place", written for the *Daily News* in 1918, he argued against the objection of "excessive" education advanced by the Federation of British Industries: " 'They would very strongly advise that in selecting children for higher education, care should be taken to avoid creating, as was done for example in India, a large class of persons whose education is unsuitable for the employment which they eventually enter.' There it is, the whole Master Class theory of society in a sentence!" Then he turned on the public schools, the bastions of upper-class tradition and the mediating factor in the rise of the wealthy middle class. Not so severe as Veblen (who had stigmatised the study of the classics for giving scholarship a sort of "talismanic virtue") he admitted their virtues: "The better among them owed much, and added much, to the practical energy, the admirable moral seriousness, the respect for the hard grind of the intellect, without fancies or frills, of Victorian England. [But] all of them, including the best, were impoverished by the feebleness of the social spirit of the same England. All of them were the victims of its pervasive class divisions, its dreary cult of gentility, its inability to conceive of education as the symbol and cement of a spiritual unity transcending differences of birth and wealth....They developed, not as partners in a community of educational effort, welcoming the obligations which such partnership imposes, and zealous to bring their contribution to the common stock, but as the apostles of an exaggerated individualism, which at first perhaps was inevitable, but which survived into an age when it was no longer a necessity, forced upon them by the backwardness of public education, but a cherished idiosyncrasy."

Others were harsher. Two Edwardian schoolmasters, Dr Norwood and Mr Hope, writing in 1909, stated bluntly, "The public schools generally produce a race of well-bodied, well-mannered, well-meaning boys, keen at games, devoted to their schools, ignorant of life, contemptuous of all outside the pale of their own caste, uninterested in work, neither desiring or revering knowledge" (*The Higher Education of Boys in England* (1909), p.187).

However the merits of the training of the nation's youth were argued, the facts of inequality of wealth were patent. Rowntree put it one way when he showed that a quarter of the population left nothing whatever when they died; others pointed out that, in a society where the average male wage was £80 a year, a High Court judge earned £5,000, and a titled family might spend £3,000 on a single ball. "Starving in the Midst of Plenty" was the title given by Glaswegian John Wheatley, of the Independent Labour Party, to a pamphlet of his published in 1913. "Public penury, private ostentation", cried Masterman in 1909: "That, perhaps, is the heart of the complaint. A nation with the wealth of England can afford to spend, and spend royally. Only the end should itself be desirable, and the choice deliberate. A spectacle of a huge urban poverty confronts all this waste energy....In England it is becoming increasingly questioned how far this wealth is providing permanent benefit to the community. It is expended in the maintenance of a life—a life and a standard—bringing leisure, ease and grace, some effort towards charities and public service, and interest, real or assumed, in literature, music, art, social amenity, and a local or national welfare. But it offers little substantial advantage in endowment, building or even direct economic or scientific experiment" (*The Condition of England*, p.68).

Tawney, in particular, developed the theme of the divorce between ownership and obligation. Once, before the days of limited liability, shareholders had had an absolute duty (if necessary, to their last pennies) to interest themselves in the conduct and management of industry and commerce. But now they concerned themselves only with dividends—as landlords did with rents, rather than repairs, and as great landowners did with royalties on the coal or minerals won from beneath their soil. Later, in 1921, when he published *The Acquisitive Society*, fruit of a decade of reflection, Tawney pinpointed property as the greatest single perversion of the just society: "Behind their political theory, behind the practical conduct which, as always, continues to express theory long after it has been discredited in the world of thought, lay the acceptance of absolute rights to property and to economic freedom as the unquestioned centre of social organisation" (*The Acquisitive Society* (1921), p.19).

How much of this struck home and contributed to the mood of doubt and uncertainty which seems to have afflicted many of the Edwardian upper class cannot be assessed. *The Queen*, a notable source of incorrigible views, noticed uneasily, "it is the fashion today to talk of Social Duty and the Right to Live; but nobody has the courage to say that we belong to different worlds". The bastions of the law remained unscathed, defending property and its rights with a severity barely tempered by the long Liberal administration. The year 1910 saw a peak in the numbers committed to prison: 179,951 (as against 149,397 in 1900, 136,424 in 1914)—most for acquisitive offences in one form or another. (The Criminal Justice Act of 1914 was specifically subtitled "An Act to reduce the number of cases admitted to prison", and the corresponding figure for 1920—not exactly a non-violent year—was only 35,439.) At the Parliamentary level, the landed interest used the Private Bill procedure to prevent the introduction of a ten-seater steam bus (invented by Sir Richard Tangye and capable of twenty miles per hour), because of its likely impact on the mobility of labourers in rural areas; while the House of Lords, in its judicial capacity, handed down, in the Taff Vale case in 1901, a judgement barely correct in law and indefensible politically, which for five years effectively castrated the trade union movement. (In the 1920s, Baldwin, by then Conservative Prime Minister, used to declare of the Taff Vale case, "The Tories should never talk of the class war—they started it!")

At the time, much was made by Lloyd George and the radicals of their political assault on the Lords and the landed interest. Yet the Liberal victory in 1911 was a Pyrrhic one: in retrospect it can be seen that the Liberal government lost, in time and energy, at least as much as it gained. The land taxes of the 1909 budget, coming on top of the death duties introduced by Sir William Harcourt in 1894, have often been held to have inspired the great sales of land during the latter part of the decade. But the sales, spectacular though they were, arose for other reasons. Death duties, after all, were levied at a maximum of 8 per cent, and then only on estates worth over £1 million. In 1909 surtax had been set at a maximum of sixpence on incomes of over £3,000 a year, and was not raised again until war broke out in 1914. These were trifling sums, given the rate of return on industrial investment. In so far as they had an effect, it was to hasten the transfer of investment (which had begun in the 1880s and 1890s) out of land and into industry, mining, and overseas opportunities. Landowners, of course, made the most of taxation in justifying themselves politically: Burke's *Landed Gentry* in 1914 blamed "hatred of the landowners" and "the nightmare of taxation" for changes probably caused more by financial stringency. Walter Long, selling off most of his Wiltshire estate in 1910, accused the government of deliberate destruction. Yet Long, like the Duke of Bedford, who put nearly half his estates on the market, seems to have been chiefly interested in what would now be called his state of liquidity and his alternative sources of income (Thompson, *English Landed Society in the Nineteenth Century*, pp.321–5).

Optimistic socialists ought to have remembered the comment of the greatest of English nineteenth-century socialists, William Morris, on the Fabians: "They very much underrate the strength of the tremendous organisation under which we live....Nothing but a tremendous force can deal with this force; it will not suffer itself to be dismembered, nor to lose anything which really is its essence without putting forth all its force in resistance; rather than lose anything which it considers of importance, it will pull the roof of the world down upon its head" (*Signs of Change* (1888), p.46). Confronting what Cobbet once used to call "the Thing", they tended too easily to put their faith in "urban democracy, the study of political economy and Socialism". Without the war to decimate and undermine the "ruling class", their essentially pacific, gradualist and educational approach might never have succeeded.

But within the ruling class itself a deep, yet almost uncharted, revulsion was taking place. Gentlemen who did not conform to, or who could not stomach, the contented plutocratic world sought escape: some, like Wilfred Blunt and Lord Dunmore, in far places; others, like Bertrand Russell and C.P. Trevelyan, in a positive commitment to the politics of equality. They shunned the twin evils of boredom and worldliness implicit in the whole organisation of polite society; like Viola, in *The Edwardians*, they woke up to a realisation that the society they lived in was composed largely of people who wanted

> to have their fun, and they want to keep their position. They glitter on the surface, but underneath the surface they are stupid—too stupid to realise their own motives. They know only a limited number of things about themselves: but they need plenty of money, and that they must be seen in the right places, associated with the right people. In spite of their efforts to turn themselves into painted images, they remain human somewhere, and must indulge in love affairs,

which are sometimes artificial, and sometimes inconveniently real. Whatever happens, the world must be served first. In spite of their brilliance, this creed necessarily makes them paltry and mean. Then they are envious, spiteful, and mercenary; arrogant and cold. As for us, their children, they leave us in complete ignorance of life, passing on to us only the ideas they think we should hold, and treat us with the utmost ruthlessness if we fail to conform.

The virtue of Vita Sackville-West's Viola, and her hero, Sebastian (as of young Jolyon in *The Forsyte Saga*), was precisely that they did break out—Viola to marry the outsider, Anquetil, and Sebastian to follow him on an expedition to discover the uncharted sources of the Amazon. And it was Anquetil who summed up Vita Sackville-West's judgement on the stifling constraints which bounded the life of the Edwardian gentleman:

My dear boy, your life was mapped out for you from the moment you were born. You went to a preparatory school; you went to Eton; you are now at Oxford; you will go into the Guards; you will have various love-affairs, mostly with fashionable married women; you will frequent wealthy and fashionable houses; you will attend Court functions; you will wear a white-and-scarlet uniform— and look very handsome in it, too—you will be flattered and persecuted by every mother in London; you will eventually become engaged to a suitable young lady; you will marry her in the Chapel here and the local bishop will officiate; you will beget an heir and several other children, who ought to have been painted by Hoppner; you will then acquire the habit of being unfaithful to your wife, and she to you; you will both know it and both, out of sheer good manners and the force of civilisation, will tacitly agree to ignore your mutual infidelities; you will sometimes make a speech in the House of Lords; you will be given the Garter; you will send your sons to Eton and Oxford and into the Guards; after dinner you will talk about socialism and the growth of democracy; you will be worried but not seriously disturbed; on the twelfth of August you will go North to shoot grouse and on the first of September you will return South to shoot partridges, on the first of October you will shoot pheasants; your photograph will appear in the illustrated papers, propped on a shooting stick with two dogs and a loader; you will celebrate your golden wedding; you will carry a spur or a helmet at the next coronation; you will begin to wonder if your son (aged 51) wants you to die; you will oblige him by dying at last, and your coffin will be borne to the family vault on a farm cart accompanied by a procession of your employees and tenants....

You inherit your Code ready-made. That waxwork figure labelled Gentleman will be forever mopping and mowing at you. Thus you would never forget your manners, but you would break a heart, and think yourse.. rather a fine fellow for doing it. You would not defraud others, but you will defraud yourself; you will never take your conventions and smash them to bits. You will never tell lies—avoidable lies—but you will always be afraid of the truth. You will never wonder why you pursue a certain course of behaviour; you will pursue it because it is the thing to do. And the past is to blame for all this ... even should you try to break loose, it will all be in vain. Your wildest excesses will be fitted into some pigeonhole. That convenient phrase "Wild Oats" will cover you from twenty to thirty. That convenient word "Eccentricity" will cover you from thirty until death.

Light years separated that world from a man, then writing, who would show one way to resolve the dilemma.

"A man's self is a law unto itself.... The living self has one purpose only; to come into its own fullness of being.... But this coming into full, spontaneous being, is the most difficult of all.... The only thing man has to trust to in coming to himself is his desire and his impulse. But both desire and impulse tend to fall into mechanical automatism: to fall from spontaneous reality into dead or material reality.... All education must end against this fall; and all our efforts in all our life must be to preserve the soul free and spontaneous.... The life activity must never be degraded to a fixed activity. There can be no ideal goal for human life.... There is no pulling open the buds to see what blossom will be. Leaves must unroll, buds swell and open, and then the blossom. And even after that, when the flower dies, and the leaves fall, still we do not know.... We know the flower of today, but the flower of tomorrow is all beyond us" (D.H. Lawrence, *Democracy—Selected Essays*, pp.91–2).

CHAPTER NINE

War

Shortly before King Edward came to the throne, Winston Churchill talked of the future with Sir William Harcourt: "I asked the question 'What will happen then?' 'My dear Winston', replied the old Victorian statesman, 'The experiences of a long lifetime have convinced me that nothing ever happens'. Since that moment, as it seems to me, nothing has ever ceased happening" (Churchill, *The World Crisis*, 1911–14 (1929), p.26). Even greater changes were already apparent before Edward VII died, as the boundaries of social convention and morality expanded, leaving the old guard on the defensive, muttering about decline and the degeneracy of the young.

By 1911 the upper class feared, quite correctly, that the tide had set against their way of life, and was running faster than they could keep ahead. Because the Great War so evidently ended their protected existence, it may seem irrelevant to say that the charmed conditions which supported it had altered. Yet the underlying trends which induced many gentlemen to sell land, move into smaller houses, let their London residences, or employ fewer servants gave as true a picture of decline as the cataclysmic blow of war. Long before 1914, land had ceased to be the passport to political power; just as the theory of upper-class leadership had ceased, *in fact*, to be the guiding principle of social existence. The war blew away the screens which had protected the upper class, and war taxation succeeded, where other measures had failed, in breaking down the distinctions—so long and sedulously preserved—between them and the rest.

The fact that many, perhaps the majority of, gentlemen had made economies in their living standards may not seem any great hardship when set against the bleak poverty of the lives of Rowntree's "submerged fifth" of the population. Yet it explains the vast sales of land in the five years before the war, and the lowering of ancient—or at least nineteenth-century—standards which compelled gentlemen of the old school to declare that "England was going to the dogs". F.M.L. Thompson has computed the finances of the Earls of Verulam at Gorhambury. In the 1870s their income was £17,000 a year (£3,500 rents, £1,300 timber, £2,500 dividends, and so on) and expenditure £19,000. Ten years later, income had fallen to £14,000, expenditure to £15,000, after a series of what were then thought to be swingeing cuts—in, for example, the allowances to the elder son, and in the size and scope of the cellar. The new Earl in 1895 kept his expenditure to £15,000 and balanced the budget; but as the twentieth century advanced this forced him temporarily to evacuate the family seat, and to speculate on the stock exchange. His family's decline was arrested, happily, by his rise in the City, and his daughter's marriage to the financier Felix Cassel.

When these figures are set against the slow but remorseless depreciation in the value of the pound (in terms of the 1880 pound, it was worth 18s 6d in 1900 and 16s 3d in 1912), the degree of constraint can be seen. Quite simply, if a gentleman did not reorder his finances, but remained dependent on rents, he would eventually drop into that peculiar sort of aristocratic penury which, after the "troubles" in the 1920s, afflicted many families in Ireland—who, while the park and roof deteriorated, lived miserably in a handful of rooms in a vast mansion, using the residue of the cellar to staunch themselves against the climate.

Instead, the more flexible and intelligent of the aristocracy and gentry diversified their interests and their capital, and, where they lacked capital, sold land to raise it. This movement, which began in the 1880s, fell off slightly in the early years of King Edward, and then speeded up enormously after the 1909 budget presaged yet further fiscal attacks on land and ownership. Many of the backwoods peers who had failed in this battle came up to London in 1910 to make a last-ditch stand against the Parliament Bill and repay the bitter debt of frustration from their long provincial exile. "Their relative impoverishment lay behind the facade of the gay and lavish life of Edwardian society, last flowering of an aristocratic world now supported by a shrunken band of the more fortunate landowners and a constantly growing contingent of the *nouveaux riches*" (Thompson, *English Landed Society in the Nineteenth Century*, p.314). The land sales between 1910 and 1914 generally show, on investigation, the transfer of wealth into more productive assets; yet, at the same time, the sales of furniture or paintings (often discreetly arranged by intermediaries like Joseph Duveen) and the number of great houses let to new millionaires show a stringency absent in the more confident Edwardian days. Walter Long told the *Estates Gazette* in September 1910, "a change is coming over the scene, and those of us who do not possess other sources of income must regulate our affairs accordingly".

Only a handful of men, like Thomas Hardy, foresaw what the war would bring. At the end of Shaw's *Heartbreak House*, as the bombing starts, Captain Shotover cries, "The captain is in his bunk, drinking bottled ditchwater; and the crew is gambling in the forecastle. She [the ship] will strike and sink and split. Do you think the laws of God will be suspended in favour of England because you were born in it?" But that was written afterwards. It was Henry James, an American, writing to a close friend the day after war had been declared, who lapsed into complete despair at "the plunge of civilisation into this abyss of blood and darkness". Now the twentieth century was proving not to be the age of improvement and betterment that he had supposed it to be, and "to have to take it all now for what the treacherous years were all the while really making for and *meaning* is too tragic for any words" (*Letters of Henry James*, ed. Percy Lubbock, vol.2, p.384).

> For all we have and are,
> For all our children's fate,
> Stand up and take the war.
> The Hun is at the gate!

Wrote Kipling, in a message more acceptable to his 1914 contemporaries than was the bleak pessimism of James.

> Our world has passed away
> In wantonness o'erthrown,
> There is nothing left today
> But steel and fire and stone!

With few exceptions Edwardian gentlemen performed as they had been taught to— leading and dying, uncomplaining, honourable, brave. They did not need strident sermons, nor patriotic lectures. Like Stalkey and Co. in Kipling's story "The Flag of Their Country", they held "jelly-bellied flag-flappers" in complete contempt— "like a lay evangelist preaching to Jesuits". They took their duties and functions for granted, without idealism or illusion.

In their letters and the occasional diary, like that kept in the trenches—against the rules—by a Coldstream Guards officer, William St Leger, they revealed their straightforward, often ruthless attachment to the code in which they had been brought up, and in which very many of them died. The total of 745,000 killed and another 1.6 million wounded and mutilated amounted to 9 per cent of the male population under forty-five; it had deep traumatic effects on the whole British society. Among the dead, however, the proportion of officers was higher: the life of a subaltern in battles such as the Somme and Passchendaele was reduced to hours rather than days. Something like 20 per cent of the first generation of volunteer officers were killed; out of Oxford University's service roll call of 14,561, the dead were 2,608; and public schools bore an even worse toll: one-third died of all the boys at Haileybury between 1905 and 1912, 427 out of 2,833 from Malvern, and 687 Old Carthusians. What this meant cannot easily be gauged from the tight-lipped references in letters home. A simple memorial in a parish church may give two names, Andrew and Thomas Margesson: the two sons of the last lord of the

manor of Findon, of a family which had held the estate since 1796. Later, at
countless war memorials, they seemed a lost, golden generation, possessed of a fame
untarnishable by the dreary discontents of the post-war years. Siegfried Sassoon
remembered his greatest friend, Dick Tiltwood, killed at Morlancourt in 1916:
"his was the bright countenance of truth; ignorant and undoubting; incapable of
concealment but strong in reticence and modesty .... He was the son of a parson
with a good family living. Generations of upright country gentlemen had made him
what he was, and he had arrived at manhood in the nick of time to serve his country
in what he naturally assumed to be a just and glorious war" (*Memories of a
Foxhunting Man*, 1942 edition, pp.218–9).

Yet behind the imagery of youthful sacrifice, blood and honour lay a second
standard. For gentlemen at home, life changed only slowly, and privation and the
trenches seemed far off. It was not they, but men already at war, who had
responded to the call, like Paul Jones, once head boy at Dulwich, killed in 1917,
who wrote, "If we are to win this war it will only be through gigantic efforts and
great sacrifices. It is the chief virtue of the public school system that it teaches one to
make sacrifices willingly for the sake of *esprit de corps*. Well, clearly, if the public
school men hold back, the others will not follow." Yet in 1916 the theatre
flourished, luxury spending scarcely diminished; and the contrast so shocked those
who came home on leave that by the end many serving officers had retreated into a
private world where the unsharable horror could be contained, free from
uncomprehending outsiders. "The profiteers are still with us", R.D. Blumenfeld
wrote in his diary in March 1917; dress sales were higher that year than they had
been in the first year of the war. Colonel Repington recorded a conversation with
Lady Ridley: "She and I discussed what posterity would think of us in England.
We agreed that we should be considered rather callous to go on with our usual life
when we were reading of three or four thousand casualties a day. But she said that
people could not keep themselves elevated permanently on some plane above the
normal, and she supposed the things around us explained the French revolution and
the behaviour of the French nobility."

Slowly, war taxation (raised 40 per cent by McKenna in 1915, and again in
1916), the rapidly rising cost of living, rationing of food and above all of petrol,
made inroads into the life still led by the upper-class. Foxhunting was generally
given up by 1917; on many estates taxes rose from 9 to 30 per cent of the rental.
An even more serious challenge came as the values by which gentlemen lived were
challenged in a way which was absent at the front line. The volunteer spirit, and the
belief that the war could be won without new methods of enforcement of authority
failed to survive the experience of total war. A Liberal government led by Asquith
was forced into compromise and finally coercion; was forced to form a coalition
with the Conservatives and finally to submit to a new Ministry led by Lloyd George,
with a War Cabinet composed of men prepared to accept any measure, no matter
how authoritarian, in order to win. Conscription was imposed, and made successful
by a series of bargains with the Labour Party and the trade union movement. The
attempt to invoke all the forces of society in the struggle led to endless calls on

patriotism, until the spirit of voluntary action was almost totally devalued. It was succeeded by propaganda, crude, violent and perverting; and, when propaganda failed, outright coercion was used, against conscientious objectors, against dissident shop stewards, against Sinn Fein in Ireland. The old guard of liberal England was broken, metaphorically, by the war; but so also was an image held by many of the upper class, of a tolerant, patriotic, self-regulating and hierarchical society.

The contrast, as so often, can be seen in popular literature: between the Richard Hannay of John Buchan's *Greenmantle*, a debonair cavalier, prepared to recognise the courage of his German opponents, and the hero of *Mr Standfast*, bigoted, ruthless in his attitudes towards von Stumm, who in the end is sent out by him into "no man's land" to be shot by his own side. Perhaps total war made it inevitable that the screen of manners should be whirled away, revealing a less attractive side beneath. Yet propaganda, in the long run, was a card of diminishing value. The Church, for example, devalued its prestige by hysterical appeals; Masterman pondered in his diary in 1918 whether or not "God is a devil who rejoices in human suffering. He may be. There's no evidence to show he isn't." In March 1917, somewhere in Flanders, Sasson remembered "that it was Easter Sunday. Standing in that dismal ditch, I could find no consolation in the thought that Christ was risen. I sploshed back to the dug-out to call the others up for 'stand-to'."

One of the most articulate of young officers, Ralph Wright, wrote a long letter back to Thomas Jones, by then Assistant Secretary of the Cabinet, showing how great the disparity between theory and practice had become:

24 May 1918.

... Seriously though, I repeat this war is lasting much too long. I am fed up. Everyone I know from general to private is absolutely fed up with thinking about the war—still worse, as far as most of us go, we know that the only thing that we must never allow ourselves to do is think about it, for then we should really go mad .... You daren't even get really fond of anyone, for if you do he gets killed. You've just got to shut yourself up, to teach yourself not to feel, to stifle completely your imagination and your sympathy .... Now look here, what you have to do is to tell me something cheerful. Tell me that all this beastly business in Parliament that seems only to succeed in chucking out good soldiers and keeping Lloyd George in power is not so base as it looks. Tell me that Northcliffe doesn't really rule England. Tell me that there is someone with enough power to see to it, at the end, that all this bloody misery is not going to lead to a beastlier England. Tell me even, though I do firmly believe it, that we are going to win. Tell me that freedom is not bad, and by freedom I mean a solid English or French thing; I mean a state of existence where anyone who is getting too fed up can tell his superior to go to hell, and go his own wise or foolish way.

Tell me that Lord Milner is not set on my doing my duty after the war according to *his* lights; tell me too that within six months after the war I shall be free to kick the hindquarters of any general who displeases me. Tell me in fact that when at last we have beaten Germany, we won't wake up to find that her spirit has beaten ours. (Thomas Jones, *Whitehall Diary*, vol. 1, pp.64–5.)

The Armistice failed him, as it failed his generation. Despite the earnest endeavours of politicians in the victor countries, the pre-war world was not restored. That marvellous society which Keynes recalled in the first chapter of *The Economic Consequences of the Peace* was doomed to become a myth, casting a long shadow forwards onto the depressed years, but irrecoverable. Physical and intellectual destruction ravaged the society Edwardian gentlemen had known. The war itself had changed its aspect: country houses had been turned into hospitals or billets, their parks ploughed up to grow crops. Afterwards many could never be restored. In Ireland, first the war between Sinn Fein and the British, and then the civil war, left dozens of great houses burnt out or desolate, and the surviving estates found the politics of the new Free State uncongenial to their style of management. In England and Scotland, decay came in more subtle ways, chiefly for lack of servants, for, despite the spur of unemployment, the armies of women and men who had abandoned domestic service for war work showed few signs of willingness to return. Servants, once the largest single occupational group after agriculture, diminished by one-third between 1914 and 1918; and for a whole generation service ceased to rank as a secure and honourable occupation. The horse, former symbol of the ruling élite, was also on the way out. With a handful of exceptions, such as Allenby's march on Jerusalem, cavalry had been proved useless in the war. Few gentlemen in the 1920s used horses regularly as a means of transport; even the great shire horses were slowly giving way to the influx of tractors.

Seemingly endless sales of land dominated the immediate post-war years. Death duties, often doubled and redoubled in the slaughter of the war, compelled the liquidation of whole estates, like the Antrobus family's lands of Amesbury Abbey. But the flow of deliberate sales also continued: Sir Francis Astly-Corbett, Lord Alington, Admiral Ernle-Ernle-Erle-Drax and Lord Pembroke were among many selling off outlying estates, the better to increase income and concentrate on compact holdings. In 1918 one firm of estate agents, Knight Frank and Rutley, handled 454,972 acres (including 250,000 for the Duke of Sutherland). Half a million acres was actually on the market before the 1919 budget, and the *Estates Gazette* predicted a revolution in landowning. In 1919 over a million acres were sold, and this record was broken in 1920. *The Times* of 19 May 1920 commented mournfully, "England is changing hands .... Will a profiteer buy it? Will it be turned into a school or an institution? Has the mansion house electric light and modern drainage? For the most part the sacrifices are made in silence. The sons are perhaps lying in far away graves; the daughters secretly mourning someone dearer than a brother, have taken up some definite work away from home, seeking thus to fill their aching hearts, and the old people, knowing there is no son or near relative left to keep up the old traditions, or so crippled by necessary taxation that they know the boy will never be able to carry on when they are gone, take the irrevocable step."

Then the sales tapered off. Hit by the agricultural depression after 1921, prices collapsed and landowners decided, often reluctantly, to carry on, however unprofitable farming might be. But in those hectic years something like a quarter of the farming land of Britain changed hands. In the majority of cases, estates were speedily broken up, and farms sold, either to sitting tenants, or to newcomers from Wales and the West Country—an influx of immigrants who bought cheaply and did well if they survived the even worse depression of the early 1930s. "Such an enormous and rapid transfer of land had not been since the confiscations and sequestrations of the civil war, such a permanent transfer not since the dissolution of the monasteries in the sixteenth century. Indeed a transfer on this scale and in such a short space of time had probably not been equalled since the Norman Conquest" (Thompson, *English Landed Society in the Nineteenth Century*, p.332).

More than anything, more even than the war and its casualties, this transfer of estates to working farmers destroyed the world which the Edwardian gentleman had inherited. Town houses and the great town estates followed in the same flood, signalling the decline of the former "season" and the handing over of Mayfair to hotels, flats and offices. The proceeds, of course, where they did not evaporate in death duties or taxes, swelled the investments of families like the Bedfords, the Cecils or the Southamptons, setting them up to survive the privations of the inter-war years. But, while the greatest families, and the shrewdest, were able to recover, these actions both weakened the basis of aristocratic leadership and destroyed the environment in which lesser families had been able to enjoy the privileges and pleasures of the upper class. In a sombre mood, the editor of Burke recorded in 1921 that many families had been included under the style "formerly of" such and such an estate; by 1937 a third of those recorded were landless. If one looks at the number of estates of more than 1,000 acres (Bateman's original definition of a gentleman's estate), the fall was acute: in Bedfordshire, for example, from forty-five in 1873 to twenty-seven in 1925; in Oxfordshire, from sixty-eight to forty-one.

In 1922 the County Landowners Association addressed the Chancellor of the Exchequer in dignified terms: "We do not ask for any special favour for landowners. We recognise that we must share, equally with others, the burden of the country's expenditure. But we are charged with the duty of presenting the case of the landowning class which has done great service to the country and has never failed in emergency" (Guttsman, *The British Political Elite* (1965), p.13). But the Great War was the last of such emergencies: the gentleman's function barely survived that Armageddon.

In political life the break came more sharply, with the fall of Asquith and the appointment of Lloyd George's coalition in December 1916—the so-called "businessman's government", which included in its range of ministers men like Sir Albert Standley, manager of the London Underground and General Omnibus Combine; Joseph McClay, a Glasgow shipowner; Lord Rhondda, a mine-owner; Lord Devonport, a grocer; and Sir Alfred Mond, a manufacturer of chemicals. If one compares the backgrounds of Cabinet Ministers for the period 1886–1916 with those of their counterparts in 1916–1935, the contrast is remarkable. The aristocrats declined from forty-nine to twenty-five, the middle class rose from forty-nine to sixty-two, and the working class from a token three to twenty-one. By 1922 even the Lords contained as many peers in the world of business and industry as it did landowners. Traditionalists like Lord Henry Bentinck might lament the change, believing that the Conservative Party was being "thoroughly commercialised and vulgarised", and the plutocracy "ennobled, decorated, knighted and enriched"; but even in local politics the long predominance of the gentry was over. In country areas, and a few towns where the prestige of local magnates survived, gentlemen could still look automatically to membership of committees, and chairmanships of councils. But increasingly their public duty was limited to voluntary service on unofficial committees, unless they chose, like the Birmingham landowner Sir Oswald Mosley, to enter the political arena as candidates for elections. Only in the great strikes of the 1920s, or when the next war came, was their service required and requested, on the host of committees which proliferated around government at national and local level.

A deeper, profounder change began in the Great War. However vigorous the critics of the gentlemanly code had been before 1914, few members of the élite actually questioned the prevailing notion that their training and qualifications uniquely fitted them to lead the nation. But the war brought the uncompromising question: if the newly commissioned, those they derisively called "temporary gentlemen", from a far wider social background, even from the working class, could serve, fight and die equally, then where lay the mystique of leadership? Sassoon noticed the phrase "temporary gentlemen" with acute distaste at training camp in England; but also that they "usually turned out to be first rate officers when they got to the trenches".

Disillusion set in about the purposes of the war, its heroics, and the society which they were supposed to be defending. An epitaph like Viola Meynell's *Memoir of Julian Grenfell* (1917) was written strictly for home consumption, with its talk of "the noble self-sacrifice of the fighter … the joy in the clash of arms …. It has fallen to him alone to express the certainty of Nature's utter sanction of the fighter, and the consciousness of the whole universe upholding him with all her mysteries." Scarcely less romantic was the reaction of Ettie Grenfell, the poet's mother: "The thought that he was dying seemed to come, go and come, but he always seemed radiantly happy and he never saw any of the people he loved look sad."

Blunden and Graves did not produce their vivid accounts of the war's horrors and the dark side of behaviour under stress until the very end of the 1920s, but the "scorching effect" (as E.L. Woodward called it) on men's minds had swept through the armies by 1917, the worst year of the war. Afterwards the cynics might ask what it had been fought for; whose England? Osbert Sitwell, demobilised at the beginning of 1919, wrote a bitter refrain (in *Le Galop Final* (1949), p.153) to celebrate the outbreak of peace:

We thank Thee, O Lord,
That the War is over.
We can now
Turn our attention again
To money-making,
Railway Shares must go up;
Wages must come down;
Smoke shall come out
Of the chimneys of the North,
And we will manufacture battleships.
    We thank Thee, O Lord,
    But we must refuse
    To consider
    Music, Painting, or Poetry.

Other voices questioned the leaders who had spurred them on.

Our captain at Wipers said us heroes should have land,
But I can't even get an allotment,
'Cos Billy Bean has father's—
The one next to the ruined Tower—
On account of a few old thistles and a trifle of back rent.
Why can't the Earl give a field
To make more plots like they have at Hordle;
I guess the Germans would have took his land
If we hadn't pushed at Wipers.

(Bernard Gilbert, "Old England", 1921.)

Others raged at a whole order which denied them a life fit for heroes to enjoy. When wages slumped in agriculture in 1921, Leonard Thompson, farmworker, "drew 27s. 6d. from the farmer and after I had given my wife 24s. and paid my Union 4d. and my rent 3s. 1d., I had a penny left! So I threw it across the field. I'd worked hard, I'd been through the war and I'd married. A penny was what a child had. I wasn't having that. I would sooner have nothing" (Ronald Blythe, *Akenfield* (1971), p.48).

For the gentleman, however, the most pervasive and probably the most demoralising effect of war was that it brought, not the equality of opportunity which the pre-war critics sought, but equalisation of income between upper and middle classes. While it remained possible to live for many years on inherited capital, the old advantage in disposable income had been eroded. At the same time, the battle against women's rights had been lost, the vote given in 1918, and society opened to all the gay abandonment of the flappers and the Bright Young Things. With money and opportunity, the middle classes erupted into the closed preserves: they bought cars, more expensive houses, fine furniture; they travelled widely in Europe, dined in fashionable restaurants, went habitually to the theatre and opera. Over a quarter of a million new passports were issued each year after 1921; total car registrations rose from 132,015 in 1914 to 482,316 in 1924, and to 1.5 million by 1933. Truly, the barriers were down, the hordes invading.

The Queen, with unconscious bathos, added its own epitaph, in an account of the state of society in 1920 (*The Queen*, ed. Quentin Crewe, p.132). Lady Great House had shut down all but the eight best bedrooms, Lady Newly Rich could not keep up such an establishment. Mr and Mrs Badly-Off were really suffering in spite of the fact that he was third son of a peer: "undoubtedly one of the trials of their life is that they cannot mix with their former associates". But by then the gentleman was in the world of Evelyn Waugh's *Vile Bodies*, and Edwardian society had gone for good.

Epilogue

There is no need to emphasise how uncongenial the geography of Europe became after the Great War to the ideal and practice of the gentlemanly life. Bolshevik revolution, strident nationalism, fascist experiments glorifying the virtues of a different sort of oligarchy, and the aspirations to power of working-class movements in what remained of the classical democracies transformed the political stage while inflation—catastrophic in Germany, overwhelming in France and Italy—undermined the economic assumptions on which that life had been based. Britain managed to remain a little apart, less affected by the repercussions of universal war, slower to react to altered conditions. Thus, in the 1930s, Baldwin made no secret of his reluctance to deal personally with what he regarded as fundamentally evil men, like the Nazis Goering and Ribbentrop, or like the French Premier, Pierre Laval; and this attitude was echoed, more pungently, by Osbert Sitwell: "Hitler belonged to the people; like Stalin, he was no gentleman—and when I say *gentleman*, I mean what I say .... Boasting, roaring, tears, dervish-like howling, fist-shaking, lying over never-ending toasts in vodka and champagne, were, by general consent, substituted for the traditional decorous voices and considerate behaviour of the old diplomacy" (*Laughter in the Next Room*, p.5).

One long-term effect of the Great War was to cut Britain off from the continent: for nearly a decade afterwards, it was unfashionable to visit Germany, and the intensity of Britain's cultural links diminished sharply. A similar sort of withdrawal can be found in the personal histories of many Edwardians after 1918, as though, in reaction against an uncomprehending and often hostile world, they were shrinking into private introspection. It is a cliché of social history that the "roaring twenties" despised what had gone before, seizing avidly on the critiques of late Victorian and Edwardian morals written by Lytton Strachey or D.H. Lawrence, and later on the bleak revisions of the real story of the war as seen by Robert Graves or Edmund Blunden. Almost the only facet of Edwardian England popular in the 1930s was that curiously archaic, stiffly conventional world of the country house portrayed in the detective stories of Agatha Christie and Dorothy Sayers, a world where crime met its just deserts at the hands of gifted amateurs like Lord Peter Wimsey, and where Hercule Poirot—epitome of the acceptable foreigner—allowed the murderers on the Orient Express to go free, because he understood the fineness of their feelings for the famous actress whose grandchild the murdered man had kidnapped and destroyed. Yet the Edwardian years left a peculiar legacy which conditioned behaviour—other than light reading—between the wars.

The legacy was the cult of gentility: not among the largely impoverished upper class, but among the vast body of the middle class which, in an age of mass production, had absorbed the privileges and perquisites of wealth, and still hankered after the less tangible essence of what had ceased to exist. It would be partly true to say that the gentlemanly ethic was used as a defence against further encroachment up the social ladder by those who had not yet tasted the material benefits; but, much more, it conferred on the "Conquerors", as Masterman had called them, the legitimacy of the old ruling élite.

Despite doubts about the traditional system of admitting recruits to the top jobs in industry, politics or public administration, reform was piecemeal, and much retarded by the war. Consequently, the gentlemanly ethic survived, when in most European countries it was destroyed; and, because it no longer corresponded to social realities, its effect was stifling on all those who adopted it. Few actually tried to break out of the prison: the satires of Evelyn Waugh, the pastiche of Edwardian life so artfully caught in P.G. Wodehouse's world of Bertie Wooster, the Drones Club, and the ineffable Jeeves, were far too amiable and indulgent to wound. The real rebels came later, like those members of the Communist Party who died in the Spanish Civil War—Christopher Caudwell, John Cornford; or the enigmatic figure of George Orwell, with his fear of an England given over to "gentlemanly semi-Fascism".

The legacy, then, was one of heightened class distinctions; sterile debates about the use of language (Nancy Mitford's peregrinations in the world of "U" and "non-U" speech); and a middle-class complacency which sat well on the prosperous south-east of England in the years of the depression. The new élite, in Orwell's phrase, "owned no land, but they felt that they were landowners in the sight of God, and kept up a semi-aristocratic outlook by going into the professions and the fighting services rather than into trade" (*The Road to Wigan Pier*, 1962 edition, p.108). The admirably flexible mechanism which had facilitated the rise to social eminence of each new thrusting group since the seventeenth century, had failed at last: partly in the face of an increasingly coherent and politically organised working class which did not aspire to those values; and partly because the "Conquerors" had assimilated themselves to out-dated stereotypes and lost the power to modify them.

Here was a great betrayal; though, for twenty years, in uniquely favourable circumstances, until 1945—and perhaps even longer—it looked like a success. It was not, of course, simply the "fault" of the public schools or of any other single factor: one generation who had known the sweet life and lost it passed on its recollections, and another, slightly later generation, which had been brought up to expect but had never actually experienced that life, attempted to console its sense of deprivation. Things as diverse as the cult of the old-school tie, the "old boy" network, and the inculcation of "standard English" by the BBC in the heyday of its Director-General Sir John Reith can be seen as fragments of a forgotten culture, shored up against the ruin of a world without class landmarks. Great areas of British life between 1918 and 1940 *were* vigorous and adaptive—if they had not been, the country could not have survived the Second World War. But many of the worst failures, the perpetuation of outmoded curricula in schools and universities, of outdated habits of industrial and business management, and of an outworn culture—music, painting, architecture, writing—can be traced back to this source.

One or two made a positive defence, seeing in the revival of an oligarchy of taste the only means to ensure the survival of civilisation. Clive Bell, in *Civilization* (1928), and T.S. Eliot, in *The Idea of a Christian Society* (1939), unashamedly argued that the future lay in recreating the past; and Waugh himself, in *Brideshead Revisited*, published in 1945, offered a lament that things could not be so. But no one dared to run counter to political evolution, in the manner of W.H. Mallock, whose sceptical analysis *The Limits of Pure Democracy* had argued that "only through oligarchy does civilized democracy know itself". In 1918 he had had the temerity to state, "In each of the three lives—that of knowledge, that of aesthetic appreciation, and that of religion—on which the quality of social intercourse in a civilized country depends, the activities of the few play a part of such supreme importance that were their activities absent, the mass of the citizens, whatever their material wealth, would be unlettered, superstitious and half brutal barbarians, as many newly enriched men on the outskirts of civilization actually are today .... The many can prosper only through the participation in benefits which, in a way alike of material comfort, opportunity, culture and social freedom, would be possible for no-one unless the many submitted themselves to the influence or authority of the super-capable few" (*The Limits of Pure Democracy* (1918), pp. 348 and 392).

Nostalgia for the last period of British and imperial greatness clouded and distorted for at least three decades the ideas held by the political élite about Britain's changing role and position in an unfriendly world. In Westminster, Whitehall, the City, the Stock Exchange, the Church, the Services—in short, in what came later to be called the Establishment—certain assumptions commanded general assent as if they had a talismanic virtue, unaffected by passing time. Most, if not all of them, can be found, stigmatised already, in Masterman's *Condition of England*, written in 1909.

But however burdensome the legacy, the ideal itself once existed and over three-quarters of a century the apparent perfection of that gentlemanly life has not lost its charm. It was as if, after the barbarian invasions of Rome, men looked back, hopelessly, to the classic age of the Antonine emperors. The price of having a golden age is that those living after it imagine it should be followed by at least a silver age; whereas the truth may well be that they exist in an age of iron.

Bibliography

Margot Asquith Autobiography
(1920)
Leo Amery My Life Vol. 1
(1953)
Maurice Baring The Puppet
Show of Memory (1922)
Andrew Boyle Montagu Norman
(1967)
Burke's Landed Gentry – 10th
to 14th editions.
Ronald Blythe Akenfield (1969)
Sir Thomas Beecham A Mingled
Chime (1973)
A C Benson The House of Quiet
(1910)
E F Benson As We Were (1930)
W S Blunt My Diaries 2 vols.
(1932)
Gerald Brenan A life of one's
own (1962)
Lord David Cecil Max. A
Biography (1964)
Sir Arthur Conan Doyle Memo-
ries (1924)
Lady Diana Cooper The Rain-
bow Comes and Goes (1958)
G K Chesterton Autobiography
(1936)

G Kitson Clark The Making of
Victorian England (1965)
Virginia Cowles Edward VII and
his circle (1956)
Blanche Dugdale Arthur Balfour
(1930)
A G Gardiner Pillars of Society
(1913) Prophets Priests and
Kings (1908)
R B Haldane Autobiography
(1929)
Frank Harris My Life and Loves
(1920) Contemporary Portraits
(1912)
S Hynes The Edwardian Turn of
Mind (1968)
Alan Hyman The Rise and Fall
of Horatio Bottomley (1972)
Henry James The Ambassadors.
The Golden Bowl. Wings of the
Dove. The Sacred Fount.
M R James Eton and Kings
(1930)
Sir L Jones An Edwardian Youth
(1956)
Edward Lucie-Smith Eroticism
in Western Art (1972)
Sir Philip Magnus Edward VII
(1964)
C F G Masterman The Condition
of England (1909)
Steven Marcus The Other Vic-
torians (1966)

Desmond Macarthy Memoirs
(1953)
Edward Marsh A Number of
People (1939)
Compton MacKenzie My Life
and Times Octave .4 (1965)
Dame Nellie Melba Melodies and
Memoirs (1925)
R K Middlemas and A J L
Barnes Baldwin a Biography
(1969)
R Nevill London Clubs (1911)
H Nevinson Changes and
Chances (1923)
Sir F Ponsonby Recollections of
Three Reigns (1951)
Princess Daisy of Pless What I
Left Unsaid (1930)
V Sackville-West The Edwar-
dians (1930)
Philippa Puller Frank Harris
(1972)

Siegfried Sassoon Memoirs of a
Fox Hunting Man (1928)
S Nowell-Smith (ed) Edwardian
England (1964)
W A Scovell Edwardian Heritage
(1949)
Lord Frederick Spencer The
Days Before Yesterday (1920)
Paul Thompson The Edwardians
(1975)
F M L Thompson English Land-
ed Society in the 19th Century
(1963)
Barbara Tuchman The Proud
Tower (1966)
John Terraine Douglas Haig.
The Educated Soldier (1963)
Daisy Countess of Warwick Dis-
cretions (1931)
Thorsten Veblen The Theory of
the Leisure Class (1899)

INDEX

The letter-by-letter system of alphabetization has been adopted.